American Women in the Progressive Era, 1900–1920

OTHER BOOKS BY DOROTHY SCHNEIDER AND CARL J. SCHNEIDER

Sound Off! American Military Women Speak Out
(Dutton, 1988)

Into the Breach: American Women Overseas in World War I
(Viking, 1991)

Sound Off! American Military Women Speak Out, rev. ed.
(Paragon House, 1992)

American Women in the Progressive Era, 1900–1920

DOROTHY SCHNEIDER
&
CARL J. SCHNEIDER

ANCHOR BOOKS
DOUBLEDAY
New York London Toronto Sydney Auckland

AN ANCHOR BOOK
PUBLISHED BY DOUBLEDAY
a division of Bantam Doubleday Dell Publishing Group, Inc.
1540 Broadway, New York, New York 10036

ANCHOR BOOKS, DOUBLEDAY, and the portrayal of an anchor are trademarks of
Doubleday, a division of Bantam Doubleday Dell
Publishing Group, Inc.

American Women in the Progressive Era, 1900–1920 was originally published in
hardcover by Facts on File, Inc., in 1993. The Anchor Books edition is published by
arrangement with Facts on File, Inc.

Text design by Ron Monteleone

Library of Congress Cataloging-in-Publication Data
Schneider, Dorothy.
American women in the progressive era, 1900–1920
Dorothy Schneider & Carl J. Schneider—1st Anchor Books ed.
p.   cm.
Originally published: New York: Facts on File, © 1993.
Includes bibliographical references and index.
1. Women—United States—History—20th century. 2. Women—
United States—Social conditions. 3. Women's rights—United States—
History—20th century. 4. Women in politics—United States—
History—20th century. 5. Progressivism (United States politics).
I. Schneider, Carl J.   II. Title.
HQ1419.S34   1994
305.4'0973'0904—dc20   93-5890
CIP

ISBN 0-385-47283-8

1   3   5   7   9   10   8   6   4   2

For Joan

*"If I were asked to designate the most thrilling years
(not of my life, but of my life as a citizeness of the United States)
from the year of my birth in 1873 to the present year,
1950, I would say the years between 1900 and 1914.
Life was full of hope and freedom.
Great movements were starting everywhere.
In the United States, the loudest voice in the land
was that of the liberal. Everyone was fighting for something.
Everyone was sure of victory."*

— Inez Irwin,
unpublished manuscript of "Adventures of Yesterday," p. 281.
By permission of The Schlesinger Library, Radcliffe College.

Contents

Preface

For the past two years we have breathed vicariously the bracing atmosphere of the Progressive Era. We've learned a lot, especially about the diversity of American women, the strength they derived from their networking with other women, and their professional and social accomplishments.

What every woman knows, and what every researcher of women's lives discovers, is that there are no ordinary women. Few of the women about whom we write are candidates for *Notable American Women*, and perhaps each of them thought of herself as unremarkable. Yet the fabric of their lives as they designed and wove it displays their times, their unique selves, and above all, the wide differences in their experiences in the America of 1900 to 1920.

Their diaries, memoirs, and letters and the recent excellent feminist scholarship on them have transported us into their times. Our work on an earlier book, *Into the Breach: American Women Overseas in World War I* (Viking, 1991), had earned us some familiarity with them. We've looked at their magazines and read the novels they were reading. We've searched out pictures of their clothes and their houses. And we've remembered the stories of our mothers and grandmothers.

Our local librarians, Anne Penniman, Mary Attridge, and Beverly Page, generously chose to regard our multitudinous requests for interlibrary loans as challenges rather than nuisances. Our friend Betty Pierson kindly allowed us to reproduce some of her early 20th-century postcards. Robert Bischoff, president of the Clinton, Connecticut, Historical Society, loaned us a photograph from its collection. Our agent, Elizabeth Knappman, as always radiated confidence and competence. Our editor, Nicole Bowen, stimulated our thinking by her insightful questions. We thank them all.

Dorothy Schneider
Carl J. Schneider
Essex, Connecticut

CHAPTER 1

Dawning of an Age of Hope and Glory

Start with the women. In 1900, the 37 million women of the United States shared no common life-style.

American women lived in dramatically different areas. Ten and a half million of them crowded into the urbanized and industrialized Northeast. Five million inhabited a largely rural and agricultural South Atlantic area still tragically struggling with its division between whites and blacks. The greatest number, 13

AN OZARK FAMILY IN A LUMBER COMPANY TOWN ABOUT 1915.   (COLLECTION OF THE AUTHORS)

million, spread across the farmlands, small towns, and great cities of the North Central area. Another 7 million dwelled in the enormous spaces of the South Central regions, from Kentucky and Tennessee to Texas and the Indian Territories. And a scant 2 million populated the Far West. Across the huge reaches of the North American continent, all these women throughout the Progressive Era, 1900–20, invented or accepted their lives in ways as different as the regions they inhabited.

They differed also in economic opportunity. In Denver Elinore Pruitt Stewart left her work as a washerwoman to move to Wyoming with her little daughter and prove her claim to a homestead. In tent shows in the South Ma Rainey, the black "Mother of the Blues," did a song-and-dance act with her husband before footlights of Coleman lanterns, with music supplied by "jug" bands. In Boston Bette Davis's divorced mother used her skills as a photographer to educate her two young daughters. In Salt Lake City Mormon Annie Clark Tanner, second of six wives, scrubbed floors and did practical nursing to support her eight children, with scant help from her authoritarian husband.[1] In New York City Jewish immigrant housewives protested in the streets against a rise in the price of kosher meat, and young Jewish women fresh from Russia labored long days in the garment industry to earn passage money to America for their families still in the Old Country. In Connecticut architect Theodate Pope Riddle learned her craft building a mansion for her wealthy parents. In Homestead, Pennsylvania, wives of steelworkers struggled to feed their families on their husbands' earnings, took in washing and boarders, and sent their children into factories to supplement the family income. In small-town Ohio middle-class women "comfortable and invaluable as mothers, but imposing and dignified women of affairs who took their world of committees seriously" devoted hours to community improvement.[2] In Washington, D.C., little black girls of 10 or 11 began work as live-in servants. Meanwhile their mothers and aunts back in the South worked seasonally in the fields or in the lowliest, dirtiest jobs in the tobacco factories. In Boston Ellen Gertrude Emmet Rand, portrait artist, exhibited at Boston's Copley Hall, where before only Whistler, Sargent, and Monet had been given solo shows. In Idaho May Arkright Hutton, cook and boardinghouse keeper, bought shares in a mine, picked huckleberries and sold pies to keep it going, put overalls on her 250-pound frame to "muck out" the mine waste, and five years later struck it so rich that she could entertain Teddy Roosevelt in her own mansion and devote her time and money to woman suffrage. In the Deep South a sharecropper's wife rose about 4:00 A.M. to get breakfast over an open fire, labored 12 hours as a field hand, and sat up at night to wash, mend and quilt.[3] In New York the eccentric Hetty Green was amassing her millions and pinching her pennies.[4] In Kansas Martha Farnsworth gardened and canned, retrimmed her old hats and refurbished her old dresses to supplement the modest wages of her postal worker husband, scrimping and saving to buy their comfortable house. Katherine Davis, her tubercular spouse, and their four children traveled for years in their covered wagon through Colorado and New Mexico, seeking health for

WOMAN TO WOMAN. THE HAIRSTYLE OF THE YOUNG HOPI NATIVE AMERICAN WILL INDICATE THAT SHE IS UNMARRIED.   (NATIONAL ARCHIVES)

the husband and father.[5] Meanwhile Mrs. August Belmont was quipping: "A private railroad car is not an acquired taste. One takes to it immediately."[6] And when Harriot Blatch's daughter was married, a newspaper commented: "The bride was Nora Stanton Blatch; they say she has money."[7]

Women's activities varied as much as their economic opportunities. Bandleader Helen May Butler toured the country with her all-woman military band.[8] In North Dakota Buffalo Woman, a Hidatsa, described and demonstrated for an anthropologist the cultivation, planting, and hoeing processes by which cooperative work groups of Indian women had long provided their tribe with food.[9] "Red Kate" Richards O'Hare was blaming capitalism for fewer marriages and more divorces: Why should a young man marry only to condemn the girl he loved to a life of poverty? In a cavelike dugout in the Far West a mother gave birth to Wyoming Benjamin Paris, the first Jewish boy born in that state. Mrs. John Kilbuck, wife of a Delaware Indian, lived in Alaska; she could reminisce about her days as a bride in Point Barrow, "where the ocean spray froze on the windowsill" and she could "hear the wild ocean roar."[10] In 1901 schoolteacher

Annie Taylor went over Niagara Falls in a barrel—the first person to accomplish this useful feat.[11] Marion Craig-Wentworth, veteran socialist lecturer on the Chautauqua circuit, having first thoughtfully provided her husband with her own replacement, left him and moved to California to become a writer.[12] Nurse Clara Louise Maas, twice subjecting herself to bites from infected mosquitoes, died a martyr to control yellow fever.[13] Frances Benjamin Johnston, pioneering photojournalist, touted in the pages of the *Ladies' Home Journal* the attractions for women of a career in photography. Marie Van Vorst for purposes of research laid aside her usual clothing—including a $40 hat, a $200 sealskin coat, a $150 dress—to don clothes that from the skin out cost $9.45 and become Bell Ballard, gummer in a shoe factory, earning $3 a week.

Times of Change and Challenge

In 1900 all these American women were living in difficult as well as interesting times, changing times. Some women inhabited a world largely unchanged from

SEGREGATE AND PROTECT! NEW TECHNOLOGY PROVIDED THE SUBWAY CAR; OLD SOCIAL ATTITUDES CALLED FOR ISOLATING WOMEN TO FEND OFF DANGERS.
(NEW YORK PUBLIC LIBRARY PHOTO FILES)

the time of their mothers or even grandmothers. Others were on the cutting edge of a changing society. But all of them felt the jolts of rapid change during the Progressive Era. "The prophecies made [at the turn of the century] by newspaper reporters of the inventions to come in the next hundred years were fantastic beyond belief," wrote Helen Hooven Santmyer. "Marconi had proved that sound could be sent over the air without wires, and his discovery could lead to a whole new system of communication; Edison had invented pictures that moved on a screen; a few inventors had succeeded in staying in the air in gliders; it was not beyond possibility that in another fifty years man would actually be flying." It didn't take fifty years: In 1911 the first American woman obtained her pilot's license. By 1914 Ford had built half a million cars, transforming the lives of their purchasers. By 1920 Americans were flocking to the movies and radios were beginning to compete with phonographs.[14]

Social developments were altering the world of American women as fast as discoveries and inventions. The urbanization that sent America's people from its countryside to its cities cost many women their established support systems. Alone, or with their husbands and children, they left behind their sisters and their mothers and their aunts, their neighborhoods where everyone spoke on the street and everyone helped her neighbors. They moved from farms or small towns where everyone knew their antecedents and status to the indifference of the city. For some, it was alienation—for others, liberation.

In either case, city life offered new ways to live. Immigrant women and their families crowded into tenements without a modicum of privacy and almost impossible to clean. Middle-class and well-off women moved from the single-family houses of their youth into apartments, or even apartment hotels that freed them from domestic cares. Amusements, ranging from dance halls and vaudeville shows to opera and art, tempted them on every side. And a myriad of shops, dominated by the great department stores, catered to them.

But though the cities attracted Americans by the millions, they repelled others, who longed to exchange the cities' mix of ethnic groups and economic classes for homogeneity, teeming streets for quiet lanes, crowds for privacy and exclusivity. The terrible San Francisco earthquake and fire of 1906 demonstrated the vulnerability of city dwellers. Many a young family found their panacea in a vision of suburban life, away from the crime and disease of the city, with their own kind, in a countryside free of city stress. And they need not even sacrifice city services and entertainments, now accessible by train and automobile.

Industrialization struck women's lives with a force equal to that of urbanization. For the 20 percent of American women over 10 who worked in gainful occupations, it opened new opportunities in offices, department stores, and the professions, but it sentenced many more to long hours and dull, repetitive labor in dead-end jobs that kept them far below the poverty level. It transformed the lives of housewives, moving production of clothing and many foods out of the home, depriving them of household help, and taking their husbands away throughout the day.

New waves of immigrants, particularly from southern and eastern Europe, enriched but also complicated life, particularly in the expanding cities and in small northeastern factory-dominated towns. Children of native-born American women went to school with first-generation Americans from 10 or 15 different countries. In 1900 almost 13 percent of America's female population—almost 5 million women—were foreign born. With their starkly different backgrounds, their "outlandish" customs, their different assumptions about women's places, they modified thinking about such issues as woman suffrage and raised questions about the future of the country. Did the teeming hordes of immigrants include radicals, even anarchists? Would America, could America, absorb all these differences and still remain America? Could all these women become *American* women?

Sometimes the nativism aroused by this sizable immigrant population operated almost as unjustly and cruelly as the racism directed against America's 4.5 million black women. Native-born white Americans expressed both attitudes

BARGAINING FOR BREAD. IMMIGRANT WOMEN SHOPPED DAILY FOR FOOD THEY HAD NO PLACE TO STORE. (NATIONAL ARCHIVES)

freely and overtly. "The American citizen," declared the editor of *American Homes and Gardens*, "is entitled to greater consideration than the foreigner."[15] Children chanted ethnic slurs. Audiences roared with laughter at minstrel shows that demeaned black Americans and vaudeville shows built on ethnic stereotypes. *Madeleine: An Autobiography*, a book that purported to be the confessional autobiography of a prostitute, alleged that average American girls from average American homes occupied the "better" brothels, but "the girls at Madame C——'s were the American-born children of the most ignorant and degraded of foreigners, brought up in the slums of the great cities, with nothing wholesome in their natures to neutralize the poison of their environment."[16] And the *Atlantic Monthly* published Margaret Deland's argument against woman suffrage: "We have suffered many things at the hands of Patrick; the New Woman would add Bridget also. And—graver danger—to the vote of that fierce, silly, amiable creature, the uneducated Negro, she would add (if logical) the vote of his sillier, baser female."[17]

The Good Old Days?

Despite all the changes being wrought by new inventions, urbanization, industrialization, and immigration, women in the Progressive Era still lived in a world that nearly 100 years later looks alien, in some ways almost primitive.

The vigilantism inherited from frontier and Reconstruction days still surged to the surface, erupting out of passion and prejudice. At its most virulent, it expressed itself in the lynchings that brutalized and scarred the nation, before the eyes of men, women, and children.

Social and political conditions were still bespattered with the results of the free-wheeling capitalism of the robber barons of the 19th century. Muckrakers like Ida Tarbell and Lincoln Steffens were filing story after story exposing the harshness of child labor, the ruthlessness and conspiratorial tactics of big business, the brutalities inflicted on striking workers and their families, the traffic in white slavery, the double-dealing of political bosses, and the machinations of the alcohol interests.

At the turn of the century, 1 percent of the population owned more of the wealth than the other 99 percent.[18] By today's standards, the middle class was small. Most people belonged to the working class—people without economic security, often living from day to day, severely affected by national financial crises like that of 1907, frequently forced to job-hunt.

Nothing more clearly delineates the differences between American life then and now than the health of the populace. Tuberculosis, dysentery, smallpox, typhoid fever, influenza, pneumonia, and diphtheria killed off people long before they came to an age to worry about heart attacks, cancer, and

Alzheimer's. The average woman's life expectancy was just a little over 48 years.[19] Sickness and accidents struck people at every turn of their lives. These afflicted the poor, of course, even more than the middle class and the rich—and the poor constituted the bulk of the population.

The rate of infant mortality was appalling: As late as 1918 the United States was 11th of 20 nations, with 250,000 infant deaths a year.[20] Elizabeth Stern, daughter of Jewish immigrant parents, chillingly recorded what this meant for some families: "Our baby was never the same baby two years in succession. The little cradle held a new burden every year, but the former occupant never lived to see its successor. Mother became a mother eleven times. Only the first four children lived." [21] In an era before clean milk was universally available, mothers still worried about getting their toddlers through the critical second summer, and they fought to protect their children against head lice, erysipelas, rickets, and milk sickness (which flourished through ignorance of the poisonous effect of white snakeroot on cattle). Most children experienced the death of a sibling.

Accidents too beset families. Workplaces, farms, and homes lacked the most basic safety guards. Report after report tells of babies and toddlers falling off beds, falling from overturning carriages, falling downstairs, falling out of windows.

Poor women often lived a long distance from the nearest doctor and/or couldn't afford to pay a physician's fees. In 1920 Mrs. H. B. Rogers of Winterville, Georgia, wrote the Children's Bureau:

> *I need advice. I am a farmers wife. Do my household duties and a regular field hand too. The mother of 9 children and in family way again. I am quarlsome when tired and fatigued. When I come out of the field to prepare dinner my husband and all the children getes in my way. I quarrel at them for being in my way. . . . What shall I do? My husband wont sympathise with me one bit but talks rough to me. If I get tired and sick of my daily food and crave some simple article, should I have it. I have helped make the living for 20 years. Should I benied [sic] of a few simple articles or money either. Does it make a mother unvirtuous for a man physician to wait on her during confinement; is it safe for me to go through it without aid from anyone?[22]*

The Children's Bureau advised Mrs. Rogers to get more rest and see a doctor.

Of necessity, women practiced a lot of home medicine, turning to the doctor only as a last resort. Take, for instance, homesteader Elizabeth Corey, who usually signed herself "Bachelor Bess." She wrote of walking several miles into town to have her foot looked at. "It is just a 'gumbile' and not the gout as I feared. The Dr opened it—cut off the corn and dressed the thing and told me how to treat it—guess it wont have to be amputated if I take good care of it. . . .

He says it was scarlet fever which I had a while back and if he had known of it I'd have been quarantined." Instead she had taught school every day![23]

Home remedies abounded. Popular magazines advertised "nostrums for complexion troubles, wrinkles, ruptures, fits, piles, bed-wetting, and tuberculosis. A new eight-tone hearing aid was featured; remedies were offered for gray hair and obesity. The heavyweight champion, Jess Willard, testified that Nuxated Iron was the secret of his victories over Jack Johnson and Frank Moral. 'John's Wife' told how John quit drinking after she slipped a few shots of Golden Treatment into his food."[24] Books like Dr. Emma Drake's *What a Young Wife Ought to Know* warned that some girls thoughtlessly and ignorantly neglected the regular evacuation of the bladder and bowels: "The result is from the fulness of the bladder long continued, a pushing of the uterus backward which may, if the habit be kept up, result in permanent displacement."[25]

Many women kept recipes for remedies along with those for food. For a sore throat Magnolia Le Guin reminded herself, "Take an onion about the size of a walnut, cut it up, sprinkle plentifully with salt and pepper, put all in a cloth and pound until it is mashed well, and bind on the throat at bed time. In severe cases the treatment should be repeated two or three times. If taken in season, this remedy will cure diphtheria."[26]

Even when women did consult doctors, they had no assurance of help. Physicians had no antibiotics to prescribe, and for many major diseases even the best of them just didn't know what to do. But the best were in short supply. In 1910, 90 percent of doctors had no college education; most of them had attended substandard medical schools.[27] Many harmed more than they helped. "I have been an afflicted woman since the first time I became a mother," wrote Magnolia Le Guin. "Dr. J. was my physician. He perhaps and no doubt did best he knew, but he came near killing me and wrecked my health in some respects for life, and he caused the death of our first born—a baby girl. As a Dr. he is unfit to visit human beings, I verily believe."[28]

Physicians incorporated old wives' tales into their advice to patients. The group of them who in 1919 published a new edition of *The Household Physician: A Twentieth Century Medica*, a tome of more than 1,400 pages, pontificated on methods of making boy babies or girl babies: For a boy,

> *Before cohabitation the husband should eat nothing but good, substantial food, take long, hard exercise in the open air, read light literature, abstain from indulgence for some time before the procreative period. The wife should abstain from animal food but should eat vegetables and farinaceous articles of diet, exercise daily until almost fatigued and pass the time with older females than herself. After pregnancy the wife should eat a great deal of meat, eggs and vegetables, but little or no pastry or sweets, and should take walks and exercise in the open air every day.*

For a girl, on the other hand,

The wife should eat the most stimulating food, should not indulge the passions and should reserve her whole vigor and strength for the desired time. The husband should take violent exercise until fatigued and a hot bath every night. After pregnancy the wife should eat little meat but should live mostly on farinaceous food and take short walks in the open air, but not enough to get tired, and should sleep as much as possible.

The same egg, the doctors allowed, could produce a boy if fertilized just before menstruation, or a girl if fertilized just after.[29]

Doctors commonly believed that during menstruation the flow of blood diverted energy from the brain, rendering women idiotic. They talked a lot about chlorosis, which they identified as a form of anemia common in adolescent girls: Girls so afflicted, they said, had trouble breathing, experienced heart palpitations, and showed a distaste for meat, which was supposed to increase the menstrual flow and arouse the passions. Some doctors used chlorosis as a reason to advise against study for young women; others thought that marriage would cure it; and still others linked it to attractiveness and high fertility.[30]

Middle-class women still had to resist the temptations of the cult of invalidism, which survived into the second decade of the 20th century. It forbade well-to-do women activity and

Be Well Without Drugs

I Will Help You to
Vibrant Health, Rested Nerves *and a* Good Figure

After my university course, I concluded I could be of greater help to my sex by assisting Nature to *regain* and *retain* the strength of every vital organ, by bringing to it a good circulation of pure blood; by strengthening the nerves, and by teaching deep breathing, than I could by correcting bodily ailments with medicines.

I have helped over 44,000 women. I can help you to

Arise to Your Best

giving to you that *satisfaction with self* which comes through knowledge that you are developing the sweet, personal loveliness which health and a wholesome, graceful body give —a cultured, self-reliant woman with a definite purpose, which makes you the greatest help to family and friends. You will be a **Better Wife,** a **Rested Mother,** a **Sweeter Sweetheart.**

I can help you to make every vital organ and nerve do efficient work, thus clearing the complexion and correcting such ailments as

Constipation	*Irritability*	*Indigestion*
Weak Nerves	*Colds*	*Dullness*
Rheumatism	*Nervousness*	*Weaknesses*
Sleeplessness	*Torpid Liver*	*Catarrh*

This work is done by following simple directions a few minutes each day in the privacy of your own room. In delicate cases I co-operate with the physician.

HOW TO BE HEALTHY THOUGH FEMALE! ECONOMICS, ISOLATION, AND THE GENERAL STATE OF MEDICAL KNOWLEDGE ENCOURAGED MANY TO GET THEIR ADVICE WHERE THEY COULD. (1910 ADVERTISEMENT FOR EXERCISES)

interests, proclaiming their physical delicacy and labeling menstruation, pregnancy, and menopause as diseases. Physicians persuaded healthy monied women of the necessity of daily visits to their offices. But the allegations of feminine delicacy did not extend to poor women, from whom society exacted brutally hard labor.

Middle- and upper-class women had also to survive popular medical advice on staying young and beautiful. A chapter of *The Household Physician* entitled "The Woman Beautiful, A Treatise on How to Keep Young" reflected the slowly changing attitudes on fat. As Louise Fischer Schneider, married in 1916, recalled, "When I was a bride, gaining weight meant that one was healthy," and 5-foot 4-inch Martha Farnsworth who in 1905 weighed 136 wanted to gain four pounds. *The Household Physician* defined dieting as "eating all you want, but of food that agrees with you." It advocated a twice-a-year, one-week all-milk diet, partly to control the weight, partly to improve the complexion: a glass of whole milk every hour all day—an intake of some 1,800 calories a day.

As for exercise, *The Household Physician* recommended for the "woman who is in fair form" the following twice-a-day workout: (1) Practicing walking correctly, the body bent forward at the belt line, taking long steps and turning the feet outward, for five minutes a session. (2) Standing on a footstool with a wand in hand, balancing first on one foot, then on the other, at the same time raising and lowering the wand above the head. (3) (To be undertaken with caution) Scampering around the room on all fours, bending backward until the hands almost touch the floor if possible; bending forward until the palms of the hands lie flat on the carpet, swaying far to one side, then the other.[31] Fortunately for them, by the turn of the century middle- and upper-class women were more and more engaging in tennis, bicycling, and other sports.

Additionally *The Household Physician* advised stirring a rose jar in the lower hallway every morning, so as to "keep away germs, insects and disease microbes, for such pests will not enter when the room is filled with sweet scents." Sweet scents particularly help "the restless woman [who] is positively soothed by a bottle of fine perfume, and should consider it a necessity instead of a luxury."[32]

The Progressive Dream

All the same, American women of the Progressive Era shared an environment throbbing with possibility. For, though their world scandalized and oppressed them with economic injustices and corporate wrongdoing and afforded many of them neither longevity nor good health, they believed in the possibility of changing it. The most popular books they read reflected their optimism: Eleanor Hodgman Porter's *Pollyanna*; the cheery-minded works of Gene Stratton Porter; and Russell Conwell's *Acres of Diamonds*, which, in addition to preaching the divine right of property, insisted that opportunity awaits in one's own backyard. Stories in union publications fantasized about enterprising young women who worked their way out of their factory jobs into the pink-collar or even the professional class.[33]

Above all, women of the time believed in progress, the uneven but sustained upward movement of the human race. They could change the environment and, by changing it, change people. Never given to abiding quietly the evils of life, Americans responded to muckraking with campaigns to alleviate or abolish the evils brought to light. They fought for legislation to punish the evildoers and prevent future wrongdoing. In "a rather widespread and remarkably good-natured effort of the greater part of society to achieve some not very clearly specified self-reformation," Americans tried "to restore a type of economic individualism and political democracy that was widely believed to have existed earlier in America and to have been destroyed by the great corporation and the corrupt political machine."[34] Filling lecture halls, Chautauqua tents, and Grange, lodge, and club meetings with talk of morality and reform, they fashioned the Progressive Era in the first two decades of the 20th century.[35]

American women, for long years imaged as the guardians of virtue and morality, and at this juncture stepping out of their homes to improve public housekeeping, had special reason to feel that by exercising their much-touted influence they could clean up the messes men had made. Mothers would improve children and, equally important, the environment in which those children lived. Settlement workers and clubwomen all over the nation believed that they could cleanse their municipal, state, and federal houses to upgrade the quality of life. Women workers turned to unions and the National Women's Trade Union League to fight for better wages and working conditions. Black women, victims of both racial and gender prejudice, sought upward mobility through education, migration, and mutual support.

American women in the early 20th century took peace pretty much for granted. They could overlook Britain's Boer War, the insurrections in the Philippines, and the Boxer Rebellion as extraneous. In the United States itself peace had reigned for 35 years. And, aside from the aberration of the four-month-long empire-building Spanish-American War, the United States had not involved itself in any foreign war for more than 80 years. Indeed, the more hopeful among them believed that Western civilization had progressed beyond the barbarities of war.

Prosperity, though coyly retreating in depressions like that of 1893-94, infused their dreams. America was famously the land of opportunity. No immigrant so alien, no black woman so downtrodden that she did not know of someone who had improved her lot. After all, the president of the United States himself, Theodore Roosevelt, the apostle of affirmation, optimism, and progress, inveighed against plutocrats, endorsed reforms, and preached the good news of progress and hope. With America's conscience awakened, the idea surged abroad in the land that government bears a responsibility to equalize opportunity, to help the poor and underprivileged.

Roosevelt's message was echoed in the social gospel of the major Protestant denominations. Protestant Christianity dominated among middle-and upper-class whites and almost all black Americans. Many of these Protestants associated Roman Catholicism with Irish politicians and housemaids or with the other immigrants flooding into the United States from southern and eastern Europe, with their strange, almost "heathen" ways. In American small towns, Protestant evangelists still conducted emotion-charged revivals, which Mary Austin described as "acute emotional crises" in which people proclaimed themselves "saved": "It was possible to feel through the whole community the ground swell of its disturbances. Night after night the people poured in . . . to be flayed in spirit, stripped, agonized, exalted at the hands of a practised evangelist, which they *liked*."[36]

Women joined in the awe of specialization, professionalization, and expertise that characterized the period. Qualified doctors, not midwives, were to birth babies. Child development experts were to tell mothers how to nurture them, and home economists to teach mothers how to cook for them. Specially trained and licensed teachers were to educate them. Scientists were to save them from bacteria and neuroses. And trained social workers were to extricate them from other troubles. When the babies grew up and went to work in factories, machines and the engineering of the assembly line would simplify their work, and efficiency experts would show them how to do it faster. Oh brave new world!

Housewives, most of whom remained amateurs despite the reams of advice specialists directed at them, found their households changing. They were having fewer children, and the ones they had were attending school longer. "The woman who married in the first decade of the twentieth century could expect to spend at least five years less caring for children than had her counterpart a century earlier and to live at least ten years longer."[37] Grown daughters now often expected to work outside the home until they married. Hired girls and cleaning ladies and laundresses and cooks were leaving for more interesting, more sociable, and better-paid jobs. Housewives themselves were less and less expected to produce, and more and more counted on to consume.

The Shifting Lives of Women

To counteract the loneliness created by the departure, at least for the daylight hours, of so many husbands, children, and servants, housewives themselves spent more of their time away from home. Socialized to form most of their personal relationships with other women, they turned naturally to their networks of women friends, which, by 1900, they had often formalized into organizations. Many women centered their social lives around their churches and Sunday school classes. Others filled their leisure with club work. In either case, they might volunteer their services to enact all sorts of reforms. Or they might dedicate their hours away from home to a favorite cause, like temperance or woman suffrage—or go shopping.

In any case, the society continued to look to them to preserve the moral order.[38] It certainly held them responsible for the conduct of their children. It even insisted that women—with their lesser temptations than those faced by the stronger sex and their natural and innate virtue—really ought to bear at least part of the responsibility for the way their menfolk comported themselves. "It has always seemed to me," confesses the male protagonist of a popular 1918 novel, "that women have— or *ought* to have!—the sort of spiritual guardianship of the world—the keys of heaven, you might say; so that through the love they give us and the love they make us give them, we find our best selves and—and— try to do better than we could ever have done alone."[39]

But standing on this pedestal was something of a strain for a mother. In 1914 Ruth S. True commented:

> *She is held to a rigorous standard which neither husband nor children are required to measure up to. We expect her to counteract the difficulties and evil influences of her environment by possessing all the known virtues of character. As a matter of fact, the worry and strain of insecurity become too great for many a woman. She grows apathetic, careless, and stolid, or she becomes querulous and neurotic. Perhaps she takes to drink.*[40]

And now and then the realities wore thin the facade of women's innocence. Clarice Richards, who described herself as a "tenderfoot bride," told a story of a cowboy so embarrassed at having inadvertently sworn in front of her that he went on a three-day drunk.[41] But Elinore Pruitt Stewart described the frustration of a man who couldn't make his team move because the presence of women precluded his swearing:

> *Mrs. O'Shaughnessy said, "Don't lay your poor driving to the women. If you drive by cussin', then* cuss. *We will stop up our ears." She threw her apron over her head. I held my fingers in Jerrine's ears, and she stopped my ears, else I might be able to tell you what he said. It was something violent, I know. I could tell by the expression of his face. He had only been doing it a second when those horses walked right out with the wagon as nicely as you please. Mrs. O'Shaughnessy said to Mr. Haynes, "It's a poor cusser you are. Sure, it's no wonder you hesitated to begin. If Danny O'Shaughnessy couldn't have sworn better, I'd have had to hilp him."*[42]

Those American women employed in gainful occupations also found their working lives shifting. Gradually new occupations and professions were opening to them (though male physicians and surgeons, startled by the presence of 7,399 women doctors in 1900, began a backlash against them). By 1900, some women were working in almost all occupations counted in the census.

Throughout the Progressive Era, more and more women took jobs away from home. Almost always, the newly employed women were taking new jobs created by economic growth or by technologic change; seldom, despite male trepidations, were women displacing men in the work force. In the elegant and prospering department stores, women cleaned and stocked the counters and clerked, but men floorwalked, supervised, and bought stock. The male office clerks of the 19th century could reasonably hope for promotion into management. The women typists and stenographers and secretaries who flooded into offices with the adoption of the typewriter and other office machines continued to type and file throughout their working days. Female telephone operators kept on providing the voice with the smile.

Most of women's new jobs, like the old, missed even the bottom rung of the ladder of upward mobility. Except for professional women, entrepreneurs, actresses, artists, and other mavericks, most working women during the Progressive Era labored at jobs with severely limited prospects—though the fiction printed in labor-union publications seemed designed to fill their heads with dreams of glory. Almost everyone assumed that women sought gainful employment only for the short term, until they married—an assumption that ignored the plight of the many black wives who worked, the wives of all races whose husbands needed help in supporting the family, the deserted wives, the women who never married, and the widows left without resources. Most of the groups that tried to help working women focused on improving safety, the work environment, job security, and better pay. Only the professional organizations spoke to the career needs of their own members.

So the Progressive Era saw many struggles, some successful, to restrict the hours of factory "girls" and to provide them with cleaner, safer places to work—especially after the holocaust of the 1911 Triangle Shirtwaist Factory fire, which killed 146 women locked in their dangerous, crowded sewing rooms. Horrors like that won public sympathy for the factory women banding into unions and public support for their strikes.

Throughout the Progressive Era, that heyday of organizing, professional women also united. Moves toward professional women's organizations usually followed a period of frustration in working through the well-established, male-dominated professional association. Women doctors, for example, organized separately only during World War I, when the American Medical Association watched blandly as the U. S. military rejected women physicians or offered them only secondary status as "contract physicians." Women librarians, who formed the great bulk of the membership of the American Library Association, never did break away. Their male officers rewarded their loyalty by contemptuously discouraging their World War I offers to work in military camps and overseas.

In any case, from 1900 to 1920, professional organizations emphasized licensing and professionalization. Partly out of concern for proper training in social work, teaching, or nursing, partly for the sake of status, partly for economic motives, they constructed elaborate hurdles for entry and promotion. More and more they claimed for themselves territory previously peopled by amateurs.

College-educated amateurs sometimes went on for graduate training in one of the professions, engaged in club work, or, often, spent some time as residents in settlement houses in situations that allowed them to hold paying jobs or to volunteer full-time for settlement work. In either case these residencies introduced them to the people and life-styles of other economic classes, provided them with remarkable women role models and mentors, and involved them in a network of knowledgeable, experienced social reformers.

Some of these college graduates, as well as other middle-class and well-off young women, were presenting society with a new cause for handwringing in the shape of the "New Woman," who emerged about 1890.[43] She was quintessentially American, a type unique to the United States. Swimming, horseback riding, golf, and tennis strengthened her body and her self-confidence. The popularity of the bicycle liberated her from her corset, shortened her skirts or clad her in bloomers, and made her mobile, free to roam through the countryside without waiting for papa's horses.[44] With more formal education than her mother, the New Woman asserted her independence.

Secure in the belief that she could earn her own living, she insisted on the freedom to conduct herself socially as she saw fit. Although only the most advanced American women smoked and drank in public, the New Woman enjoyed comradeship with young men, without benefit of chaperones. She thought her opinions worth listening to, and she considered it her duty to influence the political system. She formed personal ambitions—Helen Hooven Santmyer's college friends in *Herbs and Apples* swear a "solemn oath: 'Down with Matrimony, up with Art, Fame before Forty or bust!'"[45]

The New Woman insisted centrally on the right to live and breathe as a separate human being. "I bet I never finish on any ole gravestone as 'also Rheta, wife of the above,'" boasted the young Rheta Childe Dorr to a boy cousin.[46] And Kate Chopin's protagonist Edna in *The Awakening* dared to proclaim: "I would give up my life for my children, but not my self."

Contrast the New Woman with the 19th-century "True Woman" of whom American males dreamed: innocent, helpless, eager to please, morally strong but physically weak, displaying her virtue in willing self-sacrifice and ready acceptance of suffering—particularly labor pains. Contrast the New Woman with the 19th-century woman who took pride in immolating herself on the altar of motherhood: "I never spent a night outside my home after my first child came until you grew up. I don't see how any true woman could bear to do it."[47] Consider the rejection of "True Womanhood" implicit in the story of the young student at the Misses Fenimore Cooper's school who later became Grace Root. She participated in a coeducational ice-hockey game between her school and a boys' school, in which to compensate for their physical differences the girls wore skates but the boys didn't. Grace discovered one of her teammates cheating and physically attacked her. The Misses Fenimore Cooper sighed when they reproached Grace: "Your mother was a lady, and your sister was a lady, but we very much fear that you are no lady." To this Grace replied, "And what is it to be a lady?"[48]

But the New Woman still held claim to the superior moral insight with which legend had long endowed American women. And she did not necessarily reject matrimony—though she wanted a "companionate" (companionable) marriage rather than a patriarchal one.

"TOO MUCH DIRTY, NASTY INDEPENDENCE." AN "EMANCIPATED WOMAN" EXERCISING HER FREEDOM IN THE SMOKING CAR OF AN EARLY 1900 TRAIN. (NATIONAL ARCHIVES)

The New Woman's admirers praised her healthy attractiveness, her independence, her strong-mindedness, and her zest for living. Her detractors accused her of egotism, selfishness, self-assertion, and "too much dirty, nasty independence."[49] Where, they asked, was woman's proper spirit of self-sacrifice? Margaret Deland, in many respects so open-minded, worried about the New Woman:

> This young person—a wholesome, lovable creature with surprisingly bad manners—has gone to college, and when she graduates she is going to earn her own living, and declines to be dependent upon a father and mother amply able to support her. She will do settlement work; she won't go to church; she has views upon marriage and the birth-rate, and she utters them calmly, while her mother blushes with embarrassment; and occupies herself, passionately, with everything except the things that used to occupy the minds of girls.[50]

And Caroline Ticknor ironically hailed the New Woman: "Behold she comes apace! Woman once man's superior, now his equal!"[51]

As late as 1920, with the Woman Suffrage Amendment already passed, the *Ladies' Home Journal* was trying to control the New Woman by prescribing a credo for her:

> *I believe in woman's rights; but I believe in woman's sacrifices also.*
> *I believe in woman's freedom; but I believe it should be within the*
>   *restrictions of the Ten Commandments.*
> *I believe in woman's suffrage; but I believe many other things are vastly*
>   *more important.*
> *I believe in woman's brains; but I believe still more in her emotions.*[52]

Obviously the role of full-fledged New Woman was reserved for a relatively few women privileged by birth, education, luck, or their own endeavors. But the much-touted and talked-about symbol of the New Woman both reflected and created new modes of conduct in the society at large. Fashion took cognizance of her physically active life. After 1900 the working class provided its own breed of new women, as immigrant women from eastern Europe brought with them the radical traditions that prepared them for militant activism in unions and woman suffrage.[53] Factory girls demanded a measure of the New Woman's freedom in their few hours of playtime. Suburban housewives, especially after the purchase of their first family cars, claimed her liberty to roam the countryside. Staid and conservative clubwomen shared some of her social concerns.

All over the United States women were stepping out of their homes into club work and volunteer services, into reform movements, into new work for pay, into

PROGRESSIVE ERA MALES (LIKE THEIR GREAT-GRANDSONS) PUZZLED ABOUT WHAT WOMEN *REALLY* WANT.   (POSTCARD OF 1911, COLLECTION OF BETTY PIERSON)

politics and the marketplace. They were casting aside the limitations that had restricted their activities. Not abandoning their earlier selves, they were exercising their identities as women in larger realms. No longer confined to the private sphere, they now used their legendary powers of moral suasion and their social consciences in the public domain. Breathing the hope and optimism of the age, confident in their own abilities, they marched into the first two decades of the 20th century.

Source Notes

1. Annie Clark Tanner, *A Mormon Mother: An Autobiography* (Salt Lake City: Tanner Trust Fund, Univ. of Utah, 1976).
2. Helen Hooven Santmyer, *Herbs and Apples* (New York: St Martin's, 1987), p. 6.
3. Jacqueline Jones, *Labor of Love, Labor of Sorrow: Black Women, Work, and the Family from Slavery to the Present* (New York: Vintage, 1986), p. 90.
4. Boyden Sparkes and Samuel Taylor Moore, *The Witch of Wall Street: Hetty Green* (Garden City, N.Y.: Doubleday, Doran and Co., 1935).
5. Sharon Niederman, *A Quilt of Words: Women's Diaries, Letters and Original Accounts of Life in the Southwest, 1860–1960* (Boulder, Colo.: Johnson Books, 1988), pp. 106ff.
6. Stephen Birmingham, *The Grandes Dames* (New York: Simon and Schuster, 1982), p. 233.
7. Conversation with Rhoda Jenkins, daughter of Nora Stanton Blatch Barney, September 1991.
8. The Helen May Butler collection is in the Smithsonian Institution's Museum of American History Archives.
9. Joan M. Jensen, "Native American Women and Agriculture: A Seneca Case Study," in Ellen Carol DuBois and Vicki L. Ruiz, eds., *Unequal Sisters: A Multicultural Reader in U.S. Women's History* (New York: Routledge, 1990), p. 51.
10. May Wynne Lamb, *My Life in Alaska: The Reminiscences of a Kansas Woman, 1916–1919*, ed. Dorothy Wynne Zimmerman (Lincoln: Univ. of Nebraska Press, 1988), pp. 11–13.
11. AAA Tour Book for New York, valid through April 1988, p. 86.
12. Information provided by her daughter-in-law, Phoebe White Wentworth, courtesy of Marian Schneider Clayton.
13. Vern Bullough and Bonnie Bullough, *The Care of the Sick: The Emergence of Modern Nursing* (New York: Prodist [a division of Neale Watson Academic Publications], 1978), p. 152.

14. Helen Hooven Santmyer, " . . . *and Ladies of the Club"* New York: Putnam's, 1984), pp. 845–46. See also James D. Hart, *The Popular Book: A History of America's Literary Taste* (Berkeley: Univ. of California Press, 1963), p. 228.

15. *American Homes and Gardens* (November 1905), p. 334, quoted in Margaret Marsh, *Surburban Lives* (New Brunswick, N.J.: Rutgers Univ. Press, 1990), p. 69.

16. *Madeleine: An Autobiography* (New York: Harper and Bros., 1919), pp. 114–15.

17. Margaret Deland, "The Change in the Feminine Ideal," *Atlantic Monthly* 105 (March 1910):299.

18. Hart, p. 180.

19. Irene B. Taeuber and Conrad Taeuber, *People of the United States in the Twentieth Century* (Washington, D.C.: Bureau of the Census, 1971).

20. Richard W. Wertz and Dorothy C. Wertz, *Lying-in: A History of Child-birth in America* (New York: Free Press, 1970), p. 155. Ten percent of white babies and 20 percent of black babies died before age one. Steven Mintz and Susan Kellogg, *Domestic Revolutions: A Social History of American Family Life* (New York: Free Press, 1988), p. 104.

21. Elizabeth G. Stern, *My Mother and I* (1917; reprint, New York: Macmillan, 1941), p. 55.

22. Joan M. Jensen, ed., *With These Hands: Women Working on the Land* (Old Westbury, N.Y.: Feminist Press; New York: McGraw-Hill, 1981), p. 172.

23. Elizabeth Corey, *Bachelor Bess: The Homesteading Letters of Elizabeth Corey, 1909–1919*, ed. Philip L. Gerber (Iowa City: Univ. of Iowa Press, 1990), p. 121.

24. Sidney Ditzion, *Marriage, Morals and Sex in America: A History of Ideas* (New York: Octagon Books, 1969), p. 208.

25. Emma Frances Angell Drake, M.D., *What a Young Wife Ought to Know* (Philadelphia: Vir, 1902), p. 29.

26. Charles A. Le Guin, ed., *A Home-Concealed Woman: The Diaries of Magnolia Wynn Le Guin, 1901–1913* (Athens: Univ. of Georgia Press, 1990), p. 363.

27. Wertz and Wertz, p. 55.

28. Le Guin, p. 77.

29. Herbert E. Buffum, Ira Warren, William Thorndike, A. T. Lovering, A. E. Small, J. Heber Smith, and Charles P. Lyman, *The Household Physician: A Twentieth Century Medica* (Boston: Woodruff, 1905, 1919), pp. 459, 479. Cited hereafter as *The Household Physician.*

30. Joan Jacobs Brumberg, "Chlorotic Girls, 1870–1920: A Historical Perspective on Female Adolescence," in Judith Walzer Leavitt, ed., *Women and Health in America: Historical Readings* (Madison: Univ. of Wisconsin Press, 1984).

31. *The Household Physician*, p. 1150.

32. *The Household Physician*, pp. 1152–53.

33. Hart, p. 210. Cf. Dorothy Richardson, *The Long Day: The Story of a New York Working Girl* (1905; reprint, Charlottesville: Univ. Press of Virginia, 1990), pp. 90ff.

34. Richard Hofstadter, *The Age of Reform, from Bryan to F.D.R.* (New York: Vintage Books, 1955), pp. 5–6.

35. For the popular educational and entertainment programs of Chautauqua, see p. 95.

36. Mary Austin, *A Woman of Genius* (1912; reprint, Old Westbury, N.Y.: Feminist Press, 1985), p. 31.

37. Nancy Woloch, *Women and the American Experience* (New York: Knopf, 1984), p. 272.

38. See, for example, Mrs. Theodore Birney, "The Twentieth-Century Girl: What We Expect of Her," *Harper's Bazaar* 33 (May 26, 1900):227; Edith Summers Kelley, *Weeds* (1923; reprint Carbondale and Edwardsville: Southern Illinois Univ. Press, 1972), p. 136; Margaret F. Byington, *Homestead, The Households of a Mill Town* (1910; reprint, Pittsburgh: The University Center for International Studies, Univ. of Pittsburgh, 1974), p. 109; and Marion Harland, *The Distractions of Martha* (New York: Scribners, 1906), pp. 100–101.

39. Clara E. Laughlin, *The Keys of Heaven* (New York: George H. Doran, 1918), p. 48.

40. Ruth S. True, *The Neglected Girl* (New York: Survey Associates, 1914), pp. 26–27.

41. Clarice E. Richards, *A Tenderfoot Bride: Tales from an Old Ranch* (1920; reprint, Lincoln: Univ. of Nebraska Press, 1988), pp. 81–82.

42. Elinore Pruitt Stewart, *Letters on an Elk Hunt by a Woman Homesteader* (1915; reprint, Lincoln: Univ. of Nebraska Press, 1979), pp. 125–26.

43. Woloch, p. 269.

44. Of course women who participated in sports faced criticism. Basketball players scandalized some with their bloomers, even though these were so full that no division ever appeared however strenuous the game. And, as Elizabeth Hampsten notes, "some anti-feminists claimed women chiefly rode in order to masturbate, and in some areas women bicyclists were harassed by police for minor traffic violations." *Read This Only to Yourself: The Private Writings of Midwestern Women, 1880–1910* (Bloomington: Indiana Univ. Press, 1982), p. 220.

45. Santmyer, *Herbs and Apples,* p. 221.

46. Rheta Childe Dorr, *A Woman of Fifty* (1924; reprint, New York: Arno Press, 1980), p. 5.

47. Ellen Glasgow, *Virginia* (Garden City, N.Y.: Doubleday, Page and Co., 1913), p. 265.

48. Personal conversation between Mrs. Edward Root and the authors.
49. Martha Farnsworth, *Plains Woman: The Diary of Martha Farnsworth, 1882–1922*, ed. Marlene Springer and Haskell Springer (Bloomington: Indiana Univ. Press, 1988), p. 145.
50. Deland, "Change in the Feminine Ideal," p. 291.
51. Caroline Ticknor, "The Steel-Engraving Lady and the Gibson Girl," *Atlantic Monthly* 88 (1901), 108.
52. *Ladies' Home Journal*, August 1920, p. 191.
53. Sara M. Evans, *Born for Liberty: A History of Women in America* (New York: Free Press, 1989), p. 158.

CHAPTER 2

Women at Work: Housekeeping, Homemaking, and Mothering

Whether or not they worked for pay, almost all American women in the Progressive Era, as now, did housework. The young single women who predominated in the female paid labor force usually lived at home and were expected to help their mothers keep house—though their brothers were not. Employed married women as a matter of course did "their" housework early in the morning, late at night, and on their one day "off."[1] So did employed widows and other single heads of household.

Most of the almost 14 million married women, the 1900 census report states, did not work for pay. With some discomfort the report notes that the census did not count the farm labor of farmers' wives. Neither did it take into account the hundreds of thousands of poor women who took in boarders, sewing, and washing. Nor, one supposes, did it tally the miners' wives who "sometimes helped their husbands at the mines by clerking and even freighting and shoveling gravel at the sluices."[2] The ethic of the time shaped the census report. No matter what else they in fact did, in the eyes of society the chief business of married women was keeping house.[3]

The Help-less Housewife

Some of these women, the affluent and middle-class minority, had help— though not as many as one might suppose. Never in American history could as many as half the families afford full-time servants; by the turn of the century the numbers of household workers had already dropped dramatically, and they kept on dropping throughout the Progressive Era—as measured against the female nonagricultural labor force, the numbers fell by more than 15 percentage points between 1900 and 1920.[4] In the 1900 population of about 75 million, "only" about 1 million women were in domestic service, as maids, laundresses, cooks, companions, waitresses, and nurses.[5] About one household in 10 had live-in servants, and seven out of 10 housewives did their own work.[6] Middle-class housewives were more apt to employ part-time rather than full-time help.

Native-born white Americans looking for jobs didn't take kindly to domestic service, especially after the big waves of immigration in the 19th century, usually accepting it only as a temporary measure or a last resort. In 1900 only 26 percent of women so employed were native-born whites; 28 percent were foreign born, and another 19 percent the daughters of immigrants; and 27 percent were black.[7] As their ranks decreased from 1900 to 1920, with more industrialization and less immigration, the proportions of black and of married women servants rose. For many married women, some form of domestic service was the only option: It was what they knew how to do. So in 1910 married women constituted 55 percent of the janitors, 51 percent of the laundresses, and 39 percent of servants.[8]

All that is really just a way of saying that more and more throughout the Progressive Era only the most disadvantaged women would accept jobs as servants. And even they managed to assert themselves enough to insist on their right to their own lives and families, often refusing to live in the homes of their employers. Numbers of them undertook "day work"—

VALENTINE GREETINGS

MISS FITT DRESSMAKER

When the dressmaker comes for a stay,
She is generally paid by the day;
    She'll ruin a skirt,
    "Fits well," she'll assert,—
Gives excuses galore for delay!

MIDDLE-CLASS WOMEN WHO "DID ALL THEIR OWN WORK" OFTEN RELIED ON SEAMSTRESSES, LAUNDRESSES, AND CLEANING LADIES WHO CAME IN BY THE DAY.
(1908 POSTCARD, COLLECTION OF BETTY PIERSON)

as entrepreneurs they hired themselves out to different employers for a day or two a week, with increasing independence and control over their own schedules.

Their potential employers usually "just couldn't understand" the servant shortage. An incident at the General Federation of Women's Clubs' 1906 convention revealed the gulf between housewife and maid when a clubwoman rose to ask why, if conditions in factories were so bad, women wouldn't "come into our homes and work. We pay good wages, give them their room and board, and yet we have difficulty in getting enough help to run our houses!" Labor organizer Josephine Casey sharply responded: "If the clubwomen are not capable of running their own homes, why do they expect the working girls to do it for them?"[9] And when the Boston Women's Educational and Industrial Union members in 1897 concocted a plan to turn factory workers into domestic servants, a plan that, they reasoned, would benefit working women and give themselves servants, they found only *one* taker.[10]

The truth of the matter was that many middle-class housewives couldn't pay enough to get the polished service they dreamed of. In the sellers' market, these housewives had to put up with high turnover, sloppiness, "disrespect," and sudden departures at critical moments. A young husband in Marion Harland's novel *The Distractions of Martha* voiced the desperation of many a housewife when he described servants as "Arabs, or rather, Ishmaelites—predatory bands, their hands against employers—not working with, and for them for the common good."[11]

The clubwomen's puzzlement was genuine. After all, they told each other, we offer these "girls" nice homes and good wages—more than they can get in factories and stores. Objectively, the housewives' arguments had some truth, sometimes. As Rheta Childe Dorr reported in 1910,

> *A girl totally ignorant of the art of cooking, of any household art, one whose function is to clean, scrub, and assist her employer to prepare meals, can readily command ten dollars a month, with board. . . . The wages of a competent houseworker, in any part of the country, average over eighteen dollars a month. Add to this about thirty dollars a month represented by food, lodging, light, and fire, and you will see that the competent houseworker's yearly income amounts to five hundred and seventy- six dollars. This is a higher average than the school-teacher or the stenographer receives; it is almost double the average wage of the shop girl, or the factory girl. It is, in fact, about as high as the usual income of the American workingman.*[12]

But to the domestics' way of thinking these wages did not compensate for longer hours of work, loss of control over their personal lives, and a low-status job. The houses the domestics worked in might be nice enough, but the servants' quarters ranged from the comfortable to the hideously makeshift, usually with minimal privacy and almost certainly with no place except the kitchen—if that—to entertain. Maids slept on ironing boards propped over bathtubs, on mattresses laid over basement washtubs, on pallets spread on dining-room tables.

To the housewives' assertion that they trained their servants for marriage, one former servant countered:

> *The domestic . . . don't take the pride in her home that the shop-girl does. She has lived in such fine houses that her small tenement has no beauty for her after the first glow of married life is over. She don't try either to make her home attractive or herself, and gets discouraged, and is apt to make a man disheartened with her, and then I think she is extravagant. She has so much to do with before she is married and so little to do with after she don't know how to manage. She can't have tenderloin steak for her breakfast and rump roast for her dinner, and pay the rent and all other bills out of $12 a week—and that is the average man's pay, the kind of man we girls that work for a living get.*[13]

From the worker's point of view, who needed a job with excruciatingly long hours, no prestige, often no colleagues, and the boss peering critically over one's shoulder? By repute, and probably in fact, servants endured even more and even worse sexual harassment than other working women, the sons and sometimes the fathers of the household treating them as wanton women. From their ranks emerged more prostitutes than from any other "trade."[14] Their own families were ashamed of their jobs. Factory women snubbed them.

Rose Cohen described the psychological trauma of domestic service in a book that purported to recount her own experiences:

> *I realised that though in the shop too I had been driven, at least there I had not been alone. I had been a worker among other workers who looked upon me as an equal and a companion. . . . The evening was mine and I was at home with my own people. Often I could forget the shop altogether for a time, while as a servant my home was a few hard chairs and two soiled quilts [on which she slept in the kitchen]. My every hour was sold, night and day. I had to be constantly in the presence of people who looked down upon me as an inferior.*[15]

As Ruth Cowan has observed, "The dark satanic mills did not look nearly so dark or nearly so satanic to young women who knew what it was like to work in some of America's dark satanic kitchens."[16]

By 1920 the servant question no longer dominated the thoughts of middle-class housewives. Expectations had come into line with realities: In most parts of the country, the source of supply had dried up. Except in the Southeast, with its black domestics, and in the Southwest, with its Chicanas, most women no longer counted on household help, beyond perhaps a weekly cleaning lady or laundress. They worried less about cooks and more about gas or electric stoves.

Joy Through Household Machinery?

Though it would overstate the case to say that household machines either displaced or replaced servants, certainly industrialization was transforming housework—by 1900 in the cities, the suburbs, and some small towns an improved water supply, better sewerage, and modern plumbing were making life easier, though in most homes water heaters, bathtubs, and sinks were still to come.

Running water, a standard convenience in urban households, even in some tenements, certainly lessened what had been the gargantuan toil of doing the weekly wash. And in middle-class homes people were beginning to hitch motors to washing machines, powered by the electricity that was already lighting some houses and operating telephones. Better still, by 1900 many housewives, including even some of the poor, used the commercial laundries that in cities and in many suburban and rural areas were offering options from wet wash to fully finished laundry.

Electricity, of course, made a big difference in all kinds of household tasks. Its cost fell markedly in the first two decades of the century—far below prices abroad. Although by 1907 only eight percent of American houses were wired for electricity, 35 percent were by 1920. By 1910 electric toasters, irons, and hot water urns were becoming popular. From that year on, vacuum cleaners and all-of-a-piece electric washing machines came on the market, and by 1917 electric refrigerators and dishwashers— though these last cost too much for most folks.[17] In 1912 in Kansas Martha Farnsworth, wife of a post office clerk, exulted: "I used my new 'suction sweeper' this morning . . . ; in thirty minutes I had gotten about a bushel of dirt—(more or less, but any way, enough to astonish one) from under the carpets, and wore out the muscles of my back and shoulders and made myself lame in great shape."[18]

Most women still cooked on coal or wood stoves in 1900, though petroleum refiners were beginning to give away or sell at low prices kerosene and gasoline stoves. All the same, the cooks' tasks of food preparation were easier, and maybe more fun, than their mothers' had been. By 1900 women in most parts of America could buy commercially produced flour (for those who still baked their own bread), commercially butchered meat, and commercially canned foods, including peas, corn, tomatoes, peaches, and condensed soup. In fact, 10 years earlier the Franco-American Company had already offered them canned meals. They also had a choice of packaged dry cereals, factory-made biscuits, pancake mixes, commercially baked crackers and cookies, canned hams, and bottled

The Hard Way

Pick over the beans the day before, and soak them over night.

Boil them next day in two waters — not less than an hour and a half. Then bake them three hours.

One must keep the stove going full blast half a day — just for a dish of beans. It's about as much trouble as roasting a turkey.

Then serve the beans before they sour — the sooner the better. And serve them until they're used up.

When beans are wanted again, repeat the 16-hour process of soaking, boiling and baking.

That is the old way—the hard way.

One might as well spin her own linen, weave her own carpets, make her own soap— as they did in the olden days.

The Easy Way

Take the can from the shelf and pour the beans on a plate. Put the slice of pork on top.

The meal can be served in a jiffy.

If you want the beans hot, heat the can before opening. They'll taste then as though they came direct from the oven.

Keep a dozen cans on hand—a dozen meals always ready. When guests drop in unexpectedly there's something good to serve.

Three to five meals a week—among the best meals you have — are thus prepared without any trouble.

A skilful chef has done all the work for you, and it costs less to employ him than to do it yourself.

That is the Van Camp way.

FREE AT LAST! HOUSEWIVES IN THEIR THOUSANDS TOOK THE EASY WAY.

(ADVERTISEMENT FOR CANNED PORK AND BEANS)

corned beef. No longer need they churn butter or make cheese. Sears Roebuck mailed rural customers a 32-page grocery list with price revisions every 60 days, so that they could mail order some of their food. Refrigerated cars transported fruits and vegetables from the West Coast inland and eastward and carried oysters from the Atlantic to midwestern church socials.

But if all these products simplified cooking, the tendency toward a more varied diet complicated it. Industrialization had made it perfectly possible to feed the family with much-reduced effort, but out of pride, preference, or thrift some women committed as many hours to food preparation as their mothers, as they catered to increasingly sophisticated family tastes.

Shopping was complicated. Though chain stores were gradually opening, they didn't carry meat or vegetables. About 1900 a Massachusetts doctor's wife had to deal with a butcher, a fishmonger, an egg man, a milk man, a "provisioner" (for apples, butter, meats, potatoes), and S. S. Pierce.[19]

And people who could afford to ate a lot. The middle-class housewife had to provide big breakfasts, lunches for those children and fathers who came home, and four-course dinners. If she entered the popular competition for elaborate entertaining, demands on her time and skills multiplied—along with her desperate search for household help.

If they could afford it, women could reduce their household labors by buying commercially-made clothing. Though men's clothing was mass-produced well before women's, the advent and popularity of the shirtwaist and separate skirt early in the 20th century made fitting easier. By 1910 every article of women's clothing was available ready-made, in styles and prices to fit most purses. Although the Sears Roebuck catalog of 1894 displayed not a single item of women's clothing, by 1920 it featured no less than 90 illustrated pages. At-home "sewing of men's clothing was gone, roughly speaking, by 1880, of women's and children's outerwear by 1900, and finally of almost all items of clothing for all members of the family by 1920."[20] The electric sewing machine, it turned out, more often sent garment making out of the house than contributed to its ease at home. For a time "hand-sewing was no longer admired. On dresses and underwear it was a confession that one could not afford a sewing machine"—or "boughten" clothes.[21]

As housewives sewed less, and as they had the option of cooking less, they also found themselves relieved of much of the burden of health care. The tasks of concocting remedies (no longer did cookbooks include recipes for medicines), nursing the seriously ill, and laying out the dead were gradually being taken over by professionals. Between 1900 and 1920 the number of hospital beds doubled.[22] Improved training was professionalizing nursing. During the Progressive Era nurses gradually assumed responsibility, not only for the care of individual patients, but for health education and for many improvements in public health.

Did women of the Progressive Era then enjoy a life freer of household cares than their mothers had known? Probably, some of them did, but by no means all.

For one thing, these changes occurred very gradually and at different rates in different regions and different economic classes.[23] Many a countrywoman or small-town housewife, with or without the help of a hired girl, not only cared for her large family, but also still made their clothes and their bedding and their carpets, gardened and canned, raised chickens, kept cows, and sold milk and eggs to supplement the family income. Women like her nursed their own families and helped others in emergencies, acted as midwives, and laid out the dead.

For another, as industrialization eased household tasks, standards rose. Middle-class houses were cleaner than they had been in the Victorian era, diets were more varied, and clothes, table linen, and bed linen more frequently laundered.

Partly in consequence, cleaning tasks burdened the housewife ever more heavily, as houses grew bigger and more people became accustomed to standards of cleanliness once possible only for the rich. She picked up some new tasks, too: Traditionally, for instance, men had dealt with the problems presented by outdoor privies; when toilets moved indoors (in *urban* areas at the end of the 19th century), women usually cleaned them.[24]

Increasingly, too, housewives assumed the tasks of transportation. When, just before World War I, the automobile began to displace human feet and horses' hooves, women began to displace men as household suppliers of transportation. The Lynds in their study of "Middletown, USA" (Muncie, Indiana) noted that in the 1890s only 125 families in that city owned a horse and buggy; by 1923, there was one car for every 6.1 persons, or two for every three families.[25] Accordingly, women more and more often used the car to run the family errands and move family members where they needed or wanted to go. All that driving might be fun, but it ate up the housewife's time.

And the housewife was more likely to be doing alone what her mother and grandmother had done with servants or with members of the extended family. All in all, the housewife probably put in about as many hours in 1920 as she had in 1900. If the family had prospered, she probably allocated her work time differently, ran a cleaner household, and "produced" better-fed, healthier children. But what she gained with the washing machine, she lost with bigger washes and the departure of the laundress. What she gained with the gas stove, she lost—or threw away—with more varied menus.

Who Cooks? Who Cleans? Who Babysits?

The Progressive Era explored a lot of ways to reduce the housewife's work that just didn't pan out—sometimes inexplicably. "By what art, what charm, what miracle," sharply inquired Charlotte Perkins Gilman in 1903, brooding on the burden of individual housework, "has the twentieth century preserved *alive* the prehistoric squaw!" And Zona Gale declared, "The private kitchen must go the way of the spinning wheel, of which it is the contemporary."[26]

For a while a multiplicity of plans, experiments, and innovations made it look as though most tasks traditionally performed by the housewife might follow sewing and the care of the sick outside the home or be transferred to paid workers employed by companies, as families moved to apartment hotels, boarding-houses, model tenements, or planned communities or experimented with communal kitchens and child care. Feminists eager to free women from housework and to have the housekeeper paid for her labors sponsored some of these experiments. Gilman advocated kitchenless houses, cleaned by trained maids from a housekeeping bureau, with prepared meals sent to the door from commercial kitchens. In 1893 at the Chicago World's Columbian Exposition, so important in establishing communications among American women, MIT professor Ellen Swallow Richards exhibited a model public kitchen. Thereafter the National Household Economics Association, founded at the exposition, wrote public kitchens in poor districts into its platform.[27]

Businesspeople too were thinking about ways to lighten the housewife's load. Commercial vacuum-cleaning services became available before World War I: Large compressors on horse-drawn carts would wheel up to the door, and their drivers would uncoil flexible tubing to run into the house. More successfully, commercial laundries catered to many Progressive Era households.

The electric washing machine (and eventually laundromats) killed off the use of commercial laundries for most individual households. But why did no business that promised the delivery of cooked food on a contractual basis last more than a decade? Why did apartment hotels, some with electric dumbwaiters that delivered two meals a day, fail to survive? Why did boardinghouses, counting many married folk in their clientele, flourish from 1900 to 1920, only to decline thereafter?

And what about that dream of progressivism, communal housekeeping? From the 1880s until the mid-1920s and beyond, community dining clubs, cooperative kitchens, and cooperative laundries appeared, but they usually lasted only a short time. Thousands of women and men experienced communal living in the more than 400 settlement houses throughout the nation. The Jane Clubs, initiated by bookbinder Mary Kenney and named in honor of Addams, offered eminently sensible and desperately needed cooperative boardinghouses for single women factory workers. In Chatfield, Minnesota, farm families for a while sent their wash to a cooperative laundry run in conjunction with a cooperative creamery.

Ellen Swallow Richards's New England Kitchen, an effort to provide wholesome food and teach good nutrition, failed in its original purpose because the immigrants whom it was intended to serve hated bland Yankee food. But why did the attempt of 40 socially prominent families in Evanston, Illinois, to set up an elaborate and well-funded arrangement to provide for cooperative cooking and laundry last only two months?[28] Why did the Cooperative Kitchen of Carthage, Missouri, last only four years? It started with the committed enthusiasm of men as well as women, when "an impatient husband, an ex-senator, challenged the ingenuity of the local women's [suffrage] group, by complaining [on behalf of] his wife: 'She is always cooking, or has just cooked, or is just going to cook, or is too tired from cooking. If there is a way out of this, with something to eat still in sight, for Heaven's sake, tell us!'" About 60 people met, rented a house, hired a manager and cooks, and agreed to pay $3 a week for each person over seven, $1.50 for each child under. Husbands at first rejoiced: "Never to hear a word about the servants that have just left, or are here, or are coming to-morrow— perhaps! . . . We're *in* Missouri and we're ready for anything." "A home for the Help-less." "I'm down as a life-member."[29]

Do Americans really value their privacy and the housewife's catering to individual tastes so much as to compensate for the enormous saving in time and effort that communal cooking, cleaning, and child care would effect?

No one knows with certainty the answers to these questions. Some scholars have blamed business, which had a stake in promoting single-family households so as to sell more vacuum cleaners and washing machines. Others have theorized that men insist on individual attention from their wives. Historian Ruth Schwartz Cowan believes that Americans opt for home-cooked meals and their own household appliances in the name of family life and family autonomy. And economist Juliet B. Schor argues that since for so long married women found it difficult to get jobs, their time and labor have been undervalued. "Commercial [household] services," she writes, "were too expensive in a situation where the housewife was restrained from earning cash to pay for them. By contrast, her labor had no monetary cost; to purchase what she could produce was a waste of a cheap resource."[30]

Life-styles of Housewives

Whatever the cause, most wives in the Progressive Era, as now, labored in their own households with whatever help they could hire or extract from their families. As Cowan has noted, "The industrialization of the household did not entail, as that of the market had, the centralization of all productive processes; the household continued to be the locale in which meals, clean laundry, healthy children, and well-fed adults were 'produced'—and housewives continued to be the workers who were principally responsible."[31]

What were their work lives like? Mrs. Middle-class Housewife might be married to a high-level clerk, a railroad conductor, a businessman, or a professional man.[32] She would have been born in the 1870s and borne her three children around 1900. About 1910 the family lived in a multistoried, rambling home, perhaps in or near a big city, perhaps in a rural town with a college or university nearby. They enjoyed an annual income of $1,000 to $3,500.

She ordinarily did not work for wages, though she might keep hens and sell eggs, take in an occasional boarder, give music or French lessons, or teach fancy needlework. Often what she didn't earn she at least partially compensated for in penny-pinching. She might garden, gather wild greens for the table, put up quantities of fruit, vegetables, and meat, turn her worn sheets (split them down the middle, sew the outside edges together, and hem the sides) and the collars and cuffs on her husband's shirts, hand down clothing from child to child, make her own soap from tallow, lard, lye, and ammonia, and do the family baking.

When such a woman spoke of herself as "doing all my own work," she usually meant only that she didn't employ a live-in maid. Rarely did she do all the heavy

Get the Washer Run by Gravity!

We have harnessed the Power of Gravity to the 1900 Washer. It is the Greatest Combination known for quick, cheap, easy washing. *The Washer almost runs itself!* In just six minutes it washes a tubful of clothes spotlessly clean. Over half a million housewives have tested this and *proved it.* So can you, without spending one cent! Here is the offer:

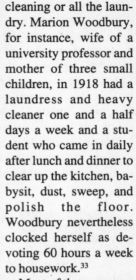

Washes a tubful in six minutes!

Washers Shipped FREE for 30 Days' Test

We make this offer to any reliable man or woman anywhere. We send the Washer by freight, at our expense and risk. That's because we absolutely *know* you will be as delighted with the Washer as the thousands who have tried it. Get one of these wonderful Washers and say "good bye" to the washboard forever. Good-bye to back-aches, worry and washday drudgery! Let Gravity Power do the *hard* work! Let the *Washer* cleanse the clothes! We sell the Washer on little payments—only 50 cents a week. It pays for itself in a hurry. Then works for you, *free for a lifetime!* Drop us a postal card for the Free Washer Book and tell us your nearest freight station. Send today. Address the

1900 WASHER CO.
592 Henry Street   BINGHAMTON, N. Y.
Canadian Address, 355 Yonge St., Toronto, Can.

FAREWELL TO WASHDAY BLUES!

(WASHING MACHINE ADVERTISEMENT OF 1910)

cleaning or all the laundry. Marion Woodbury, for instance, wife of a university professor and mother of three small children, in 1918 had a laundress and heavy cleaner one and a half days a week and a student who came in daily after lunch and dinner to clear up the kitchen, babysit, dust, sweep, and polish the floor. Woodbury nevertheless clocked herself as devoting 60 hours a week to housework.[33]

Most of these women probably started marriage cooking on a coal or wood stove and lit their houses with gas or kerosene. If they lived in the city, they probably had running water, which they heated in the reservoirs of their stoves; if they lived in towns or in the country, they might still have to pump well water. The design of their kitchens, with little or no counter space, cost them many a step, from the kitchen table, where they did much of their work, to the pantry, where they stored their dishes and food, back to the kitchen sink and stove. Though urban dwellers had iceboxes, countrywomen cooled their food in the well or in a cisternlike 10-foot-deep hole in the basement floor, into which a dumbwaiter with shelves was lowered and raised by a chain on a pulley.

Housework followed a strict daily and weekly routine. Every day required the conscientious housewife to dust, sweep, and make the beds—sometimes still featherbeds or even straw ticks. Monday she tackled the washing, perhaps trying to get the worst over early in the week. She might have a washing machine, most often hand powered, but even so she probably boiled the clothes before they went into the machine and transferred them to separate tubs for rinsing, at each stage wringing them with a hand wringer, and finally hung them out to dry. Tuesday she ironed—everything, in those natural-fabric days—with flatirons, with the handle cast in one piece and padded with a piece of blanket, or with a removable wooden handle. Wednesday she mended, Thursday she sewed, Friday she housecleaned, and Saturday she baked.

Gradually from 1900 on families added improvements that eased housework *or* made life more pleasant. Railroad conductor L. R. Dodge installed a bathroom in 1904 (most middle-class households had one by 1912), and in 1913 he bought a gas range and hitched it up to the gas main. By World War I, most middle-class families had central heating and electricity and were acquiring electric irons, vacuum cleaners, and fans.

These middle-class housewives didn't have to spend much of their time running errands. Marion Woodbury in 1918 phoned in her order for groceries, to be delivered to her door; she went to market only every other week. Laundries picked up and delivered. Deliverymen brought ice and milk to homes. Doctors made house calls. Knife sharpeners and pot menders peddled their services through neighborhood streets. Commuting husbands brought home needed items from the city to

THE TELEPHONE CONNECTED THE HOUSEWIFE WITH THE WORLD—AND THE GROCERY STORE.

(1911 POSTCARD, COLLECTION OF BETTY PIERSON)

suburban wives; some New York department stores arranged to leave telephone-ordered goods at Grand Central Station for husbands to collect and take home. Department stores in most cities delivered over a wide area and even picked up articles to be returned.

When they did visit the elaborately decorated department stores, ladies

> *could open Charge Accounts, have their clothing Cleaned and Dyed, and put their furs into Cold Storage. The store had its own Chiropodist, Dental Parlor, Electrolysist, Hairdresser, Manicurist, Notary Public, Optician, and Physician—and he was backed by his own Prescription Service. . . . You could buy Gymnasium Equipment at Berliner's. You could get a Harness for your horse, or a Hercules Fireproof Safe for your money, or a Lace Portiere for your doorway. You could buy a Player Piano complete with Music Scrolls, rent more from the Music Scroll Exchange Library, get a Piano Scarf to drape over its top and a Piano Tuner to fix it up if it got wonky, all without leaving the premises of this one magnificent emporium.*[34]

With the post office's introduction of Rural Free Delivery in the 1890s even country folk could order just about anything they wanted from the magic catalogs of Sears Roebuck.

But most married women couldn't afford any such luxuries. What with layoffs, seasonal work, and generally low wages, Mrs. Working-class Housewife knew little security. (Not until 1920 did a more stable form of blue-collar life emerge, thanks to labor legislation and union negotiations.)[35] A working-class family in 1910 might live in a tenement in a large urban area, a dilapidated frame house in a small city, a row house in a company town, a collapsing farmhouse on a small plot, or a log cabin in the woods. Such a family had to cram into their homes not only their several children, but also other members of their extended families, orphaned children, and often some boarders. Family members and lodgers lived in one, two, maybe four multipurpose rooms, sharing or sometimes rotating beds, some cooking while others slept.

Clearly in such crowded conditions, with almost no room for storage, keeping a tidy house, let alone a clean one, presented a major challenge, one that defeated many a woman. Housewife or child had to carry water from a well or in the city from a central faucet in the yard and fetch fuel for the cookstove, which also provided the only heat. In such circumstances most women perforce fed their families monotonous diets, mostly bought already cooked: bakery bread, sausages, salamis, salted fish, cheese, beer, canned goods, and macaroni. What cooking they did consisted mainly of one-pot meals—gruels, stews, or soups that could be boiled on top of the stove. Otherwise they relied on the frying pan to prepare bacon, fish, or occasionally chops. Poor country people often had no time to make their own gardens, subsisting mainly on cornmeal mush, bacon, game, and fish.

THOUSANDS OF WOMEN AGRICULTURAL WORKERS "KEPT HOUSE" IN BUILDINGS LIKE THESE, THREE OR FOUR FAMILIES TO A BUILDING: ONE ROOM ABOVE, ONE BELOW, WITH AN OUTDOOR DINING ROOM ON THE SIDE. (NATIONAL ARCHIVES)

Washday in these homes must have made the strongest women shudder. Housewives had to carry the water, heat it, carry it to the tubs, scrub on washboards the cheap, heavy fabrics that were all that they could afford, wring them out, empty and refill the tubs once or twice to rinse the clothes, wring them out again, and carry them outside to hang up. Baths required not only hot water but also what was even harder to get, a modicum of privacy. So the poor seldom bathed and seldom changed their clothes.

Whether the husband was a tenant farmer, a miner, a day laborer, or a factory hand, his income probably did not suffice to provide even the necessities dependably, so other family members had to work, sometimes from a very early age. The wife and mother had to contribute too—usually (though not always) from work she performed at home for a bit of money: cooking, cleaning and washing for boarders, taking in washing or sewing, or doing sweated piecework.

Not surprisingly, the poor frequently fell ill. Yet the mother had no way to isolate a sick child, no means to prepare special food, no way even to furnish the child with the luxury of quiet. Employers neither compensated workers for sick days nor guaranteed their jobs during illnesses.

The lot of the poor housewife was not a happy one. Worst of all, too often she had to watch her children go hungry, watch them go out to work too young and for too long hours, watch them drift into lives of crime and prostitution, watch them suffer with illnesses she could neither prevent nor adequately treat, watch them die.

Enter the Expert—Preaching

The way poor women had to live often made it impossible for them to learn and exercise the skills required by the new demands of "educated motherhood." But middle-class women, now bearing fewer children than in the past, had more time to think about how to raise them and to seek advice. For motherhood, like housewifery, was being argued over and redefined by the new experts. No longer was the biological fact of birthing supposed to endow a woman with the wisdom to educate, the moral standards to inculcate ethics, and the medical skills to nurse her children through diphtheria, tuberculosis, and the thousand other dangerous ills that pre-antibiotic flesh was heir to.

Motherhood, like so much else, was being professionalized. After decades that equated motherhood and infallible saintliness, suddenly mothers heard that they needed training to raise their children properly. Women's colleges, eager to justify their own existence, leaped on the bandwagon of the professionaliza-tion of motherhood. What task, they rhetorically asked, was more important than forming a child's mind? And did such an undertaking not require the best possible training?

Enter the experts, with or without credentials, but all enthusiastically rushing to tell mothers what to do and how to do it: how to keep children and their environment sanitary, how to feed them, how to educate them, how to control or modify or influence their behavior. Systematize child rearing, the experts adjured. Put babies on strict schedules. Don't play with them. A Children's Bureau pamphlet of 1914 warned that infants are born with strong autoerotic, masturbatory, and thumb-sucking impulses that must be curbed. Tie their feet to opposite sides of the crib so they can't rub their thighs together. Sew sleeves over their hands. Use suppositories to toilet train them—early.

People were to think of their offspring, said the experts, not as small women and men, but as children, of whom different reactions and responses had to be expected. Charlotte Perkins Gilman admonished mothers in 1911 that it was their duty to ensure their children "an ever longer period of immaturity," by extending their education as long as possible.

The experts usually tugged behind them a cargo of guilt to deliver to parents. For at the same time that they bestowed information, they robbed parents of confidence. Not only did they demand that a mother scientifically keep records, follow rules, understand each stage in a child's development, and gear her responses to the child's needs, but they also told her that she was to judge herself by how well her child turned out. What's more, scientific motherhood, they said, should lead to the improvement of the race, so if they didn't rid mankind of selfishness, drunkenness, and criminality, mothers would have failed.

The experts' emphasis on the need for sanitation and pure milk and water saved the lives of thousands of babies, but it also induced near hysteria in some mothers. In her novel *Edith Bonham* Mary Hallock Foote lampooned a young woman who, her "blue ecstatic eyes fixed on sterilization," her imagination fed "not on poetry but germs," exhausted herself and exasperated her parents by trying to reform the milking process on their farm.[36]

But the experts of one period sometimes look like the bunglers of another. Take breast-feeding. Doctors contributed to the growing impression that bottle-feeding was more scientific, more modern—even more American. What a boon—a chemical formula worked out for the precise needs of the individual infant—a formula, of course, that needed constant re-adjustment! Luckily for their children, most poor women perforce stayed with the means of feeding that came with the baby.

The threat implicit in so much expert advice became explicit when Dorothy Canfield Fisher, writing in 1916 about the Montessori method of education, warned mothers, "If all this sounds too troublesome and complicated, let it be remembered that the Children's Home looms close at hand, ominously ready to devote itself to making conditions exactly right for the child's growth, never impatient, with no other aim in life and no other occupation but to do what is best for the child. *If we are to be allowed to keep our children with us*, we must prove worthy the sacred trust."[37]

And, backing up the threat, schools and social workers began to take over some of the responsibilities and the authority traditionally assigned to parents. How could it be otherwise in a society where millions of immigrants struggled to enter a new and largely unknown world, where science, technology, and efficiency experts were making discoveries that turned grandma's cures and theories into witchcraft and nonsense? Courts increasingly intervened in family life, "even depriving parents of custody if it could be determined that the relationship was harmful to the child."[38]

If motherhood grew suddenly complicated for the native-born, middle-class mothers whom the experts saw as the most likely source of "educated mother-hood," think of the quandary of the immigrant mother. Her husband, at work for his long day in the factory or on the streets with his pushcart, might or might not be learning English, but he was certainly learning the ways of the New World. In the schools her young children were taught not only English but also new behavior and modes of thought by teachers determined to make little Americans of them. Her older children in domestic service or in factories learned English, dressed themselves as far as they could afford in American fashions, yearned after American modes of recreation, and cast aside her standards of conduct as Old World and outmoded. Meanwhile mama usually stayed home, most often in a neighborhood where she heard little English, in a community of women like herself. How was she to give advice, let alone impose authority, for children living in a world of which she stood only on the verge?

Interestingly enough, pressures for educated motherhood pushed many women out of the home, to unite with other mothers in Mothers' Clubs and the National Congress of Mothers, founded in 1897. In organizations like these, they fought for legislation to give mothers equal guardianship with fathers over children, to protect dependent and deviant children, to abolish child labor, to establish juvenile courts, to provide widows' pensions, to find foster homes. They raised money for kindergartens and playgrounds. They supported Lillian Wald and Florence Kelley in their successful lobbying for a national Children's Bureau (established in 1912) to promote the health and welfare of America's children.

While child-rearing experts and educators were instructing woman-as-mother, nutritionists and professors of domestic science were handing down the law to woman-as-housewife, to make her "as proficient in her realm as the businessman is in his." [39] Experts defined the ideal kitchen as a "combination of laboratory, machine shop and studio" where the housewife must be mistress of all trades and jack of none. She must command

> *the difficult art of cookery, adapting her menu to the welfare of a group of people of all ages and with all kinds of needs. She must be washwoman and laundry woman, cleaning and scrub woman. She must know all the proper chemicals to be applied to the cleansing of different kinds of metal, cloth, wood, and every sort of surface painted and unpainted. She must be food expert, and textile expert, medicine and poison expert. Besides all this, she must be teacher, instructor, and entertainer, the encyclopedia and gazetteer, a theological and philosophical professor.*

The kitchen, burbled Martha Foote Crow, ought not be a place to which the housewife is condemned, but a place she is "going to love because it is a laboratory where science has sway, where aseptical cleanness reduces every process to a fragrant dream, and the laws of processes appear as miracles of nature controlled at last by the art of man."[40]

A small but growing legion of experts stood ready to offer information, teach housewives, and train young daughters in the mysteries of scientific management of the home: domestic science departments at state universities, the Grange, extension services, bureaus of the federal government, settlement house workers, writers for women's magazines. The Department of Agriculture in the 1910s was signing up 125,000 young girls each year to participate in its canning clubs, where they learned not only to preserve food but also to garden and to raise poultry and cattle. "The Tomato Club has meant more to me than I am able to tell," wrote 15-year-old Myrtle Hardin of Camden, Tennessee. "My two years' experience has taught me how to prepare nice things for the table, how to beautify the home, and how to make life in the country attractive and happier.

A NURSE, A HOME DEMONSTRATION AGENT, AND A COUNTY AGENT TAKE THEIR EXPERTISE INTO RURAL ALABAMA. (NATIONAL ARCHIVES)

Nothing has done more to train my mind than our Club work."[41] In 1914 Congress passed the Smith-Lever Act to fund 2,000 home demonstration agents to train housewives in homemaking, budget management, and child rearing.

When in 1897 the Boston Women's Educational and Industrial Union established a School of Housekeeping, though it failed to attract the working girls whom it had hoped to turn into superior domestic servants, it did enroll middle-class housewives who aspired to expertise in "household administration." They signed up for courses in household sanitation, chemistry of foods, home economics, home sociology, house architecture, principles of housework, marketing, and sewing.

The hardy new domestic science experts even undertook to indoctrinate tenement dwellers. Mabel Kittredge, for example, wanted "to instill a clock-like regularity and discipline to tenement living through the re-education of the mother. The imposition of the clock would enable women to develop a daily schedule, consistent repetition would inculcate habits that would promote order and efficiency; by adopting an assembly-line approach, mothers could become model workers." No wonder one of the women visited by such teachers reported, "By pictures and lectures she shows us poor people how we should live without meat, without milk, without butter, and without eggs. Always it's on the tip of my tongue to ask her, can't you yet learn us how to eat without eating?"[42]

It is easy to chuckle and to sympathize with the reactions of the "many women, particularly southerners and immigrants, [who] considered the rationalization of housework both alien and undesirable—especially when its precepts were associated with self-righteous Yankees and meddling middle class do-gooders."[43] One feels for the poor woman who after eating Swallow's New England Kitchen food allegedly moaned, "I'd rather eat what I'd rather. I don't want to eat what's good for me."[44] A wiser woman than she knew, for the "New Nutritionists" were calculating caloric and protein needs much too high (as high as 7,000 calories a day for a 70-kilo man at hard labor), preaching the wisdom of ingesting lots of fat, advising people to eat more white flour, denigrating most fruits and vegetables, dismissing tomatoes as without food value, advocating the use of condensed milk only, and boiling vegetables to a fare-thee-well. "In short," comments Harvey Levenstein, "if America turned *en masse* to follow their advice, rickets, beri-beri, scurvy, and other vitamin-deficiency diseases may have reached epidemic proportions."[45]

Of course, the stage of scientific knowledge limited expertise. After all, until about 1911 no one had heard of vitamins. Just as experts today with each new study change their minds about the virtues or evils of aspirin, coffee, and alcohol, so Progressive Era experts erred.

All the same, the domestic scientists introduced higher standards of cleanliness and efficiency and made life more pleasant and easier for thousands of families. They raised concern for children's nutrition and inaugurated school lunches. With ecology still not established as a separate science, they reduced pollution and fought for pure water.

The Grace Notes: Home Decoration, Personal Care, Recreation

Despite all the difficulties housewives confronted, now and then they had time for frills or for themselves.

Well-off and middle-class women rejoiced in home beautification. For the superrich, Elsie DeWolfe as exponent of the new profession of interior decoration was creating drawing rooms of startling simplicity—simplicity, that is, as contrasted with those of the overstuffed Victorian era. For the modish, fashion dictated curio cabinets, etchings, and engravings, "aesthetic motifs reflected even in the wash basins." Hannah Solomon recalled, ". . . a real artist was engaged to paint friezes on the walls, to festoon the ceilings with posies or to lend a woodsy touch by means of flocks of birds and hovering butterflies! And sometimes, as a finishing, enterprising touch—the epitome of decorative elegance—would be added an entire scene, all in the favorite Delft blue of the day!"[46]

Even tenement dwellers tried to decorate their homes. Lillian Wald described their "real heroism [in] scrubbing rotten floors and polishing brass in rooms which could never catch the light of the sun."[47] May Mabel Kittredge marveled at "the hemming and the hanging of ruffles over every door, around every shelf and even around the tubs . . . at the tarletan festooned around the chandelier and over the pictures . . . the dozens of calendars collected and pinned on the walls."[48]

No dwelling was so primitive as to suppress the urge to ornament. In a tar-paper-covered tent in a boom-town gold camp, Anne Ellis struggled to make a home:

> *Our beds are made of bed springs which during the day can be closed against the wall; in one corner is a tiny inkstand stove; between the foot of the bed and table is one trunk, which two children can sit on while they eat. (On wash days this trunk is used for a bench.) The big box is unpacked and used for a dresser, lending quite an air when it is draped with a piece of Battenberg [lace] on top, with the old mirror hanging above. I hemstitch curtains for the*

MRS. MOTTO SPENT MOST OF HER TIME MAKING ARTIFICIAL FLOWERS WITH HER FAMILY AND WRESTLING WITH THE IMPOSSIBLE HOUSEHOLD TASKS INFLICTED BY TENEMENT OVERCROWDING. BUT NOTE HER EFFORTS TO BEAUTIFY HER HOME.
(NATIONAL ARCHIVES)

one window and door, and after the books are unpacked and put on a
shelf, and the few pictures tacked up, we are quite cosy.[49]

Those women not too weighed down by cares and financial woes to think about their own bodies were at least as likely to want to gain as to lose weight. Many still accepted the old idea of plumpness as a sign of good health. Not until 1918 did the newer idea of restraint at the table really win out. Harriet Hubbard Ayer in her 1902 book on health and beauty offered extraordinarily sound advice to those who exceeded even her rather generous standards of weight: limit sleep to seven hours; eat fruit and rare meat; limit fats, starches, and sugar; and exercise.

More and more women were indeed exercising, leading active lives, and abandoning the advice offered by a physician to 33-year-old Helena Richie, the protagonist of Margaret Deland's novel of 1905, to stay abed late of mornings, since she was not "strong."[50] Younger and better-off women took the lead in bicycling, golfing, playing tennis, and boating. Women's colleges, eager to belie the allegation that study ruined women's health, had for some time required their students to exercise. But physical culture was also being urged on farm girls, and rural high schools boasted girls' basketball teams. Kansan Martha Farnsworth loved to skate, bicycle, camp, swim, drill with her prize-winning women's drill team, and above all dance—even though an evangelist had denounced dancing as "hugging set to music." Farnsworth indignantly replied, ". . . a respectful young man would no more hug a young woman in a dance, than at church or anywhere else. A *respectful* young man will be respectful *in the dance* and a *disrespectful* young man, will be disrespectful, wherever he is."[51]

Just as popular as physical culture was cultivating one's mind. Women joined clubs where they read papers, listened to speakers, held spelling contests, and debated. They constituted the major readership of many magazines and journals. They took lessons from "the tribe of 'Perfessers' who circulated through mid-America offering tidbits of cultural technique, elocution, voice-training, conversation, penmanship, character-reading, and the principles of success."[52] They attended the entertainment/education sessions of Chautauqua and subscribed to Chautauqua's home-study courses.

Some hard-worked women isolated on their farms had no time for recreation. Magnolia Le Guin mourned, "Oh, what a *great* loss it is to me to be denied of the pleasure of taking my little boys out and talk with them about Gods beautiful sunshine, beautiful frost, beautiful balmy weather. . . and beautiful colored trees etc etc. We've had this pleasure only once this fall."[53] She, poor lady, went for five years without ever leaving her home farm.

But most farmers' wives when they could went visiting. Sometimes they "put on sunbonnets or shawls, took their sewing, and walked across the fields to visit neighbors," often with children in tow. Sometimes they and their husbands picked up all the children and, usually without warning, descended on relatives or friends for the whole day. (Happy hostess—with an additional eight or 10 mouths to feed!)

"The procedure was always the same," wrote Edith Summers Kelley in her novel *Weeds*. "Everybody, men, women, and children, came out to the wagon to welcome the visitors. There would follow a few moments of general kissing, hand-shaking, comments on the weather, and mutual inquiries concerning health." While the men unhitched and retired to the barnyard to talk and the children played hide-and- seek, the women cooked. After they served dinner, washed up, and swept the kitchen floor, "they sat down stiffly on straight-backed chairs, smoothed their aprons and talked about the price of calico, the raising of chickens," illness and death. "The only break in what would seem to an outsider an interminable stretch of tedium was the dinner. This usually consisted of salt hog meat, fried or boiled, potatoes and some other vegetable, followed by a heavy-crusted apple pie or a soggy boiled pudding. If it were summer or autumn there would likely be a big platter of 'roastin' ears,' sliced ripe tomatoes, or sliced cucumbers and onions in vinegar."[54]

Small-town housewives said to neighbors, "What are you doing tomorrow afternoon? Bring over your scrap-bag and let's just spend the whole afternoon cutting out quilt patches." As they cut, they reminisced about the various pieces—from a particular dress, worn at a particular occasion. More formally, they had quilting bees, husking bees, country parties, and dances; on Friday evenings they went to spelling matches, box suppers, lectures, and political speeches in their neighborhood schoolhouses; Sundays were given to church services and to all-day visits, picnics, basket dinners. In many communities, social activities centered around the churches, which held poverty socials ("Wear Your Oldest Clothes!"), pound socials ("Entrance Fees by Weight!"), and box socials, where the men paid for the privilege of eating with ladies by bidding on the decorated lunch boxes the women had prepared.

In short, recreation varied as much as women themselves. Woman suffragist Mrs. Clarence Mackay, clad in silver lamé with a train carried by pink-brocaded black boys, attended a party at Sherry's in New York given by James Hazen Hyde at a cost of $100,000. Private trains transported guests from Boston, Philadelphia, and Washington, to be entertained by the Metropolitan Opera orchestra and corps de ballet and by the Parisian actress Mme. Réjane, who brought along her own scenery to perform in a bedroom farce. Two suppers, one at midnight, one at 3:00 A.M., and breakfast were served among marble statues and trickling fountains.[55]

In the tenements, married women socialized mainly by visiting relatives, and they looked forward to big celebrations at weddings. Sometimes they were lured to club meetings and parties at a settlement house. "*Rushing-the-can* like the men," wrote one poor soul, *that's all the pleasure the poor women had in that time. In the summer when it was so hot you couldn't stay in those buildings, the women and the boys and girls and babies were sitting down in the street and alley. All the women would bring down their chairs and sit on the sidewalk. Then somebody would say "All the women put two cents and we'll get the beer." So everybody did and the children would run by the saloon and get the can of beer. The saloon had ice and they kept that beer ice cold. So the women, and children too, were drinking beer to get cool. . . . That's all the pleasure we had—the cool from the beer in summer. Even when we started the club in the settlement, the women in the alley were drinking beer.*

Members of settlement women's clubs reported that settlement workers "used to tell us that it's not nice to drink the beer, and we must not let the baby do this, and this. . . . So after we had about an hour, or an hour and a half of the preaching, they would pull up the circle and we'd play the games together. All together we played the games—the Norwegian, the German, the English, and me [an Italian]. Then we'd have some cake and coffee and the goodnight song."[56]

Source Notes

1. See, for example, Charlotte Baum, Paula Hyman, and Sonya Michel, *The Jewish Woman in America* (New York: Dial, 1976), p. 109.
2. Elliott West, "Beyond Baby Doe: Child Rearing on the Mining Frontier," in Susan Armitage and Elizabeth Jameson, eds., *The Women's West* (Enid: Univ. of Oklahoma Press, 1987), p. 185.
3. See, for example, Charlotte Perkins Gilman, *What Diantha Did* (New York: Charlton, 1910), p. 31.
4. Elyce J. Rotella, *From Home to Office: U.S. Women at Work, 1870–1930* (Ann Arbor: Univ. of Michigan Research Press, 1981), Table 2.12.
5. Nancy Woloch, *Women and the American Experience* (New York: Knopf, 1984), p. 232. The figure for domestic servants is very soft, partly because of the number of part-time and temporary workers, partly because of the way the census sorted out workers. Dolores Hayden, for instance, gives the number of domestic servants in the United States in 1900 as 1.5 million. *The Grand Domestic Rovolution: A History of Feminist Designs for American Homes, Neighborhoods, and Cities* (Cambridge: MIT Press, 1981), p. 170.

   Many employers rated governesses as upper-class menials, ill paid, ranking somewhat below clerical workers. Martha Bensley, an experienced college-trained teacher, investigated the governesses' plight by applying for various posts herself. Employers, concerned mainly that she agree to wear a uniform, took little interest in her qualifications or references. Martha Bensley, "Experiences of a Nursery Governess," *Everybody's* (1905), quoted by Arthur W. Calhoun in *A Social History of the American Family from Colonial Times to the Present* (Cleveland: Arthur H. Clark, 1919), vol. 3, 134–36.

6. Hayden, p. 21. Sheila M. Rothman, *Woman's Proper Place: A History of Changing Ideals and Practices, 1870 to the Present* (New York: Basic Books, 1978) gives the number of families in 1900 hiring a full-time servant as one in 15.

7. Woloch, p. 232.

8. Rothman, p. 89.

9. Agnes Nestor, *Woman's Labor Leader: The Autobiography of Agnes Nestor* (Rockford, Ill.: Bellevue Books, 1954), p. 74.

10. Susan Ware, *Partner and I: Molly Dewson, Feminism, and New Deal Politics* (New Haven: Yale Univ. Press, 1987), p. 36.

11. Marion Harland, *The Distractions of Martha* (New York: Scribner's, 1906), p. 222.

12. Rheta Childe Dorr, *What Eight Million Women Want* (1910; reprint, New York: Kraus Reprint Co., 1971), pp. 252–53.

13. Lucy Maynard Salmon, *Domestic Service* (New York: 1897), pp. 149–50, quoted in David M. Katzman, *Seven Days a Week: Women and Domestic Service in Industrializing America* (New York: Oxford Univ. Press, 1978), pp. 278–79.

14. Rheta Childe Dorr reported an 1888 study by the Massachusetts Bureau of Labor Statistics, which showed that 30 percent of the prostitutes surveyed had previously been domestic servants. Dorr, *What Eight Million Women Want*, pp. 196–97.

15. Rose Cohen, *Out of the Shadow* (New York: George H. Doran, 1918), pp. 180–81.

16. Ruth Schwartz Cowan, *More Work for Mother: The Ironies of Household Technology from the Open Hearth to the Microwave* (New York: Basic Books, 1983), p. 124.

17. Ibid., pp. 93–94.

18. Martha Farnsworth, *Plains Woman: The Diary of Martha Farnsworth, 1882–1922*, ed. Marlene Springer and Haskell Springer (Bloomington: Indiana Univ. Press, 1988), p. 211.

19. Harvey A. Levenstein, *Revolution at the Table: The Transformation of the American Diet* (New York: Oxford Univ. Press, 1988), p. 62.

20. Cowan, p. 78.

21. Rose Wilder Lane, *Old Home Town* (1935; reprint, Lincoln: Univ. of Nebraska Press, 1985), p. 19. But women were expected to know how to

sew: "In those days, most little girls had a needle put in their hands at 5 and were given their first lessons in sewing and fancywork." Gladys S. Douglass, *Oh Grandma, You're Kidding: Memories of 75 Years in Lincoln* (Lincoln, Neb.: J and L. Lee, 1983), p. 97.

22. Cowan, p. 77.

23. See, for example, Hayden, p. 12, Douglass, p. 4, and Joan M. Jensen, ed., *With These Hands: Women Working on the Land* (Old Westbury, N.Y.: Feminist Press; New York: McGraw-Hill, 1981), p. 165.

24. Cowan, pp. 88–89.

25. Robert Lynd and Helen Lynd, *Middletown: A Study in American Culture* (New York: Harcourt Brace, 1929), pp. 252–54.

26. Hayden, p. 17.

27. Ibid., p. 151.

28. Cowan, pp. 115ff.

29. Hayden, pp. 207–08.

30. Juliet B. Schor, *The Overworked American: The Unexpected Decline of Leisure* (New York: Basic Books, 1992), pp. 101–2. Dolores Hayden speculates on the complex answers to these questions in *The Grand Domestic Revolution*. So does Harvey A. Levenstein in *Revolution at the Table*. Today the fast-food industry flourishes, workmen pick up sandwiches at the nearest store instead of carrying lunchboxes prepared by loving hands at home, and retired people go to live in communities that clean their apartments, launder their linens, and prepare for them at least one meal a day—all of these attempts to resolve the question of who cooks.

31. Cowan, p. 100.

32. For descriptions of the housework of the typical middle-class housewife and the typical poor housewife, we draw heavily from historian Ruth Cowan. In her composites Cowan used many materials, among them John B. Leeds's 1912–14 study of 60 middle-class families, the account books of railroad conductor L. R. Dodge (1889–1945), prewar women's magazines, and the *Journal of Home Economics* (established 1908). We have added details from other sources.

33. Marion Woodbury, "Time Required for Housework in a Family of Five with Small Children," *Journal of Home Economics* 10 (1918): 226–30, quoted in Cowan, p. 160.

34. Meredith Tax, *Rivington Street* (New York: William Morrow, 1982), p. 339.

35. Steven Mintz and Susan Kellogg, *Domestic Revolutions: A Social History of American Family Life* (New York: Free Press, 1988), p. 105.

36. Mary Hallock Foote, *Edith Bonham* (Boston: Houghton Mifflin, 1917), pp. 21–24.

37. Italics ours. Dorothy Canfield Fisher, *A Montessori Mother* (New York: Henry Holt and Co., 1916), p. 138.

38. Mintz and Kellogg, p. 129.
39. Lydia Ray Bladerston, instructor in housewifery and laundering at Columbia University's Teachers College, quoted in Jane Stern and Michael Stern, "Neighboring," *The New Yorker*, April 15, 1991.
40. Martha Foote Crow, *The American Country Girl* (1915; reprint, New York: Arno Press, 1974), pp. 137, 134, 150, 139.
41. Ibid., p. 190.
42. Elizabeth Ewen, *Immigrant Women in the Land of Dollars: Life and Culture on the Lower East Side, 1890–1925* (New York: Monthly Review Press, 1985), pp. 160, 78.
43. Jean Gordon and Jan McArthur, "American Women and Domestic Consumption, 1800–1920: Four Interpretative Themes," *Journal of American Culture: Studies of a Civilization* 8 (Fall 1985):42.
44. Levenstein, p. 56.
45. Levenstein, p. 57 and p. 235, n. 21.
46. Hannah G. Solomon, *Fabric of My Life: The Autobiography of Hannah G. Solomon* (New York: Bloch, 1946), pp. 66–67.
47. Robert L. Duffus, *Lillian Wald: Neighbor and Crusader* (New York: Macmillan, 1938), pp. 77–78.
48. "Housekeeping Centers in Settlements and Public School," *Survey* 30 (1913):189, quoted in Ewen, p. 157.
49. Anne Ellis, *The Life of an Ordinary Woman* (1929; reprint, New York: Arno Press, 1947), p. 249.
50. Margaret Deland, *The Awakening of Helena Richie* (New York: A. L. Burt, 1905, 1906), p. 128.
51. Farnsworth, pp. 203–04.
52. Mary Austin, *Earth Horizon* (Boston: Houghton Mifflin, 1932), p. 134.
53. Charles A. Le Guin, ed., *A Home-Concealed Woman: The Diaries of Magnolia Wynn Le Guin, 1901–1913* (Athens: Univ. of Georgia Press, 1990), pp. 54–55.
54. Edith Summers Kelley, *Weeds* (1923; reprint Carbondale and Edwardsville: Southern Illinois Univ. Press, 1972), p. 10.
55. James Brough, *Princess Alice: A Biography of Alice Roosevelt Longworth* (Boston: Little, Brown, 1975), pp. 159–61, passim.
56. Marie Hall Ets, *Rosa: The Life of an Italian Immigrant* (Minneapolis: Univ. of Minnesota Press, 1970), pp. 222–23.

CHAPTER 3

Women at Work: Outside the Home

In 1900 the census enumerated as workers in gainful occupations 5,829,807 American women—18.8 percent, one in five of the female population over 10 years of age. They constituted almost a fifth of the total work force. By 1920, their numbers had increased to 8,202,901—24 percent, one in four of females over 10.[1]

Who Went Out to Work?

Most of these women whom the census counted as workers were young and single.[2] The others were widows, divorcees, poor married women, and a relatively few well-to-do married women.[3] The frequent economic depressions of the late 19th and early 20th centuries bolstered the general feeling that married women, who *theoretically* were adequately supported by their husbands, ought not take jobs that "rightfully" belonged to men. Although statistics in the years before World War I show only 10 percent of married women as employed, this low percentage nonetheless represents a lot of women—more than 1,384,000 of them. In poor and black communities, of course, the figures ran much higher. Overall, in 1900 a fifth of the female labor force was married, and a third was over 35. Their numbers rose throughout the Progressive Era.[4]

The myth lingered: Married women didn't/shouldn't work. But some did. As one of Sinclair Lewis's characters says, "I'm typical of about ten thousand married women in business about whose noble spouses nothing is ever said."[5] Or perhaps business women were supporting disabled spouses, or had married avant-garde spouses.

To their impossibly long factory workdays, these married workers and their even more unfortunate widowed or divorced sisters who headed families had to add hours of labor at home. Women learned early, the novelist Marion Harland observed, "that housekeeping is every woman's profession, no matter what other business she may follow. It's the *sine qua non* for her."[6] The journalist Rheta Childe Dorr reported the plight of factory women:

The women of the mills went on working. They cooked and served meals, washed dishes, cleaned the house, tucked the children into bed, and after that sewed, mended or did a family washing. Eleven o'clock at night seemed the conventional hour for clothesline pulleys to begin creaking all over town. . . . In Fall River a woman in the mills and at home worked an average of fourteen hours a day and had babies between times. The babies could not be taken to the mills, and as soon as the mothers were able to leave their beds they relegated the care of the babies to some grandmother, herself a broken down mill-worker, or to the baby-farms in which the town abounded. Of course the babies fared ill under this system, the mortality rate among them being very high.[7]

In 1900, 11.9 percent of all working women headed families, and 16.4 percent of all working women were the sole providers for their families.[8] The contemporary Pittsburgh Survey noted the plight of a widow in a Pennsylvania steel town whose husband had died after eight years of semi-invalidism caused by an accident at his mill. She lived in a two-room tenement with her four children, whom she tried to support by taking in sewing and washing. "The kitchen was small and hot and the younger children noisy, and the not unnatural consequence was that the oldest girl drifted to the streets, mixed with a gay crowd, and eventually became a charge of the Juvenile Court."[9] In such circumstances more than one woman despaired—like a pregnant paper-box maker, deserted by her husband, who tied her two children to her body and jumped into the river.[10] Even middle-class widows had a hard time. Carrie Jacobs Bond and her small son almost starved and at times were six months behind on their rent. She resorted to taking in boarders, painting china, and performing songs she had written. Only the success of her songs "I Love You Truly" and "Just a Wearyin' for You" gave her the money to establish her own publishing company and freed her from debt.

Moreover, young though most women workers were, almost a third of the female labor force was 35 or older,[11] a significant figure, particularly when the average length of a woman's life was less than 50 years. Hard as was the life of the working young, think what it meant for older women to stand all day in laundries shaking out heavy wet sheets in rooms made torrid by steam.

In 1920 the female nonagricultural labor force was older than in 1900. Thanks to child labor laws and better educational systems, the percentage of girls aged 10–15 had fallen from 6 in 1900 to 2 in 1920. Working women 16–24 had dropped from 43 percent to 39 percent, while women 25–44 had risen from 37 percent to 41 percent, and women over 45 from 13 percent to 17 percent. Married women had increased their representation from 13 percent to 21 percent.[12] While the percentage of black and foreign-born white women employed hardly changed, more native-born white women went to work as clerical and professional jobs opened up: In 1900, 17 percent of these women worked, and in 1920, 23 percent.[13]

Who Did What?

As the number of paid women workers mounted, many men feared that women would take their jobs or would lower their wages by being willing to work for less. Already threatened by the New Woman and alarmed by politicians' ravings against the dangers of the rising divorce rate and the falling birthrate, men clung to the domestic ideal, reassuring each other about the God-given nature of woman's place. As an editorial writer at the *New York Times* asserted in 1906: "A nice girl. . . is not thinking about spending her life in commercial employment."[14]

These men worried unduly, for most of the women entering the marketplace did not displace men but took newly created jobs. And women lowered wages for each other much more than for men. Still, the men's fears had some basis. Women were increasing the labor supply and thus, like immigrant men, keeping wages low or making them lower. Unpracticed in the ways of the business world, most women employees meekly accepted the conditions imposed upon them. Relatively few thought of building a career or even considered the possibility of upward mobility. Many looked upon themselves as temporary workers, supplementing the family income rather than providing its sole support. In that they were hard to organize and they tractably accepted indecent working conditions, they did threaten men's standards of employment.

And what did all these women do to earn their pay? The range and variety of their work as described in the 1900 census astound those who think of all women a century ago as homebodies. Many have heard of the professional women: the 1,010 lawyers counted in the 1900 census, the 2,193 journalists, the 3,405 clergy, the 787 dentists, and the 7,399 physicians and surgeons. And anyone can explain away as mavericks the 18 stevedores, the 84 engineers and surveyors, the 95 theatrical managers, the 100 architects, the 409 electricians, even the 1,365 miners and quarriers. But who were those 8,246 women whom the census designated as "hunters, trappers, guides and scouts"? And what about the 307,788 women listed as "farmers, planters and overseers"—a figure that does not include farm wives, pickers, and field hands?

The numbers of working women in unexpected occupations took aback even their feminist contemporaries. Nearly 3,000 women, wrote labor organizer Agnes Nestor, worked in the Chicago stockyards, "in the canneries, in the chipped beef rooms, in the packing rooms, packing, weighing, and painting cans, and sewing the bags for the hams."[15] Lydia Commander bragged in 1907, "There are 946 commercial travelers, 261 wholesale merchants, 1,271 officials of banks, 100 lumbermen, 113 woodchoppers, 84 civil engineers and surveyors, 1,932 stock raisers, 143 marble cutters, 595 butchers. There are even 10 wheelwrights, 8 steam boilermakers, 2 roofers and slaters, 1 well-borer, and a licensed pilot on the Mississippi."[16] By 1907 women held nearly a quarter of the highly skilled jobs of core making in Pittsburgh foundries.[17] In short, feminists pointed out, by 1900 women could be found in 295 of the 303 occupations listed in the census.

Why Women Worked

What probably mattered even more than the variety of women's occupations was that women's working for pay became commonplace. As Elizabeth Sears wrote, most women employees then, as now, worked because they had to. "What reasonable person," Sears cogently inquired, "will believe that a girl will crowd to work every morning, rain or shine, because she wants extra pin-money that she has no time to spend?"[18]

At the same time, women's attitudes about paid work were changing. Sinclair Lewis's Golden family, too poor to send their daughter to college but too respectable to permit her to take a job, began to seem old-fashioned.[19] Popular writers like Edna Ferber were setting before their readers the joys and benefits of earning one's own living: Ferber's skirt saleswoman Edna McChesney thanked fortune "that [she] wasn't cursed with a life of ease. These massage-at-ten-fitting-at-eleven-bridge-at-one women always look such hags at thirty-five."[20]

New Women turned away from the prospect of staying submissively at home as good daughters until they moved to other homes as good wives. "All the girls in my town expected to earn their own living," wrote a midwesterner. "Most of us went to work as soon as we were graduated from college or high school, or from the condensed form of instruction known as the business college. . . . No girl dreamed of remaining at home as a burden to the family to support. . . . When we met a new girl, we did not ask, 'Who is she?' We inquired, 'What does she do?'"[21] Women like these might not be able to move into their own apartments without damaging their reputations, but they could and did go into settlement houses. Or they could respectably set up housekeeping with other women.

As more women attended college (85,000 in 1900; 283,000 in 1920), many of them began to think about building careers, with or without marriage.[22] Not only did college professors, particularly at women's colleges, provide impressive role models of working women, but many of them also told their students that as educated women the students had an obligation to contribute to society through their work. The students who listened to this gospel would eventually wield influence, for most of them came from families in a position to give them a good start in life and in a career. Take Molly Dewson, for instance, an 1897 graduate of Wellesley, who studied under mathematician Ellen Hayes, a feminist and temperance advocate; historian Elizabeth Kendall, a lawyer and world traveler; economist Katharine Coman, an associate of a Boston settlement house—not to mention the pacifist Emily Greene Balch, social reformer Vida Scudder, and poet Katharine Lee Bates. Mentored by the social activist Elizabeth Glendower Evans, Dewson went on to become an adviser to Franklin Roosevelt and America's first woman political boss, known throughout the Democratic Party as "More Women Dewson" for her insistence on more and more important jobs for women within the party and the government.

By no means did all women college graduates undertake professional work outside the home. Many slid gracefully from the protection of their parents' roof to their husbands', rejoicing in the theory that their college educations made them better wives and mothers. Others reverted to the primary role of daughter: Status as "daughter" was "at least as important amongst this social circle as professional achievement." Alums reported: "Occupation: being a daughter, and doing all sorts of things for church, hospital board and other organizations" and "still single . . . making 'sunshine in the home' for mother." A surprising number of those who did work for pay outside the home still lived with their parents, and many of them "took their roles as daughters more seriously than they did their professional pursuits." In response to a request for "offices of trust and honor held," a Wellesley alumna whose activities included being a real estate manager, administrator, and political appointee listed first being the "elder daughter" at home.[23] Even women of as independent mind as Vida Scudder and Molly Dewson maintained the closest of relationships with their mothers as long as those mothers lived.

At the same time for young women with more modest education and ambitions, pink-collar jobs were opening up in the thousands. Booth Tarkington's Alice Adams could not have considered factory work without loss of status; in her family's financial crisis she turned, however reluctantly, to clerical work.

With all these new opportunities, from 1900–1920 the participation of native-born American women in the labor force increased at a faster rate than that of foreign-born women. Some middle-class families encouraged their daughters to work rather than to jump into unwise marriages. Suffragists like Mary Livermore reasoned that women's entrance into the work world would help to introduce desirable feminine qualities into society. Gradually the idea was building that for her own self-respect an able-bodied single woman needed to support herself.

Trends in Employment

Three important trends in employment for women dominated the Progressive Era. First, women redistributed themselves, moving, whenever they could, out of domestic service and factory work into jobs with more status—though not necessarily with more pay. Not that most individuals enjoyed much upward mobility—only very able and very lucky women made the jump from blue to pink or white collar. But some young black women whose families sent them from the South to Washington, D.C., to take jobs as domestic servants saved enough money to launch themselves as independent contractors who did house-work by the day rather than live in as full-time maids. And gradually the daughters of some immigrants were able to stay in school long enough to prepare themselves as typists and stenographers.

Second, professional women assumed for pay tasks earlier performed by volunteers. These professionals brought to their undertakings a new expertise that earned them recognition and respect. They raised the standards for their own education and performance. As they discerned unmet needs, they broadened the concept of their fields. In a word they professionalized their work. Social workers, nurses, and home economists knew the excitement of creating new professions and transforming the lives of the people they served.

Third, the work of women in factories and in offices, by contrast, was "de-skilled," broken into its component parts, each of which could be quickly learned. Such jobs both deadened the senses of the women who performed them and dead-ended.

Clearly, women at opposite ends of the class hierarchy experienced their work differently. For most women work was a grim necessity, not a challenge and a liberation. Indeed, most of them hoped that marriage would free them from working for wages.

The Work Experience: Farm Workers

The 1900 census counted almost half a million women employed as agricultural laborers. More than half of them were apparently field hands and vegetable and fruit pickers, toiling, all too often with their young children, under miserable, hopeless conditions. Of these, almost three-fourths were black: In 1900 over half of all black Cotton Belt households hired out at least one daughter 16 or younger as a field laborer.[24] German-American, Swedish-American, Mexican-American, and Japanese-American women also tilled the fields across the United States.

Another 300,000 women, mostly white, were farmers, planters, overseers—apparently women of property or at least of considerable responsibility and authority. Some inherited a family farm. Others bought land for themselves. Here and there in fugitive records they show up: "[An Oregon] girl bachelor, being weary with working for others at housework and sewing, now lives alone, on a few acres of land, and depends upon the revenue from two cows, one sow, and a hundred hens. Two women in the Willamette Valley do all their work on a large farm, except the plowing. They raise registered cattle and sheep, and have a few acres in native huckleberries. One old lady gets her pin money from three acres in cherry trees and currant bushes."[25] Among them was Lavisa McElroy, at 25 a widowed mother of four. With her husband she had homesteaded in Oklahoma. After his death and the subsequent birth of her twins, she abandoned her sod hut there for a log house on a 40-acre farm in Arkansas.

THE DAILY GRIND. FARM WIVES, UNCOUNTED BY THE CENSUS AS FARM WORKERS, CONTRIBUTED UNTOLD HOURS OF LABOR. (NATIONAL ARCHIVES)

Among these "farmers, planters, and overseers" were also the women who homesteaded their own land, for unmarried women filed 12 percent of claims. Sarah Show Wisdom, for example, a widow with four children who homesteaded in Nebraska in 1886, proved her claim by working it as a farmer and rancher even while she went to school to earn a teaching certificate. She remarried, but when her second husband died leaving her pregnant with her fifth child, she joined his claim to her own, went on teaching, and later claimed another 320 acres.[26]

By 1920 the census found a total of almost 900,000 women engaged in agriculture, a sizable increase over the 1900 figure. But much of the increase came from population gain: With continuing urbanization and industrialization

HARVEST TIME! WIVES AND DAUGHTERS OF WELL-OFF FARMERS HELPED REAP THE
ABUNDANCE—AS ON THIS OKLAHOMA FRUIT RANCH. (NATIONAL ARCHIVES)

women agricultural workers had dropped from 3.3 percent of all employed
women in 1900 to 2.6 percent in 1920.[27]

The Work Experience: Factory Workers

Factory work was just one step up from domestic work. In 1900, factories
employed about a quarter of women workers—almost 1,250,000.[28] Most of
them were young, single immigrants—75 percent of them were foreign-born or
the daughters of foreign-born parents. Much of their work was seasonal. They
knew no security: According to a survey by the Women's Trade Union League,
most of them held two to five different positions during a year.[29]

They worked in many industries. They stripped tobacco and rolled and packed
cigars. They assembled paper boxes. They dipped and wrapped candies. They
made artificial flowers and feathers. They processed and canned food. Almost
40 percent of them labored in the needle trades, some in an "inside shop" that
did cutting and sewing, some in a "contracting shop" that hired workers to finish
garments, and some in their tenement dwellings as home workers. No one knew
how many women toiled at home in such jobs, with or without the help of their

BUT AMERICA'S FOOD SUPPLY ALSO DEPENDED ON FAMILIES LIKE THESE. THE
TWO-YEAR-OLD IN THE STROLLER HULLED STRAWBERRIES ALONG WITH HIS MOTHER
AND SIBLINGS.   (NATIONAL ARCHIVES)

families; they were paid on a piecework basis. The New York State Department
of Labor in 1901 put the number in that state at 30,000, mostly Italian women.[30]
About all that home workers and inside shop workers had in common were
miserable working conditions.

Descriptions of factory conditions of the day at first horrify and eventually
numb the reader by their sheer inhumanity and general hellishness. A food-pro-
cessing plant in Pittsburgh:

> *The women who fill the cans work, four at a machine, in a dark room,
> where floor and walls, machines and girls, are sticky with the exudations
> of syrup, and a visitor can scarcely walk without being fastened like a fly
> to what ever spot he touches. . . . Molasses comes in a continuous stream
> from the spout of the machine and spatters the girls as well as every
> exposed spot of floor or wall nearby. One girl pushes the cans under the
> spout, another takes them out and puts the tops on, a third clamps the top
> at another machine, and a fourth puts the can on a chain which takes it
> to the labeling table. The machine which puts the tops on the cans is
> difficult to adjust, yet if it is a sixteenth of an inch out of gear, the molasses
> splashes all over the girls and the floors.[31]*

A Milwaukee brewery, described by the labor organizer Mother Jones:

*Condemned to slave daily in the wash-room in wet shoes and wet clothes,
surrounded with foul-mouthed, brutal foremen . . . the poor girls work in
the vile smell of sour beer, lifting cases of empty and full bottles weighing
from 100 to 150 pounds, in their wet shoes and rags. . . . A [pregnant]
mother told me with tears in her eyes that every other day a depraved
specimen of mankind took delight in measuring her girth and passing . . .
comments.*[32]

A sweatshop for artificial flower making, described by Mary Van Kleeck in
1913: In a tenement lives a family of seven—father, mother, grandmother, and
four children. All but the father and two babies make flowers. They earn 10
cents a gross, and among them they can make about a gross an hour. This work
is seasonal, lasting only seven months a year. "The three year old girl picks apart
the petals; her sister, aged four years, separates the stems, dipping an end of each
into paste spread on a piece of board on the kitchen table; and the mother and
grandmother slip the petals up the stems." In another tenement Van Kleeck
found an 18-month-old child at this work.[33]

Only occasionally does a description of a model factory lighten the murk of
hardship and abuse. Elizabeth Butler in her 1907 study found just one laundry
with good working conditions. Its clients—the Pullman company, towel companies, and restaurants—required perfect work. This laundry, Butler reported,
attracted efficient workers who, with proper ventilation and protection against the
heat that throbbed through most laundries, could work faster and better.[34] Marie
Van Vorst, a journalist who changed her identity to work in a series of industrial
jobs, wrote of the Plant shoe factory in Boston with its eight-hour day, fire safety,
model ventilation, and new machinery. But these were rare exceptions.

Far more typical, sadly, were the cotton mills where Van Vorst toiled in South
Carolina for 13 hours a day. "This is chaos before order was conceived," she
wrote, "more weird in that, despite the din and thunder, everything is so orderly,
so perfectly carried forth by the machinery." The youngster who taught Van
Vorst to "spool" (attach yarn to spools) offered her snuff; her colleagues dipped
and spat, so that the floor was always wet. The air was white with cotton,
respiratory diseases like tuberculosis and pneumonia constant scourges. Fights
broke the monotony. One woman knifed a man who was sexually harassing her:
"And that gyrl told Min that she couldn't help knife the men, they all worried
on her so! 'Won't never leave me alone; I just have to draw on 'em; there ain't
no other way.'"[35] Children as young as six worked there, wearing the same
clothes summer and winter, often going barefoot all winter. One little boy told
Van Vorst that he washed his hands on Sundays. Underfed, filthy, and constantly
exhausted, the children chewed tobacco, swore, and fought.

"The mill-girl is happy, isn't she?" everyone asked Van Vorst after her factory
experiences:

"A MOMENT'S GLIMPSE OF THE OUTSIDE WORLD" FOR A SMALL COTTON SPINNER OF NORTH CAROLINA. (NATIONAL ARCHIVES)

I thank Heaven that I can say truthfully, that of all who came under my observation, not one who was of age to reflect was happy. . . . The most sane and hopeful indication for the future of the factory girl and the mill-hand is that she rebels, dreams of something better, and will in the fullness of time stretch toward it. . . . Nothing is provided for them that they can use, and they turn to the only thing that is within their reach— animal enjoyment, human intercourse and companionship. They are animals, as are their betters, and with, let us believe, more excuse [than their betters].[36]

In such work most women could not earn a living wage. Indeed most male factory workers had trouble supporting their families, in 1905 averaging $400 yearly when $800 was considered the minimum needed for a family of four.[37]

Employers usually paid women a quarter to two-thirds of what men earned.[38] Sometimes they argued that women needed no more, since they could look to their husbands or fathers for support. Anyway, they said, women were only working temporarily, until marriage. In fact, uncontrolled by minimum-wage laws, employers paid only what they had to. Worse still, they eroded even the pittances they paid by such mean devices as forcing waitresses to pay for

IN THIS INDIANA WOOLEN MILL WOMEN STOOD ALL DAY AT KNITTING MACHINES ON FLOORS STREWN WITH THREAD AND LITTER. (NATIONAL ARCHIVES)

unsatisfactory food which customers sent back to the kitchen or requiring glove makers to buy their own machines, charing as much as $65 for a machine that cost them only $35. Fringe benefits, of course, did not exist. No sick days: sometimes women even gave birth on the mill floor between the looms.[39]

On the $5 or $6 a week that the average *experienced* factory woman earned for her 60-hour week, she almost had to live at home with her family. Most of the "women adrift," as the society called working women living alone in boarding houses or rented rooms, barely eked out enough for room, board, and clothing even though they earned higher-than-average wages. All of them scrimped, sleeping three to a bed, skipping meals. Yeddie Bruker from her relatively munificent $7 a week paid $4 for room and board, $2 for clothing, and all of $0.10 for theater tickets. Rita Karpovna sacrificed breakfasts, lunches, and decent clothing (in 18 months she spent a total of $20 for clothes) for union dues and the "Woman's Self-Education Society."[40] Truly desperate women without families had to resort to 10-cent-a-night beds in strictly regulated dormitories sponsored by charitable organizations—if they could find them.

So most young single factory women lived at home. Almost all of them turned over their unopened pay envelopes to their mothers. Working sons more often paid their parents room and board or at least kept for themselves a considerable portion of their own wages, but parental expectations of daughters differed. As flower maker Theresa Albino explained, "But you know how it is with a boy. He wants things for himself." Mothers also required that their daughters help with housework and look after younger brothers and sisters, while their working brothers after their day's work took their leisure.[41]

Her family made plain to 23-year-old box maker Lucy just how much she owed them when they turned down in her behalf a "good offer" of marriage, telling her that she must help support them until her younger brother was old enough to work.[42] Lucy was only one of thousands of young women whose birth families felt they had first claim on her services. Sons might marry and set up separate households or seek better jobs elsewhere, but in the minds of many families daughters were forever. Mothers and fathers, prematurely aged by overwork, left off earning and looked to their daughters for support. "When these girls began to marry . . . the old father and mother were left facing stark poverty, in some cases the almshouse. Bitterly many parents resisted the marriage of their daughters. The fathers raged and the mothers pointed to their own married lives as warnings against a similar fate."[43]

Their parents usually allowed young women like these $0.25 or $0.50 a week, supposedly to pay for their carfare and lunches. Of course at their age, longing for fun and pretty things, the girls often walked to work and, at risk of censure for their behavior, visited saloons for the free lunches.

Heaven Won't Protect the Working Girl. We Will!

The plight of working women, especially the many young among them, outraged reform-minded middle-class women, particularly when they considered that these working women were the mothers-to-be of future Americans, and they roused themselves to action. But these reformers did not escape the rampant nativism of the population. Nor did they always show good sense. The looks, clothes, speech, heritage, and way of life of the young working women often struck them as outrageously foreign and wrong-headed. Reformers, not revolutionaries, the middle-class women tried to teach workers their own values.

To shield young women from the evils of the big, bad city, they established benevolent organizations like Travelers' Aid and the Working Girls' Clubs, a national network started by Grace Dodge to develop good work habits and genteel femininity. YWCAs, concerned particularly for the well-being of young women moving from farms and small towns to cities, built dormitories as safe havens for those working women who could afford them, kept lists of cheap but respectable boardinghouses, and ran employment agencies.

Settlement houses tried to help in dozens of imaginative ways. They mediated between working girls and their parents, many of whom did not even know where their daughters worked, let alone the conditions they faced every day. Settlement workers talked to bewildered, non-English-speaking immigrant mothers about New World ways, took them to visit their daughters' workplaces, explained the daughters' need for clothing and a bit of fun, and tried (often unsuccessfully) to keep them from disowning a misbehaving daughter. They ran craft fairs at which the mothers could display the skills they had brought from the Old Country and earn a bit of respect from their daughters, all too prone to look down on mothers who dressed, spoke, and acted in old-fashioned, Old World ways that embarrassed their children. They established recreational clubs to keep young women away from the theaters, saloons, and dance halls where, they feared—often with reason—the young women might get drunk, be seduced, be led into prostitution.

More liberal middle-class reformers focused on unionizing women and passing legislation to protect them, moving away from the condescending attitudes of Lady Bountiful toward real cooperation between working-class and middle-class women. They set themselves no easy task, for different value systems, an economic abyss, and much sharper class distinctions than Americans accept today arbitrated against its accomplishment. Working women suspected the motives and methods of their would-be middle-class sisters. Even those like Rosa Schneiderman who worked most closely with middle-class reformers seesawed between trust and suspicion. The reformers resented accusations that they simply didn't know enough about what working women needed or how to achieve it. That these efforts succeeded as well as they did is a credit to every woman, working class or middle class, who ever walked a picket line, to every clubwoman and factory woman who lobbied a state legislator for a minimum wage.

Of all the attempts at cooperation, that of the Women's Trade Union League (WTUL) worked best. The small group of reformers who founded it in 1903 staked its life on the idea that nonindustrial women could help women in industry. Workers, they believed, should staff and run the WTUL, with the help of middle-and upper-class women "allies"—better known to workers like Rosa Schneiderman as "the mink brigade." Workers would organize women and, if necessary, strikes. Allies would support these efforts, educate the middle class about the virtues of trade unionism, try to persuade American Federation of Labor officials to make unionizing women a priority, and represent working women's needs to middle-class suffragists.

During the WTUL's glory days, from 1904–20, the focus gradually shifted from unions to protective legislation. Workers and allies alike floundered in their efforts to organize women. No wonder. Employers powerfully opposed them. Governmental authorities usually supported employers. Men's unions didn't want to admit women or organize separate women's unions or support women's strikes. Most frustrating of all, few of the unskilled, poorly paid, irregularly employed women workers understood what a union was all about or had the energy for the day-to-day work necessary to keep a union alive. By mid-1913 the WTUL began to concentrate on passing woman suffrage and protective legislation like the minimum wage, restrictions on the amount of weight women could be required to lift, and prohibition of night work for women.

Worker Leonora O'Reilly and ally Margaret Dreier Robins epitomized the WTUL's

ROSA SCHNEIDERMAN. (NATIONAL ARCHIVES)

small but remarkable membership. O'Reilly, daughter of a widowed factory worker who brought home sewing at night, herself began work in a collar factory when she was 11. Somehow her mother surmounted exhaustion to take her to labor meetings. Encouraged by socialist friends and middle-class reform-minded women, at 16 Leonora organized the Working Women's Society. With the help of well-off friends who recognized her talent and her achievement, she educated herself vocationally and liberally, in sewing and sociology. Meanwhile she supported herself in jobs from forewoman in a shirtwaist factory to union organizer to teacher at the Manhattan Trade School for Girls. She helped to found the National Association for the Advancement of Colored People. She chaired the industrial committee of the New York City Woman Suffrage Party. She represented the WTUL at the International Congress of Women, which in 1915 tried to end World War I. But always she centered her life on unionizing women. With the WTUL, she had a love/hate relationship. Sometimes culture clashes between workers and allies drove her to despair. Most of the time she fervently believed in the WTUL's power to forward the interests of working women. She personally recruited into the WTUL Margaret Dreier Robins.

That Robins and O'Reilly should ever have met testifies to the existence in the Progressive Era of the closest approach to a sisterhood that America's women had ever achieved. For while O'Reilly was born and raised in poverty's ghetto, Robins grew up in a well-to-do German-American family, a family with a sense of discipline and civic responsibility. While still in her teens, she began her work for social justice, which eventually involved her with the Women's Municipal League. She didn't marry until she was 37; when she did, she chose a wealthy man but a crusader whose zeal matched hers. Of her own money Robins said, "I never earned a dollar of it and I recognize that I hold it in trust."[44] As a matter of conscience she and her husband chose to live in a cold-water tenement in Chicago, making friends of labor leaders, ministers, anarchists, trade union women, and the Hull House crew. From 1907-22 she was president of the WTUL. She was willing to do anything and everything, from standing on street corners telling hotel and restaurant employees on their way to work about the new 10-hour-day law to editing the WTUL's official publication. She worked untiringly to support strikers. She contributed and helped to implement ideas, like a training program that prepared some 40 young working women for local trade union leadership. But most crucial in that cross-class organization, she helped workers and allies get along together.

The WTUL did not succeed in unionizing large numbers of working women. Since it cooperated with other reform groups to secure protective legislation, no one can isolate its very real achievements in that area. But its support of workers' strikes involved its middle- and upper-class allies directly in workers' causes. Its imaginative programs to train workers as union leaders changed their lives and strengthened them in their struggles. And, despite many a bitter misunderstanding between workers and allies, it helped these women communicate with each other, face together the bruising bullies who attacked them on the picket lines and the judges who savaged them in the courts, and work together for a common cause.

Union Now? Ever?

Industrial women needed all the help they could get. In the early years of the century, labor unions must have seemed the most likely source. Women could see union men in the same shops getting off work at noon on Saturdays while they themselves were forced to work on. Yet by 1900 only 3.3 percent of industrial women were unionized, and in the next decade their numbers actually dropped, as union men "vowed to check this most unnatural invasion of [their] firesides" and the public attacked union women as communists, revolutionaries, prostitutes, and "unsexed female incendiaries."[45] Even in 1920, though for the past two decades women had been enrollng at a rate twice that of men, only 6.6 percent, one in 15, belonged to a union.[46]

Yet union membership could make an enormous difference in a woman's life. Scrubwomen in downtown Chicago office buildings once had their own union, affiliated with the elevator men and janitors. Though that union was later destroyed by the people who had organized it, it did give its women members their first sense of fellowship and protection. At a Hull House meeting the president of one of its locals

> told first of the long years in which the fear of losing her job and the fluctuating pay were harder to bear than the hard work itself, when she had regarded all the other women who scrubbed in the same building merely as rivals and was most afraid of the most miserable, because they offered to work for less and less as they were pressed harder and harder by debt. Then she told of the change that had come when the elevator men and even the lordly janitors had talked to her about an organization and had said that they must all stand together. She told how gradually she came to feel sure of her job and of her regular pay, and she was even starting to buy a house now that she could "calculate" how much she "could have for sure."[47]

Consider too what a union achieved for women in Illinois state institutions, where the WTUL found a woman who after 26 years of work had reached the top salary bracket of $30 a month, nurses who earned only $35-$40 a month, and an average salary for women of $20 a month. The WTUL organized them and secured for them a minimum wage of $30 a month, one day off a week, and an eight-hour day.[48]

Meanwhile thousands of women were involving themselves in men's strikes. "Mother" Mary Harris Jones, the relentless and indomitable heroine of striking coal miners, counted on their wives to spearhead many a protest. She herself attained an almost mythic status as she disguised herself as a peddler to collect information, led a pitiable group of working children from Pittsburgh to Washington, D.C., in a crusade to dramatize the evils of child labor, endured repeated imprisonment, defied the thugs hired by mine owners, and, at the age of 89, fought in the thick of the 1919 steel strike. Often at mine sites she would recruit miners' wives to keep scabs from operating the mines during a strike, but, she said, she never had to teach them what to do: They already knew how to fight. They used bucket-and-broom brigades to paint the scabs with excreta and tin-pan noisemakers to frighten off the mine mules. If arrested, the women took their babies to jail with them and kept them awake and crying all night by singing, until the guards could stand the racket no longer. No wonder Jones said that every strike she had been in had been won by women. Women persuaded their striking husbands to stay home while they themselves walked the picket lines, on the shaky and often-disproved theory that scabs and police would not assault women. They did; sometimes they killed them.

And what greater courage than that of a striker's wife whom a WTUL visitor found lying in bed with her newborn baby beside her and three other small children in her unheated room: "It is not only bread we give our children," she said. "We live by freedom, and I will fight till I die to give it to my children."[49]

The dramatic "Bread and Roses" strike of 1912 against the Lawrence, Massachusetts, textile industry involved both women and men workers. There, where half the children worked in the mills, where women were sometimes scalped when their hair caught in the unguarded machinery, where almost a fifth of babies born live died in their first year, where more than a third of the mill workers died before their 26th year, 20,000 workers struck. When employers' ruffians assaulted mothers *and their children* as they tried to send the starving youngsters out of Lawrence, a nationwide protest forced the employers to settle—a short-lived victory for the unions, though, for soon one of the frequent economic recessions of the era cost the unions most of their gains.

Brave and desperate industrial women were also stirring by themselves on their own behalf. Indeed, if older women or black women or married women wanted union representation at all, they almost had to bestir themselves, since neither the WTUL nor most labor unions took much interest in

REMAINS OF THAT "MOST DEPRAVED ACT OF SAVAGERY," THE LUDLOW (COLORADO) MASSACRE. IN APRIL 1914, IN THE ABSENCE OF STRIKING MINERS, THE MILITIA FIRED ON THEIR TENTS. SOME OF THEIR FAMILIES FLED IN A HAIL OF BULLETS; OTHERS LAY ON THE EARTH WITHIN OR IN PITS DUG UNDERNEATH THE TENTS. LATER THE MILITIA SET FIRE TO THE TENTS, ASPHYXIATING A DOZEN WIVES AND CHILDREN. (NATIONAL ARCHIVES)

them but focused instead on young single white women. It took a lot of courage. Women union organizers had to outface not only accusations of being communists but also personal attacks. Leaders like the outspoken anarchist Emma Goldman, who announced that "women need not always keep their mouths shut and their wombs open," frightened off potential union members.

All the same, from 1895 to 1905, women conducted 83 strikes completely on their own.[50] Between 1900 and 1917, New Jersey women cigar makers struck 24 times.[51] In 1900 San Francisco laundry workers rebelled against a system that forced them to stand for as long as 17 hours a day at mangles just above the washroom with hot steam pouring up through the floor, "breathing air laden with particles of soda, ammonia, and other chemicals," and to live in dorms with four beds to a room, denied food after 6:00 P.M., though they often worked until midnight, for a wage of $8.10 a month plus room and board. Secretly unionizing, they won elimination of the boarding house system, shorter hours, higher pay, holidays, overtime, and a regular lunch hour. Their union thrived for years.[52]

Michigan corset makers won a Pyrrhic victory when a sympathetic boycott to their strike drove their company out of business. Women bookbinders, mostly native-born, comparatively well-educated whites, managed to unionize a quarter of their 14,000-member work force. Their unions, which functioned as hiring halls and insisted on closed shops, protected them against the twice-a-week 24½-hour workdays common in non-union shops.

"We STRIKE for JUSTICE! We don't want to WASTE our lives in Making Waists Only!"[53]

Of all women's strikes in the Progressive Era, those of the garment workers in New York and Philadelphia attracted most attention. They began in New York, where the labor force included thousands of Russian Jewish women. More politically sophisticated and less passive than many immigrant women, they spearheaded the strikes in which women from many other ethnic groups courageously joined. Take Clara Lemlich, for instance. In 1903, when she was 15, she fled Russian pogroms, having already, against her father's wishes, learned to read and acquainted herself with radical literature. In New York she went to work making shirtwaists and in 1906 helped to found Local 25 of the International Ladies' Garment Workers Union.

From August 1909, trouble was brewing in the shirtwaist industry. By November, Lemlich had already participated in a series of walkouts and been arrested 17 times; sometimes she was beaten. At a meeting in Cooper Union on November 22, Lemlich galvanized the crowd with a passionate speech, in Yiddish, making a motion for a general strike. The crowd, roaring its approval, took the Jewish oath: "If I turn traitor to the cause I now pledge, may this hand wither from the arm I now raise."[54]

Twenty thousand shirtwaist makers immediately walked out; within a week 30,000 had struck.[55] Women without savings, women whose families depended on their earnings, women whose fledgling unions had no strike funds risked their livelihoods and their safety.

To their support came the WTUL, already experienced in conducting strikes and ready to lend their expertise, furnish "respectable" pickets to walk the lines with the strikers, provide middle-class or wealthy observers to bear witness in court to strikebreaker and police brutality, solicit money for bail and a strike fund, and attract public sympathy—as in this report of a picket-line incident by the *New York Sun*'s McAlister Coleman:

> *Of a sudden, around the corner came a dozen tough-looking customers, for whom the union label "gorillas" seemed well-chosen.*
> *"Stand fast, girls," called Clara [Lemlich], and then the thugs rushed the line, knocking Clara to her knees, striking at the pickets, opening the way for a group of frightened scabs to slip through the broken line. Fancy ladies from the Allen Street red-light district climbed out of cabs to cheer on the gorillas. There was a confused melee of scratching, screaming girls and fist-swinging men and then a patrol wagon arrived. The thugs ran off as the cops pushed Clara and two other badly beaten girls into the wagon.*
> *I followed the rest of the retreating pickets to the union hall, a few blocks away. There a relief station had been set up where one bottle of milk and a loaf of bread were given to strikers with small children in their families. There, for the first time in my comfortably sheltered Upper West Side life, I saw real hunger on the faces of my fellow Americans in the richest city in the world.*[56]

Within a few days the strikers had brought the industry to a virtual halt, and owners of small factories began to capitulate. By the end of November about half the strikers were back at work at more than 300 factories, their wages upped by 12 percent to 20 percent, and their union recognized. But the larger and more powerful employers refused to sign and began hiring scabs, including the black women to whom their doors had always been closed.[57]

Gradually, as the hungry, thinly clad workers shivered on their picket lines, their strike became a cause célèbre. The factory owners fed the fires with the barbaric methods common in union disputes of that era. The journalist Rheta Dorr, walking arm-in-arm with a frail shirtwaist maker, watched in horror while a foreman struck her companion in the face, knocking out several teeth. Police arrested the strikers—some 723 of them between November 22 and December 25 (and sometimes, to official embarrassment, their socially prominent allies)—and judges sentenced them to the workhouse. "You are on strike against God,"

CONDITIONS LIKE THESE LED TO THE TRIANGLE FIRE AND TO THE GARMENT WORKERS'
"RISING OF THE 20,000." (NATIONAL ARCHIVES)

one magistrate roared from his bench at a shirtwaist maker, who had not recognized the Deity in the figure of her exploitative employer.[58]

The WTUL saw to it that editors were aroused and reporters and photographers were on hand to record what was going on. They hired well-known lawyers to defend arrested strikers. They staged a huge march on city hall, led by three recently arrested strikers and three allies, to present the mayor with a petition of grievances. They sent out pairs of allies and waist makers to address women's groups. Wellesley students raised strike funds; Vassar and Bryn Mawr students picketed. So did Anne Morgan, sister of J. P. Morgan. Anna Howard Shaw, president of the National American Woman Suffrage Association, spoke to an enormous rally at the Hippodrome. Alva Belmont organized a motorcade of her own cars to circulate through the Lower East Side and ran a fund-raiser at the exclusive Colony Club, where one striker told how her employer covered the face of the clock to get more time out of his workers and another described how a priest visited her shop to warn Italian girls that if they struck, they would go to hell.

When the manufacturers shipped their unfinished work to Philadelphia, the strike spread there. Just before Christmas 15,000 waist makers, almost all women, went on strike. The WTUL set up another headquarters there. Mother Jones arrived in time for their rally at the Philadelphia Opera House. Philadelphia clubwomen mobilized, and the Equal Suffrage Association protested police brutality.

By December 23, 1909, union officers thought they had an agreement with the manufacturers, who consented to lower the work week to 52 hours; provide "free" needles, thread, and appliances; institute several paid holidays; rehire all strikers; not discriminate against union members; receive and deal with grievances—but would not recognize the union. New York and Philadelphia strikers rejected the contract.

The strikes ended not with victory but with whimpers. Union officials and the WTUL wavered. Holdout manufacturers farmed out their work to factories that had signed with the union. Finally in February the unions yielded and made peace with some manufacturers, without the recognition for which they had fought. Worse still, the strike ended with no contract at all with large manufacturers like the Triangle Shirtwaist Company.

But this Rising of the 20,000 inspired other strikes elsewhere and boosted union membership. By 1910 women workers were organized in many other trades and were being admitted to a dozen national unions. By 1914 the International Ladies' Garment Workers Union was one of the largest.

Even so, the most optimistic unionists hardly saw a millennium at hand. While many looked to the unions as their only bulwark against exploitation and abuse, other industrial women workers and their friends and allies sought protection through legislation, arguing that women, mothers or future mothers of the nation, needed special defenses. In an argument that still has not ended, they encountered opposition even from the most staunch defenders of women's rights. Harriot Stanton Blatch raised objections: "Was it perhaps woman's proverbial logic," she inquired, "to demand special protection and at the same time insist on 'equal pay for equal work'?"[59]

Often, though, it was easier to push through protective legislation than to win a strike. Working men supported it because it reduced competition: It counterbalanced women laborers' advantages of cheapness and exploitability and shut women out completely from many kinds of work. "We cannot drive the female out of the trade," proclaimed a union leader in the cigar industry, "but we can restrict [her] through factory laws."[60]

Reformers saw protective legislation for women as an opening wedge for the protection of all workers. Time and again the courts had defeated efforts to limit the workday. But in 1908 the U.S. Supreme Court upheld an Oregon law providing a 10-hour day for women, directly stating that "sex is a valid basis for classification." Half a loaf was better than none. If reformers could not immediately protect all workers, they could now begin to protect women.

Between 1909 and 1917, 41 states wrote or revised laws for women regulating hours, limiting night work, and restricting the weights women could lift.[61] States forbade women to work in physically dangerous places like mines or morally dangerous places like bars. During World War I, reformers and unionists alike fiercely defended protective legislation, especially hours laws, against pressures exerted by the demands for more goods for the war effort.

The female factory worker of 1920, as compared with her sister of 1900, had benefited to a limited extent from union gains and in a major way from the new protective legislation. She still faced severe sexual harassment; she still earned a fraction of a man's pay. But no longer could her boss legally order her to scrub the factory floor on Saturday afternoon without recompense.

Counter Arguments

In 1900 almost 216,000 women worked in stores; by 1920 their numbers had more than doubled, to about 527,000.[62] Though most of them also came from the working class, they considered themselves a notch or two above industrial workers. Middle-class women scorned their tedious and low-paid jobs, but many a working-class girl yearned for them, attracted in part by being near the goods the stores sold, which they coveted but could not afford. The stores happily hired women, especially neatly dressed and well-spoken women, but only, of course, for the lower ranks. Male floorwalkers, much better paid, supervised them.

In 1891 a store employee's usual 12-hour days stretched on weekends and during the Christmas rush from 7:45 A.M. until 11 P.M., or later. After hours she had to take stock and rearrange goods without pay, though she was docked if she came to work more than 15 minutes late the next day; indeed, at some stores that much tardiness cost her half a day's pay.

The work took its toll physically. Although officially the stores allowed her 20 minutes to eat lunch, the savvy saleswoman knew better than to take more than 10 minutes during the rush season. The five minutes allowed to go to the bathroom offered her no relief in stores like one in Baltimore that had only one toilet on the third floor of its annex for all customers and the 282 women it employed—and so much the worse for her kidneys.[63] She was forbidden to sit down or to lean on her counter. If she fainted from the long hours of standing, she was stretched out on the concrete floor of a damp subbasement lunchroom or sent home with no pay for the time she missed. She got no pay for legal holidays or for vacations. In slow times she might be laid off. Floorwalkers, petty tsars, could deny her permission to leave her counter or instruct her that she was insufficiently well dressed. How was she to dress better on her $6 or $7 a week? That was her problem, but didn't she know any male customers . . . ? The store reduced her wages if she damaged, lost, or broke any of their wares. "One little cash-girl was fined for knocking off a vase which had been placed too near the edge of a counter. Her pay envelope at the end of the week contained, therefore, but twenty-five cents."[64]

In these dismal conditions, help came from middle-class women. The Working Women's Society, founded in the 1880s, which recruited many members from department stores, appealed to customers to help women store employees improve their circumstances. Customers of conscience, like Josephine Shaw Lowell and Dr. Mary Putnam Jacobi, were appalled at what they heard. The shopgirls' plaint transformed the life of Maud Nathan, heretofore a comfortable young matron. For after all, her life as a consumer and those of the saleswomen converged in the store. Once alerted, she could not ignore them. Out of her concern and that of women like her grew in 1890 the remarkable New York Consumers' League (CL), later a national organization of 60 leagues in 20 states.

The league cooperated with the Working Women's Society in campaigns to enact protective legislation. In New York, for instance, CL helped to pass the Mercantile Inspection Act of 1896 limiting work hours, prohibiting child labor, and requiring seats behind counters and sanitary facilities. Better still, it harried the state and the stores to get these provisions enforced, when necessary providing unpaid inspectors from its own membership, only after a dozen years handing the job over to the state.

The CL also supported saleswomen's efforts to unionize, particularly by trying to sway public opinion. Union members lost the 1913 New York City strike, despite all that socially prominent CL members could do to help: distributing literature on New York's busiest corners, making sure to block traffic, getting themselves arrested, and then granting interviews to reporters. Elsewhere strikes went better. In Buffalo a strike beset by violence on the picket line earned a settlement for 4,000 retail workers, 80 percent of whom were women. In 1916 Lafayette, Indiana, clerks won a minimum wage and shorter hours.

But its use of consumer clout most distinguished the league. Its longtime executive secretary, Florence Kelley, as a child had been impressed by the example of a great aunt who refused to use cotton and sugar because slave labor had produced them. Kelley understood the league as a means to enact wage and hour laws and eliminate child labor through consumer pressure.

The organization based its influence on its potential to boycott—a potential that it chose not to exercise overtly. Rather than advising customers to avoid stores (and manufacturers) that violated its principles, it placed on its "White List" those that agreed to conform to them.

Its standards in some respects were modest, in others revolutionary. To make its White List, stores had not only to agree to CL's minimum wages, maximum hours, and vastly improved conditions of work, but also to survive inspection tours by CL's members. The first White List in 1891 had only eight stores, but the list grew after CL published it in a newspaper ad, and CL members visited unlisted stores to close their accounts—though this ploy evoked from some store owners the cogent question of how the customers would like it if the store owners inspected their homes to see how they treated their servants. All the same, by the end of 1893 the list had 24 names. Eventually it weighed so much with merchants that some of those omitted from it threatened to withdraw their ads from papers publishing the list—whereupon CL shifted to ads in theater programs, buses, subways and elevated trains, waiting rooms of hotels, and White List stores. And in time CL had to get injunctions to prevent manufacturers from reproducing its white label without its authorization.

The league tried to be fair to merchants; after all, its middle- and upper-class members shared many of the store owners' assumptions about life and work. CL leaders like Vida Scudder recognized the buying public's ultimate responsibility for fair labor practices. So the White List included the names of stores whose employment practices conformed to CL standards even if the stores would not sign the CL pledge.

What's more, CL would offer a fair exchange. For instance, if the stores would give their employees compensatory time off when they kept open late, CL would try to educate customers to shop earlier. Much of their other consumer education also benefited the stores, as they taught customers to pay bills promptly so that the stores could pay wages promptly, discouraged customers from sending home goods for inspection and then expecting the store to pick them up for credit, and asked customers to specify that packages could be sent the next day.

The status of some CL members and the people they could influence helped the cause along. The wife of an ex-governor of New York, for instance, saw a saleswoman faint, followed her when she was carried to a basement and laid on the floor, took her home, and learned that she had been nursing her sick mother and had fainted from fatigue exacerbated by having to stand all day long. Next day the governor's lady visited the head of the firm: "Seats behind counters for salesgirls or I withdraw my account!" When CL pressured stores to provide employee restrooms, one merchant furnished a disgracefully tatty cubbyhole and refused CL's requests to improve it. Thereupon Maud Nathan took the merchant's wife for a drive and suggested tactfully, and with the desired result, that women understood such things better than men.[65]

CL members got their reward when a young saleswoman naively told one of their inspectors, "Oh, yes, now we have seats and the floor-walker sees us sitting on them and doesn't tell us to get up. And we are no longer told to hurry our luncheon and return to the counter in ten minutes . . . There is a bunch of society women working for us now, and they'll never know the amount of good they've done!" [66]

Best of all for the retail-store workers, CL became a kind of ombudsman for them. As its fame spread, workers began to write in to complain about sexual harassment and working conditions. When, for instance, the league arranged an unpaid vacation for an exhausted saleswoman, the store fired her. The CL member who then called upon the manager emerged with his $40 check to pay for the vacation and an offer to rehire the employee, for whom, fortunately, the league had already found a place elsewhere.[67]

Pink Collars and Coffee Cups

Clerical workers, the elite of working-class women, were a comparatively new breed. They too were mostly young, mostly single, but they numbered few immigrant, black, or Jewish women. Theirs is the story of the entry into the work force of large numbers of white native-born women, usually the daughters of native-born parents. Their numbers grew from 7,000 in 1880 to 187,000 in 1900 to 1,421,000 in 1920.[68]

Their very status in the hierarchy of money-earning women inflicted hardship on them. They were not the kind to think of unionizing. Their clinging to the status of "ladies," identifying with the bosses rather than with other workers rendered them vulnerable. Witness what happened at the Curtis Publishing Company in 1912: After *Ladies' Home Journal* editor Edward Bok saw 15 women dancing the turkey trot during their lunch hour, the company fired them, and they had no recourse.

These clerks and "typewriters" were not displacing men, though men often aggrievedly thought they were. In reality industry was expanding, introducing machines, and applying the principles of "scientific management" to get the work done faster, more easily, and cheaper. In 1919 an officer of a sugar company boasted that one bookkeeping machine operator could take the place of three men. And who would operate these machines but women—women who in the popular view were tolerant of routine, careful, manually dexterous, docile, untroubled by thoughts of upward mobility. By preference employers hired young, attractive women to adorn the office; unmarried women with no prattle about the need for more wages to support families; above all, women who would work for far less money than men.

The very definition of clerical work was changing. Scientific management atomized office work, simplified it, and robbed it of interest. It deprived the new women clerks of control and opportunity, reducing them almost to robots, easily substitutable one for another, and not worth much pay. Always assign a task to the lowest-paid worker possible, scientific managers preached to employers, and don't worry about turnover at the lower levels. If Susie performed unsatisfactorily or quit, Mabel could easily take over. The clerical work that in 1871 had required "knowledge of languages, skills in accounts, familiarity with even minute details of business, energy, promptitude, tact, delicacy of perception" by 1910 in many large offices took little more than the ability to pound a typewriter or file.[69] So the jobs the new women clerks took were quite different from those previously assigned to male clerks. Many male clerks had been and still were aspiring and upwardly mobile, in training for management positions. But the female clerks might stay in the typing pool indefinitely.

Not so the private secretary—by its nature her work was too diverse, too personal in its relationships, too subject to the notions of her boss to be analyzed and mechanized. She had status: She expected file clerks and typists to call her "Miss." To some extent she could decide for herself when to do what. But her boss expected from her in the office some, if not all, of the personal services he expected from his wife at home. Often her pay did not adequately recompense her for the responsibilities she bore. And like her sister office workers she could aspire to no higher job.

Like private secretaries, office workers in small businesses performed more diverse tasks and exercised more control over their own work, especially in one-woman offices, than in large corporations. Indeed, then as now they often knew more about the business than the men to whom they reported, but only

"Look! the boss has a WOMAN to write his letters"

THE OPENING WEDGE. (NATIONAL ARCHIVES)

rarely could they overcome the gender prejudice that denied them commensurate wages and promotion.

In short, men of comparable ability could make more in other jobs than in clerical work, but women could make more in clerical work than in other jobs. For both in status and in money, women office workers fared better than women in factories, stores, and domestic service. In the late 19th century when they first began to infiltrate offices, some women clerical workers had even outearned teachers. The gap between clerical workers and other women narrowed as more women entered the lowest ranks of clerical work, legislation and unionization improved the lot of factory women, and store workers' and teachers' pay rose with their standards of education. All the same, investing in a commercial education paid off. Even if women learned their office skills in the more prestigious private schools, they paid tuition as low as $10 a month, perhaps for as long as nine months, after which they could expect to start with wages of $10 a week.[70]

So young women flocked to business schools. In Providence, Rhode Island, Katharine Gibbs, a widow with two small sons, took courses at Simmons College, sold her jewelry to get capital, opened her school to teach office skills and "professional development" (respect, promptness, dependability, loyalty, and modesty of dress), and made so much money in two years that she could open branches in Boston and New York.[71]

Office jobs marked the point in time and in kind of labor where middle-class and working-class women met. They attracted women from both groups. They offered a kind of upward mobility to working-class women and a safe haven to middle-class women just entering the work force.

Of all "women's jobs" in the Progressive Era, office work changed fastest. Its numbers bounded higher and higher. It created thousands of "respectable" new jobs for women. It became what it still remains, a female ghetto and a refuge. As management de-skilled the work available in the typing pools and file rooms, it sentenced women to "no-exit" jobs. At the same time office work provided a kind of insurance for women who dropped in and out of the work force or needed to move from one city to another as familial demands changed.

TRIMMING CURRENCY.   (NATIONAL ARCHIVES)

Professional Women

Working-class women worked because they had to, only when they had to. But middle- and upper-class women more often worked because they wanted to, and they had wider choices in the kinds of work they did.

They differed from working-class women in all sorts of ways. Though they clustered in large cities, they were geographically mobile. Politically aware, they were strikingly active in reform work. They undertook all sorts of responsibilities in medicine, law, journalism, science, business, the arts, education, and sometimes paid positions in club work and reform activity. And, of course, they had more money than working-class women.

The middle-class women who chose to work outside the home were still fighting the Victorian value system that had imprisoned them by telling them that they were too delicate to work, that they needed rest and more rest, often reducing them to ill health and uselessness, robbing them of interests. Physicians like Dr. Edith Lowry warned especially against exercising the brain, advising that girls should be guarded from too much exertion during puberty by removing them from school and teaching them housework! Under such a system some women came close to being literally bored to death. Rheta Childe Dorr wrote of her days as a young society matron, "I made something like fifty calls a month on women who differed from one another no more than peas in a pod. . . . The men who came to our house. . . treated me like a nice child. . . . We all lived in dolls' houses and I for one wanted to get out into the world of real things."[72]

Those who opted out of the system faced lots of difficulties, but they found lots of opportunities, many of which they developed for themselves. In the professions that they entered in increasing numbers, they had to battle the usual societal disapproval, sexual harassment, inequitable status, and pay and gender discrimination, particularly in such situations as that of physicians, where their numbers in an overcrowded field frightened male doctors into unscrupulous retaliation. Almost as often as not, they had to deny themselves marriage if they wanted a career. And only about a quarter of them dared to indulge themselves in what so many men have long taken for granted, the combination of satisfying professional work and a family.[73]

But these gutsy and lucky women enjoyed the advantage unusual among women workers of exercising control over their own work. Better still, as women's presence and influence increased, they began to create their own conditions, even their own professions and their own professional associations. It's hard to be first, but it's also fascinating.

It was fascinating for Alice Hamilton, who explored and tilled the virgin field of industrial medicine. Harvard and her colleagues there, after appointing her their first woman faculty member, neglected her and underpaid her, but by then she had earned such a reputation in the world of industry as to frustrate some of their attempts to take her work from her. When a group of businessmen approached Harvard with a proposition to fund a large research project in her field, the men in her department told her they would take care of it, but the businessmen refused to pay unless she was included—the very woman, mind you, who had insisted that these same businessmen eliminate dangerous conditions in their factories.

It was fascinating for the journalist Rheta Childe Dorr. Having left her more-than-comfortable home, with a young son and his nanny to support, she had to fight her way in the world of newspapers and publishing, where a few women had preceded her, "altho [she] never knew with what burglar's tools they broke in." It took her three years of free-lancing, handing in her copy to supercilious office boys, selling her diamonds, and pawning her family silver. Eventually she established enough of a reputation to be offered a position on the *New York Post*, for which she was required to furnish evidence of good character—a requirement that, she tartly pointed out to the editor, could not have been met by the paper's founder, Alexander Hamilton. Once well launched, she asked for a raise, only to be told that naturally women were paid less than men; men after all had families to support—a reply that didn't change when Dorr pointed out the obvious: "I know personally five women who are exactly in my position, widows or abandoned wives with babies to support." Furthermore, her editor told her, "You have no future. There is no position open to you better than the one you now hold. You know yourself that a woman could never be a city editor, much less a managing editor."[74] But by no means would Dorr have chosen to escape these hardships and insults by forfeiting her hard-won expertise on women in industry, about whom she published a series of articles; her intimacy with the British suffragist Mrs. Pankhurst, whose autobiography she helped write; or the knowledgeability that won her a trip to revolutionary Russia and a visit to the front lines with the Russian women's Battalion of Death.

Their work fascinated women like these partly because of its own interest, partly because of the new worlds to which it introduced them, and partly because it made them pioneers. Sometimes they pioneered in pushing back the boundaries of knowledge, like Lucy Sprague Mitchell, who throughout her lifetime experimented with progressive schools and the study of children as individuals.

Sometimes they pioneered in changing the conditions of work within a profession, like Henrietta Rodman and her associates. When they came to it, teaching was a profession cribbed, cabined, and confined with restrictions. In the rural areas academic standards hardly existed. Fifteen-year-old Frieda Ware was only one of thousands of youngsters who took on the education of a whole farm community of "children"—including students sometimes older and often bigger than she. But small towns across America held the teacher to standards of behavior more suitable to convents than to secular communities: In some places she could be fired for getting into a carriage with a man other than her father or brother, dressing in bright colors, dyeing her hair, loitering downtown in ice cream stores, wearing dresses more than two inches above the ankle, not being home between 8:00 P.M. and 6:00 A.M.—indeed, for any reason the local school board chose, or none.[75]

Even in New York City in 1900 marriage meant automatic dismissal, except that the married teacher might become a permanent substitute, at lower pay. In 1901 Brooklyn teacher Mary Murphy married, only to be charged with misconduct and fired. Her suit failed, but she won on appeal, the judge apparently finding himself unable with a straight face to call marriage "misconduct." In 1913 Rodman acted as point woman in a fight to let pregnant women and mothers with children keep their jobs, charging the New York City Board of Education with "mother-baiting." "Virtuous motherhood," so much touted by the moralists of the day, at last won also in the courts.

Almost inadvertently, middle-class women workers created new professions, notably in home economics. A couple of forces pushed them toward it. Infatuated with expertise, Americans turned to science to answer their questions and solve their problems—why not domestic science to improve housekeeping and mothering? And male scientists, unwilling to admit women to their own fields but unable to deny the abilities of some of the extraordinary women who earned degrees in them, happily relegated these women to something that at least had to do with where they belonged—at home.

What these women discovered in their new departments of home economics in the universities and in their government offices was translated into practical applications for housewives by women like Atalanta Pummill. A teacher from the age of 17, she earned her bachelor's and master's degrees the hard way, by year after year of summer school. Married, with a child, she taught countless young women in the Missouri Ozarks how to improve their families' nutrition, clothe them less expensively and more attractively, and make their homes more appealing. Once her daughter had grown, she went where she was needed. Her school superintendent husband would remark: "They need a home ec teacher over at Birch Run." "Now, Joe," she would warn, "I don't want to go off and leave you another winter." "I know, Lanty, but what are they going to do over at Birch Run?" And she would be off for another year of boarding at the local "hotel" and commuting home on weekends.[76] Women like her (and men like him) changed the lives of thousands of people.

Something similar happened in social work. As women in volunteer or paid jobs, particularly women in settlement houses, grew to recognize the complexity of social problems, they felt the need of more expertise. Take Katharine Bement Davis, for instance. Unable to afford a college education until she was 30, Davis studied at night and taught by day, earned her way through Vassar, directed a model workingman's home at the Columbian Exposition of 1893, and then took charge of a settlement house in a Philadelphia neighborhood of black and immigrant families where she established model apartments. Four years later she resigned to work on her Ph.D. in political economy; she received it in 1900, when she was 40. She then won a civil service appointment as superintendent of the new Reformatory for Women at Bedford Hills, New York; she created a distinguished 13-year record there, improvising as she went, developing a cottage system and inaugurating a program to identify and help potentially reformable women. She left only to become commissioner of corrections in New York City and later chair of the New York City parole board, winding up her brilliant career at the Rockefeller Foundation. Penology, famine relief, treatment of sex offenders, parole policy, research in narcotics addiction and the white slave trade, presidential campaigning, woman suffrage—she involved herself with all of these. Not much room for boredom.

This kind of need to know, this search for expertise gradually professionalized workers. Among the most absorbing examples is the story of public health nursing.

Toward the end of the 19th century, the American public awoke to the dangers of contagion. Robert Koch had demonstrated in 1882 that tuberculosis was catching, and in the 1890s the public panicked over the germ theory of disease. No longer could the middle and upper classes console themselves with the belief that good stock survives and prospers. In the first five years of the new century articles in popular magazines blared "Books Spread Contagion," "Contagion by Telephone," "Infection and Postage Stamps," "Disease from Public Laundries," and "Menace of the Barber Shop."[77] Publicity by Consumers' League about diseased food handlers and the filthy tenements in which garments were sewn, conditions that menaced the health of customers, spurred efforts to reduce illness among the poor. By 1910 most municipalities had been harassed or otherwise persuaded into adopting such public health measures as removing garbage, providing pure water, building sewers, improving housing, controlling contagious diseases, and testing the milk supply.

The next step was to teach people how to care for their families and themselves. Late in the 19th century, wealthy women in New York, Boston, Philadelphia, and Buffalo had hired nurses to visit the poor, not only to care for the sick, but to teach hygiene, nutrition, and disease prevention. Organizations began to pick up this obviously good idea, forming visiting nurses' associations. Nurses worked six days a week, eight to 10 hours a day, visiting perhaps a dozen families a day.

Demand for public health nurses soared, and their duties multiplied. They worked for clubs, factories, insurance companies, boards of health and education, hospitals, tuberculosis associations, settlement houses, milk and baby clinics, playgrounds, charity organizations, dispensaries, and churches. In 1901 only 58 groups employed these women; by 1914 almost 2,000 clamored for their services.[78] The 200 public health nurses of 1900, multiplied to an estimated 3,000 by 1912.[79]

Nurse–settlement worker Lillian Wald shrewdly persuaded New York City to hire nurses by demonstrating that this move would reduce absenteeism. And,

THE CONSUMERS' LEAGUE ALERTED THE PUBLIC TO THE FILTHY CONDITIONS UNDER
WHICH FOOD WAS PREPARED FOR PUBLIC CONSUMPTION IN SLUM HOMES. HERE A
MANGY CAT WANDERED OVER CRACKED NUTS, AND WORKERS COUGHED AND BLEW
THEIR NOSES AS THEY PICKED THE NUTS FROM THEIR SHELLS.   (NATIONAL ARCHIVES)

arguing that such a technique would save the company money in death benefits
paid out, she sold the mammoth Metropolitan Life Insurance Company on the
idea of providing the services of visiting nurses as an additional benefit to its
industrial policyholders. Three years later, in 1914, the Met was paying for a
million visits a year.[80]

The nurses' work required them to go everywhere, into the poorest and
filthiest of tenements, at all hours of the day and night. Apparently their uniforms
protected them, for many tenement dwellers owed their lives to these brave
women. They soon learned not to wear tight corsets and to reduce the usual
number of undergarments—too many stairs to climb, too many blocks to walk,
too many all-night vigils. Never, Rosalind Gillete Shawe advised the public
health nurse, should she enter a room of contagion hungry; in fact, she should
always nurse on a full stomach. They carried with them the supplies they needed:
thermometers, aprons, mutton tallow melted with rose water (as a hand lotion),
vaseline, measuring glasses, a stick of nitrate of silver, catheters, a map of the
city and a street directory, a list of charitable institutions, and names, addresses,
and office hours of all doctors in the district.

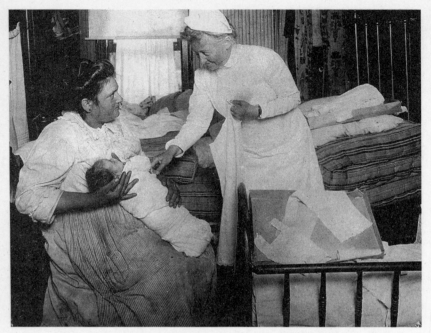

WOMAN TO WOMAN, EXPERT TO MOTHER. A PUBLIC HEALTH NURSE HELPING AND
TEACHING. (NATIONAL ARCHIVES)

The decision about whether or not to call a doctor, and which one to call, often rested with the nurse. Sometimes she would deliver a baby herself. She had to improvise, in circumstances where even keeping the patient clean was a triumph and providing the patient even a modicum of privacy an impossibility.

Her work did not end with her medical duties. She cleaned house, if only to set things to rights enough that she could care for her patient decently. She cooked, for how could she let her patient or the children in the family go hungry? Often she needed a strong stomach, for, as Shawe warned,

> Any one may theoretically love little children; to love little children who are sick, dirty, and unwholesome, and possibly covered with sores and vermin, to clean these same little children with her own hands, and to perform the same offices for children of a larger growth, the sick, ignorant, dirty adults, who have never properly learned the uses of soap and water, needs a person with a love for humanity amounting almost to a reverence.[81]

Besides these immediate tasks, the nurse sought to help her patients and their families to better health over the long term, by showing them how to improve their homes, instructing them in personal and household hygiene, and—teaching them habits of thrift! This last task suggests just how easy, perhaps inevitable, it was for a nurse to involve herself deeply with the families she visited. Often she assumed duties we today would assign to a social worker—at least to the extent of calling in the agency that could effectively tackle the problem. And, Shawe adjured her, she should teach not only the importance of regular bowel movements, but also "wrongfulness of excess in all ways, and the wickedness of indulgence in unlawful passions."[82]

All in all, what the visiting nurse did aside from her medical duties depended on her own personality and the philosophy of her particular agency. Some kept scrupulously away from influencing patients politically or religiously; others consciously undertook to act as Christian missionaries. Some gave food and clothing, and others insisted that such gifts destroyed the characters of the recipients. Some wanted to help only those they found "worthy," but one brave organization deliberately searched out the unworthy, apparently for the challenge they provided!

A case described by Lillian Wald illustrates what the visiting nurses were up against. One nurse encountered an Italian man paralyzed below the waist, suffering from three large bedsores, lying on a hard cot with a sheet over him and rags beneath. His wife cared for him in the intervals of doing sweated work finishing knee pants—the sole support of the family. The nurse got her patient an air bed and loaned him bed- and nightclothes. She recruited friends to supplement his diet with eggs and milk, and she herself went twice a day to change his dressings. She appealed to her employer, the Association for the Improvement of the Condition of the Poor, for help with the rent; to a woman's club for eggs and groceries; to the Centre Street Dispensary for milk; to the Nurses' Settlement for sheets, pillowcases, and dressings; and to a neighbor for a couch. Meanwhile his wife sewed all day and washed his linen when it became too dark to sew. When her double duties had exhausted the patient's wife, the nurse arranged for household help. The poor old fellow "lived only a few weeks longer, but died, as he wished, at home."[83]

With the wild mix of public and private support for the public health nurses, turf fights broke out. Municipal health departments and school health services wanted to mark out preventive work for themselves. Visiting nurse associations naturally resented this effort to cut them out, particularly as they had pioneered the preventive work; they reasoned that the nurse who visited the sick in their homes could best identify the sources of infection and best teach prevention.

Some physicians also were worrying about their territorial rights. Early on, to save their own time and that of the doctors, the nurses began to obtain blanket orders applicable in given situations, rather than waiting for a physician to write an order to treat a specific patient. As a result the visiting nurses became far more independent of physicians than were hospital nurses or nurses on private duty. Public health nurses generally, as they recognized their need to know more, sought more training, rendering themselves more threatening to "below-average" doctors. At the same time the visiting nurse grew more sophisticated, and perhaps more formidable, as she came to know her way around her territory, the legal system, and the network of private charities and public institutions where she could find help for her patients.

Sometimes she had to go head-on with a doctor, as in a case cited by Lavinia Dock, where a nurse diagnosed an illness as smallpox and the doctor denied that it was a contagious disease. After 24 hours, she gave in to her conscience and reported it to the authorities, only to be dressed down by the doctor for reporting it and by the authorities for delaying to report it. Dock, a thoughtful and insightful nurse, administrator, scholar, and feminist, commented that in large cities poor people often drew below-average doctors and above-average nurses. What's more, the doctor usually looked only at the sick person, the nurse at the whole family.[84]

Opposition to the visiting nurses was aggravated by the oversupply of doctors. Male physicians scrambling for a living eyed suspiciously women doctors, midwives, and visiting nurses, who might preempt some of the trade that should by rights and tradition be theirs. As visiting nurses raised their standards and their sights, physicians tried harder to put them in their place (under the physician's thumb).

Although such opposition no doubt kept the visiting nurses from what they might otherwise have achieved, one hates to think what the state of America's health would have been without them, in an era when so much of the population was poor, ill nourished, and ignorant of the basic principles of health; in a time when it was sometimes as dangerous to enter a hospital as to go without medical care. School nurses and industrial nurses descend from them. Thousands of newspaper and magazine articles have echoed their emphasis on preventive medicine. Remnants of their associations survive and grow in importance with the aging of the American population; they check blood pressure and cholesterol in drugstores and enable many a chronic patient to stay in her or his own home.

The difference they made in the United States is clearly implied in the annals of those public health nurses who went to France in World War I. Women like Elizabeth Ashe, chief nurse of the Children's Bureau of the American Red Cross, were horrified by the conditions they found in that country, which had not enjoyed the blessing of public health nurses. They itched to roll up their sleeves and get to work, flinging open the windows of stuffy rooms, instructing caretakers *not* to feed several babies from the same spoon, educating French mothers in better prenatal care and infant care and feeding, fighting tuberculosis, cleaning up children covered with impetigo and lice, teaching children to play.

In many ways the course of the public health nurses typifies the progress of other American professional women in the first two decades of the 20th century. Though they usually were not the first American women to do their work, they took over and professionalized work previously done by amateurs and volunteers. They expanded their fields. They undertook all sorts of responsibilities for the public welfare. They raised the educational standards in their profession. They insisted on licensing. They formed their own professional organizations. And, again like other professional women, they encountered, and now and then overcame, a good bit of male resistance and harassment. As Franklin Roosevelt's secretary of labor Frances Perkins remarked, "I don't think people realize how much professional and cultural life women had if they wanted it before the days of women suffrage."[85]

On Their Own

Of all working women in the Progressive Era, those who ran their own businesses may be the hardest to track. All sorts of women undertook entrepreneurial miniventures. Wives supplemented the family income by selling milk and eggs or taking in boarders or doing piecework. Domestics transformed themselves into day workers, freeing themselves from the tyranny of the hovering housewife and the necessity of wearing uniforms, supplementing their income with part-time jobs sewing or serving at parties. Private-duty nurses also hired themselves out by the day, though they depended heavily on physicians' recommendations. By 1900 more than 3,500 women worked as professional photographers, many of them specializng in portraits. Women operated dressmaking and hatmaking businesses from their homes or in small shops. Women ran two-thirds of the employment offices in big cities from their homes. They peddled goods on pushcarts.

One stumbles across vagrant references. Anne Ellis bid on and won a contract to feed the 75 men at a shearing camp.[86] "One woman is making $6,000 a year from an ostrich farm; another $3,000 by growing violets. A Western woman raises animals for menageries; an Eastern one designs unique and attractive advertisements."[87]

Otherwise, although there must have been several failures and many modest successes for every triumph, the entrepreneurial record is confined mostly to those whose success earned them fame or wealth. For instance, in Texas Jessie Daniel Ames and her mother operated a local telephone company. Gene Stratton-Porter, nature writer and sentimental novelist, wrote her first story in secret, renting a post office box to conceal the rejections she expected: Her novel *Freckles*, about a poor, pure-hearted, ecologically-minded youth, sold 10,000 copies in the original edition and 1,400,000 in a cheap reprint. In 1902 Fannie Farmer opened her School of Cookery in Boston and transformed home cooking by specifying exact measurements and emphasizing the nutritional values of food. Her publisher so doubted the success of her book that he insisted that she pay publication costs; it has sold almost 4 million copies.

Elsie deWolfe flourished first as an actress and then as an independent interior decorator. Her housemate Amy Marbury, who had begun her business career by raising poultry, went on to become a theatrical and author's agent. Illustrator and author Rose Cecil O'Neill in 1909 created the first Kewpies, which eventually earned her royalties amounting to some $1.5 million. In Richmond, Virginia, in 1899 Maggie Lena Walker rescued from near-bankruptcy a cooperative insurance venture founded in 1867 by ex-slave Mary Prout and sustained and enlarged it throughout her lifetime; she was the first woman bank president.

Another pioneer black businesswoman, Madame C. J. Walker, metamorphosed herself from a washerwoman into a millionaire philanthropist with her invention and marketing of the "Walker Method" of hair products. By 1910 she employed 5,000 black women all around the world. By miracles of fund-raising, poet-journalist Harriet Monroe founded in 1912 *Poetry: A Magazine of Verse*, arguably the most influential magazine of poetry of the 20th century. Rose Markward Knox, co-founder and later sole operator of the gelatin company, spoke for many women when she commented, "I just used common sense—a man would call it horse sense—in running my business. But from the first I determined to run it in what I called a woman's way."[88]

Other women acted entrepreneurially not for themselves, but for the public weal. Oregonian Mary Lord, for instance, pressed for a flax industry in her native state. She spoke to individual farmers, to granges, to farmers' institutes, and, perhaps most important, to the Portland Woman's Club, which formed the Women's Flax Association and a stock company to promote the production of flax.[89]

Woman's work is never done, and never adequately described. This chapter can only suggest, rather than record, the variety, daring, and perseverance of women in the world of paid work in the Progressive Era. Most who entered it found it unwelcoming, harassing, inhumanly demanding. Only a lucky few (usually with strong bodies and extraordinary energy and determination) broke through to enjoy the rich rewards in achievement and satisfaction it had to offer.

Society had not yet internalized women's need and right to work for pay. In her testimony before the National War Labor Board in December 1919, Dr. Anna Howard Shaw still found it necessary to insist: "The time has come when we women have a right to ask that we shall be free to labor where our labor is needed, that we shall be free to serve in the capacity for which we are fitted. No human being can tell what another human being can do until that human being has had the opportunity to test himself. And so it has been with women."

Source Notes

1. These figures do not purport to represent the totality of female labor. They do not even include the farm labor of farmers' wives. Inevitably, the census

takers missed many intermittent laborers, like those married women who resorted to paid employment outside the home when husbands were not working or times were hard. Nor did they count housework or the labor involved in doing sweated piecework at home, taking in boarders, and the myriad other small entrepreneurial ways in which married women supplemented the family income. Bear in mind also the significant amount of work contributed by women as volunteers.

2. This statement needs reading with a grain of salt, in the form of the recognition of the youth of the population as a whole, and the shortness of the life span. The average length of life implied by the death rates of 1900 was 46.3 years for males and 48.3 for females. Irene B. Taeuber and Conrad Taeuber, *People of the United States in the Twentieth Century* (Washington, D.C.: Bureau of the Census, 1971). The census of 1900 recorded only 37 percent of all females as married, 55 percent single, 7 percent widowed, and 0.3 percent divorced.

3. Thirty-five percent of widowed and divorced women worked. A 1914 study showed that of 370 working women on the West Side of Manhattan, 43 percent were widows and deserted wives. A similar study in Philadelphia indicated that of 728 married women at work, 237 were widows, 146 were deserted wives, and 12 were divorced. Mimi Abramovitz, *Regulating the Lives of Women: Social Welfare Policy from Colonial Times to the Present* (Boston: South End Press, 1988), p. 191.

4. Cindy Sondik Aron, introduction to Dorothy Richardson's *The Long Day: The Story of a New York Working Girl* (1905; reprint, Charlottesville: Univ. of Virginia Press, 1990), p. xviii. See also Carl N. Degler, *At Odds: Women and the Family in America from the Revolution to the Present* (New York: Oxford Univ. Press, 1980), pp. 410–11; Abramovitz, pp. 189–90; Ruth Schwarz Cowan, *More Work for Mother: The Ironies of Household Technology from the Open Hearth to the Microwave* (New York: Basic Books, 1983), p. 170; and Sara M. Evans, *Born for Liberty: A History of Women in America* (New York: Free Press, 1989), pp. 156–57.

5. Sinclair Lewis, *The Job: An American Novel* (New York: Grosset and Dunlap, 1917), p. 172.

6. Marion Harland, *The Distractions of Martha* (New York: Scribner's, 1906), p. 86.

7. Rheta Childe Dorr, *A Woman of Fifty* (1924; reprint, New York: Arno Press, 1980), pp. 188–89.

8. Margery W. Davies, *Woman's Place is at the Typewriter: Office Work and Office Workers, 1870–1930* (Philadelphia: Temple Univ. Press, 1982), p. 75.

9. Margaret F. Byington, *Homestead, the Households of a Mill Town* (1910; reprint, The University Center for International Studies, Univ. of Pittsburgh, 1974), pp. 109–10.

10. Dorr, *A Woman of Fifty*, pp. 188–89, 201.
11. U.S. Department of Commerce and Labor, Bureau of the Census, *Statistics of Women at Work* (Washington, D.C.: Government Printing Office, 1907), p. 168.
12. Elyce J. Rotella, *From Home to Office: U.S. Women at Work, 1870–1930* (Ann Arbor: Univ. of Michigan Research Press, 1981), Tables 5.4 and 2.8.
13. David M. Katzman, *Seven Days a Week: Women and Domestic Service in Industrializing America* (New York: Oxford Univ. Press, 1978), app., Table A-14.
14. January 17, 1906, quoted in Judith Freeman Clark, *Almanac of American Women in the 20th Century* (New York: Prentice-Hall, 1987), p. 9.
15. Agnes Nestor, *Woman's Labor Leader: The Autobiography of Agnes Nestor* (Rockford, Ill.: Bellevue Books, 1954), p. 63.
16. Lydia Kingsmill Commander, *The American Idea* (1907; reprint, New York: Arno Press, 1972), p. 132.
17. Barbara Meyer Wertheimer, *We Were There: The Story of Working Women in America* (New York: Pantheon Books, 1977), p. 210.
18. Elizabeth Sears, "Business Women and Women in Business," *Harper's Monthly* 134 (January 1917):276.
19. Lewis, *The Job,* p. 5.
20. Edna Ferber, *Personality Plus: Some Experiences of Emma McChesney and Her Son Jock* (New York: Frederick A. Stokes, 1914), p. 61.
21. Sears, p. 274.
22. Barbara Miller Solomon, *In the Company of Educated Women: A History of Women and Higher Education in America* (New Haven: Yale Univ. Press, 1985), p. 63, Table 2. In other words, the percentage of all women 18–21 years old attending college rose from 2.8 percent in 1900 to 7.6 percent in 1920. Solomon, p. 64, Table 3. In 1900, 8,104 women graduated from college; 16,642 in 1920. Rotella, Table 2.
23. Joyce Antler, *The Educated Woman and Professionalization: The Struggle for a New Feminine Identity, 1890–1920* (New York: Garland, 1987), pp. 171, 176, 178.
24. Degler, p. 409, and Jacqueline Jones, *Labor of Love, Labor of Sorrow: Black Women, Work, and the Family from Slavery to the Present* (New York: Basic Books, 1985), p. 91.
25. Mary Osborn Douthit, ed., *The Souvenir of Western Women* (Portland, Oreg.: Anderson and Duniway, 1905), p. 170.
26. Degler, p. 410. See also Martha Foote Crow, *The American Country Girl* (1915; reprint, New York: Arno Press, 1974), p. 111, and Anna Langhorne Waltz, "West River Pioneer: A Woman's Story, 1911–1915, Parts Three and Four," *South Dakota History* 17 (1987):242–48, 285–95, reproduced in Carol Fairbanks and Bergine Haakenson, eds., *Writings of Farm*

Women, 1840–1940: An Anthology (New York: Garland, 1990), pp. 221–240.

27. Joseph A. Hill, *Women in Gainful Occupations, 1870–1920* (Census Monographs 9. Washington, D.C.: Government Printing Office, 1929), p. 19, Table 12.

28. Nancy Woloch, *Women and the American Experience* (New York: Knopf, 1984), p. 235.

29. Nancy Schrom Dye, *As Equals and As Sisters: Feminism, The Labor Movement, and the Women's Trade Union League of New York* (Columbia: Univ. of Missouri Press, 1980), pp. 212, 73.

30. Ibid., pp. 18, 19.

31. Wertheimer, p. 217.

32. Ibid., p. 218.

33. Ibid., p. 224.

34. Ibid., p. 215.

35. Mrs. John Van Vorst and Marie Van Vorst, *The Woman Who Toils, Being the Experiences of Two Gentlewomen as Factory Girls* (New York: Doubleday, Page and Co., 1903), pp. 221, 272.

36. Ibid., pp. 267, 269.

37. Byington, p. 79.

38. Wertheimer, p. 214; and Andrew Sinclair, *The Emancipation of American Women* (New York: Harper and Row, 1935), p. 306. "Economist John Commons estimated that only 25 percent of all female wage earners made a living wage in 1914—a figure placed at $8. a week." Alice Kessler-Harris, *Women Have Always Worked: A Historical Overview* (New York: Feminist Press, 1981), p. 63.

39. Nestor, p. 158; Dorr, *A Woman of Fifty,* p. 123; and Wertheimer, p. 358.

40. Kathy Peiss, *Cheap Amusements: Working Women and Leisure in Turn-of-the-Century New York* (Philadelphia: Temple Univ. Press, 1986), pp. 52, 53.

41. Ibid., p. 68. See also Elizabeth Ewen, *Immigrant Women in the Land of Dollars: Life and Culture on the Lower East Side, 1890–1925* (New York: Monthly Review Press, 1985), pp. 107–108.

42. Peiss, p. 68.

43. Dorr, *A Woman of Fifty,* p. 190.

44. Quoted in Mary E. Dreier, *Margaret Dreier Robins: Her Life, Letters, and Work* (New York: Zenger Pub., 1950), p. 31.

45. Abramovitz, p. 189.

46. Degler, p. 400. In 1920, though women constituted 20 percent of the work force, they made up only 8 percent of organized workers. Woloch, p. 241.

47. Jane Addams, *Twenty Years at Hull House, with Autobiographical Notes* (1910; reprint, New York: Macmillan, 1934), p. 226.

48. Nestor, p. 139.

49. Eleanor Flexner, *Century of Struggle: The Woman's Rights Movement in the United States* (Cambridge, Mass.: Belknap Press of Harvard Univ. Press, 1968), p. 244.
50. Wertheimer, p. 204.
51. Patricia Cooper, "Women Workers, Work Culture, and Collective Action in the American Cigar Industry, 1900–1919," in Charles Stephenson and Robert Asher, eds., *Life and Labor: Dimensions of American Working-Class History* (Albany: State Univ. of New York Press, 1986), p. 201.
52. Wertheimer, pp. 214ff., passim.
53. Motto on badge worn in the Rising of the 20,000.
54. Evans, p. 159.
55. Helen Marot of the WTUL estimated that only about 6,000 of these were men. Woloch, p. 209. We draw much of our information on this Rising of the 20,000 from Woloch's dramatic account.
56. Woloch, pp. 207–08.
57. Of the tiny number of black women already working in the garment industry, a few courageously joined the strike. Wertheimer, p. 307.
58. Informed of this *obiter dictum* George Bernard Shaw commented: "Delightful. Medieval America always in intimate personal confidence of the Almighty." Flexner, p. 243.
59. Harriot Stanton Blatch and Alma Lutz, *Challenging Years: The Memoirs of Harriot Stanton Blatch* (1940; reprint, New York: Hyperion, 1976), p. 287.
60. Woloch, p. 244.
61. Abramovitz, p. 188.
62. Katzman, Table A-3.
63. Wertheimer, p. 239.
64. Maud Nathan, *The Story of an Epoch-Making Movement* (Garden City, N.Y.: Doubleday, Page and Co., 1926), p. 12.
65. Ibid., p. 39.
66. Ibid., pp. 43–44.
67. Ibid., p. 56. For the fascinating story of the expansion of CL work, readers may turn to Nathan's book and to Josephine Goldmark's *Impatient Crusader: Florence Kelley's Life Story* (Champaign: Univ. of Illinois Press, 1953).
68. Margery W. Davies, *Woman's Place is at the Typewriter: Office Work and Office Workers, 1870–1930* (Philadelphia: Temple Univ. Press, 1982), Table 4.
69 Rotella, p. 70.
70. Valarie Quinney, "Office Workers and Machines: Oral Histories of Rhode Island Working Women," in Charles Stephenson and Robert Asher, eds., *Life and Labor: Dimensions of American Working-Class History* (Albany: State Univ. of New York Press, 1986), p. 265.

71. Ibid., p. 265.
72. Dorr, *A Woman of Fifty*, pp. 55–56.
73. Degler, p. 385.
74. Dorr, *A Woman of Fifty*, pp. 74–75, 83, 99, 127.
75. Wertheimer, p. 248.
76. Atalanta Pummill was Dorothy Schneider's aunt and role model.
77. Barbara Ehrenreich and Deirdre English, *Complaints and Disorders: The Sexual Politics of Sickness* (Old Westbury, N.Y.: Feminist Press, 1973), p. 53.
78. Karen Buhler-Wilkerson, ed., *Nursing and the Public's Health: An Anthology of Sources* (New York: Garland, 1989), pp. unnumbered, but supporting note #9 cites Josephine Goldmark, *Nursing and Nursing Education in the United States* (New York: Macmillan, 1923), and Yssabella Waters, *Visiting Nursing in the United States* (New York: Charities Publication, 1909).
79. Vern L. Bullough and Bonnie Bullough, *The Care of the Sick: The Emergence of Modern Nursing* (New York: Prodist [a division of Neale Watson Academic Publications], 1978), p. 143.
80. Buhler-Wilkerson, Introduction.
81. Rosalind Gillette Shawe, *Notes for Visiting Nurses* (Philadelphia: P. Blakiston, Son and Co., 1893), in Buhler-Wilkerson, pp. 11–12.
82. Ibid., p. 110.
83. Lillian D. Wald, "The Treatment of Families in Which There Is Sickness," in Buhler-Wilkerson, p. 158.
84. Lavinia Dock, "As the Nurse Sees It," *Charities and the Commons* 16 (April 1906):10-12, in Buhler-Wilkerson, p. 164.
85. Susan Ware, *Partner and I: Molly Dewson, Feminism, and New Deal Politics* (New Haven: Yale Univ. Press, 1987), p. 12.
86. Anne Ellis, *The Life of an Ordinary Woman* (1929; reprint, New York: Arno Press, 1974), pp. 108–11.
87. Commander, p. 34.
88. *New York Times*, May 23, 1937, quoted in *Notable American Women, 1607–1950: A Biographical Dictionary*, ed. Edward T. James, Janet Wilson James and Paul S. Boyer (Cambridge: Harvard Univ. Press, 1971), vol. 2, 344.
89. Douthit, pp. 128–31, passim.

CHAPTER 4

Cleaning Up Society: Local, State, and National Housekeeping

"The old notion that woman was intended by the Almighty to do only those things that men thought they ought to do is fast passing away. In our day and in this country, a woman's sphere is just as large as she can make it and still be true to her finer qualities of soul." So wrote the black club woman and lecturer Fannie Barrier Williams in 1904, highlighting women's determination to widen their horizons even while they hung on to their status as guardians of conscience and morality.[1]

The New Brooms

Middle-class women used this traditional guardianship to claim the right, even the duty, to move out into society and clean it up. The more they found out about the public sphere, the more clearly they saw how messy it was. It cried out for good housewifery. They stood ready, willing, and able to air the society thoroughly, sweep it out, scrub it down, and polish it to the high luster of the cleanliness that is next to godliness.

"A woman's duty and responsibility," wrote Maud Nathan, "are not bounded by the four walls of her home. . . . [Her capabilities] belong not alone to herself to be used solely for the benefit of her loved ones, they also belong to the world outside the sheltering walls of home, and must be used for the benefit of others in the community. Every department of

the home is but a reflection in miniature of the broader departments of the municipality and the world beyond."[2]

Were women not to undertake such tasks, how could they properly perform the duties everyone acknowledged to be theirs? How could they keep their houses clean if the streets outside were filthy with uncollected garbage? How could they feed their families properly if the stores sold contaminated food? How could they raise healthy children in a city without playgrounds? And didn't the lack of protective labor legislation impede them in their religiously imposed responsibility to care for the poor? "Having learned that effectively to 'swat the fly' they must swat its nest," wrote Mary Beard in 1915, "women have also learned that to swat disease they must swat poor housing, evil labor conditions, ignorance, and vicious interests."[3]

If women were truly the guardians of morality, they could not tolerate the saloons that tempted their menfolk to drink and the brothels that tempted them to infidelity and infected them with disease. For that matter, they ought to try to rescue their sisters, the prostitutes woefully sunk in sin. They could not ignore the white-slavery conspiracy that threatened the virtue of their daughters. The good woman "had to supervise the moral standards of her community, or wickedness would destroy the home she had uplifted."[4] The Women's Trade Union League adopted the motto: "The Eight-Hour Day. A Living Wage. To Guard the Home," and its seal bore the image of a goddess extending a protective hand to a woman holding a baby.

The more middle-class women thought about such matters, the more they felt they must involve themselves in public affairs. And they could hardly avoid thinking about them. For magazines and books bore into their homes the writing of muckrakers like Lincoln Steffens and Ida Tarbell, laying bare civic and social ills. Well-to-do ladies like Marie and Bessie Van Vorst disguised themselves as factory hands and exposed the shocking conditions they encountered in shoe factories and cotton mills. Parsons preached a social gospel that stressed the Christian's responsibility to protect the weak and helpless by reforming society and on the Sunday before Labor Day lent their pulpits to labor representatives who described the horrors of the working woman's life. Popular fiction reinforced the message. Ellen Duvall, writing in the *Atlantic Monthly* (whose readership included more women than men), criticized male authors' portrayals of women: "For most men the world of women is divided into two classes, those who prey on men, and those who pray to men. . . . Where is the civic and social conscience of these fair ladies?"[5] Edith Stokely and Marian Hurd in *Miss Billy: A Neighborhood Story* featured a noble 16-year-old heroine who organized the children of a poor immigrant neighborhood into a civic improvement society. Literature, the popular press, and the pulpit reinforced the call to women to take on social responsibilities.

Almost without realizing the import of their actions, women involved themselves in municipal and state affairs. Doing so didn't take a college education. Look, for instance, at Albion Fellows Bacon. The daughter of a Methodist minister, she grew up in rural Indiana, attended high school in Evansville, and worked as a secretary for her uncle, a judge. Marrying at 23, she devoted herself for 10 years to her husband and four children, refusing her friends' appeals to join them in working for civic betterment and charity. But after her children were all in school, she read Jacob Riis's *How the Other Half Lives* and was moved to investigate her own town. When she found there slums just as bad as those Riis described in New York City, she proposed a housing ordinance for Evansville that grew into a bill for state regulation of tenements. Once she had lobbied that through the legislature in 1910, she immediately campaigned to broaden its coverage, an effort that succeeded in 1913, thanks to the support of the State Federation of Women's Clubs, whose housing committee Bacon by this time chaired. Bacon's progress from housewife to lobbyist followed a path well-worn by other American women before and after her.

The Ladies of the Clubs

Naturally with women like these around, women's clubs all over the country moved away from acquiring culture toward doing something about the world's problems. Many of these clubs had sprouted from the zeal for self-improvement that pervaded the late 19th and early 20th centuries. In those days a magazine called *The Mentor* urged its readers to "Learn One Thing Every Day." Julius Haldeman published an inexpensive popular series of "Blue Books" with which readers could educate themselves on every conceivable subject. Chautauqua tent shows educated people in small towns every summer, and Chautauqua courses gave them study materials in the long winter evenings around the kitchen tables. And for a time the ladies of the clubs read papers to each other on literature and the fine arts.

In the old days in the clubs, wrote Helen M. Winslow in her 1906 novel, "the word 'culture' comprehended our broadest meaning, and a book was our symbol. One would imagine that society had no ailment, spiritual or moral, that could not be relieved by a good strong dose of culture, administered in a book capsule. Dooley's picture of Carnegie handing out a library to a starving man on his back door-step would have served as a portrait of our club idea." But those days had prepared the way for the club of the early 20th century. "[Now] the true remedy," wrote Winslow, "the present club spirit as evidenced in the altruism of our various lines of work, dealing with the root of evil, proves that the club movement is not a fad with us, but a splendid force for righteousness whose future is intertwined with the destiny of nations. . . . [Now] we prefer

Doing to Dante, Being to Browning."[6] Jane Addams put it another way: "Lumbering our minds with literature only served to cloud the really vital situation spread before our eyes."[7]

Clubs, the impetus that in the 19th century had propelled women out their front doors into meetings in their churches and other public places, now were pushing them to confront public problems. Men who supposed their wives and daughters still to be idling around the less sophisticated edges of "culture" received some rude shocks—like the patriarch who learned that his daughter's club had provided an audience for the anarchist Emma Goldman. Clubwomen discussed the writings of Havelock Ellis and Ellen Key on modern marriage and flocked to the lectures of Charlotte Perkins Gilman, who impassionedly argued women's need for economic independence. Orators like Dr. Anna Howard Shaw included mothers' clubs and church Ladies' Aid societies on their lecture circuits for woman suffrage. Factory owners' wives listened to a glove makers' unionist present the case for a closed shop. Such practices discomfited the National Association of Manufacturers, whose president warned his membership about 1909: "Soon we shall have to fight the women as well as the unions."[8]

Next the club members took the obvious step of investigating the matters their speakers talked about. Much of the research they undertook on their own. In time, though, for major projects they sometimes hired professional scholars and sought expert advice. And experts aplenty, many of them women, could be

WITH PICTURES LIKE THESE, THE WTUL ROUSED CLUBWOMEN TO OPPOSE CHILD LABOR. (NATIONAL ARCHIVES)

tapped to define problems and suggest solutions: Dr. Alice Hamilton, the pioneer of industrial toxicology and champion of the victims of industrial disease; attorney Crystal Eastman, early advocate of industrial safety; attorney Florence Kelley of the Consumers' League, with her multipronged attack on child labor through factory inspection, compulsory school laws, and organized pressure from the buying public.

From research the club members soon turned to action, to clean up the municipal, and eventually the state and national houses, in an easy, almost inevitable progression. For instance, at one point the General Federation of Women's Clubs asked each club in the United States to report all the working children under 14 in its vicinity. Members of a Florida club, amazed and horrified by the number and tender age of Cuban children they found working in sugar mills, began to lobby for protective legislation.[9] Of course, children had sweated in those mills for years without anyone's trying to help them, but the clubwomen's own research localized the problem and precipitated their action.

The process that took women into the public arena was all so gradual, so unthreatening. Look at the Granges, which were for farm families what clubs were for city women. They relieved the terrible isolation of the farm woman. The Grange encouraged farm families to study. Soon farm women, wanting education for their daughters as well as their sons, were pushing their state colleges to admit women. Their studies informed them of the monstrous conditions in the city slums, and they initiated a program to give city women and children a country vacation.

Similarly all over the country around the turn of the century many—though by no means all—clubwomen simply began to insist that their cultural interests benefit their homes and communities as well as themselves. That, of course, necessitated good libraries, so with donated books that they cleaned and repaired, or books they bought with the funds they raised, they created makeshift libraries in schools, churches, stores, town halls, hospitals, prisons, asylums, and lumber camps, as well as traveling libraries to fill in the gaps. Then it occurred to them to turn to their states for funds. In tiny Rhode Island, by 1911 women's clubs had established 109 libraries; at this juncture the state took over the whole project.[10] Americans owe their unparalleled community libraries, it would seem, not only to Mr. Carnegie.

If club members saw the need for libraries, they also wanted good schools. The 1896 General Federation of Women's Clubs convention passed a resolution urging clubs to investigate all aspects of education in their communities. And at the 1910 convention they invited the director of the New York Bureau of Municipal Research to teach them how to inspect their schools and whom to contact to correct abuses. After the clubwomen had looked, they demanded improvements: better heat, light, ventilation, drinking water, drainage, seats, desks, fresh paint, pictures on the walls, and playgrounds.

But physical improvements didn't suffice. They advocated vacation schools, schools for the handicapped and the delinquent. They lobbied for free kindergartens. They asked the schools to institute new programs, like manual training and domestic science, social hygiene and temperance. They demanded medical inspections for school children and hot lunches. They put women on school boards. And they raised money for scholarships to send young women to college.

From establishing libraries and improving the schools there was no turning back, and clubwomen, energized by their successes, undertook to improve public health services, protect the country's environment, encourage better household economics, ensure the purity of the food supply, reform the civil service, and ameliorate industrial conditions for women and children who labored.

When club members moved their sights from study to action, support from like-minded women was ready all across the country. For middle- and upper-class women, club membership had become commonplace. The small city of Portland, Maine, in 1890 had no fewer than 50 women's clubs.[11] Club membership had been steadily climbing throughout the latter part of the 19th century, and in the 20th it soared. It had indeed reached a critical mass, a potentially powerful lobby. True enough, these lobbyists had no vote, but within their families and in the public arena they had a voice.

Womanpower Through Federation

When clubwomen nationwide united, they multiplied their influence. The General Federation of Women's Clubs (GFWC), founded in 1890, both strongly encouraged women's turn from self-improvement to public affairs and provided the instrument through which they could extend their clean-sweep housekeeping from their municipalities to their states, and eventually to their nation.

Women who concentrated on single issues had long enjoyed the advantages of national organizations, the women's rights enthusiasts in the National American Woman Suffrage Association and its predecessors, and the prohibitionists in the huge Women's Christian Temperance Union. Now the GFWC banded together the more moderate women of the literary clubs, women often of a conservative cast, women who in church ladies' auxiliaries formed the backbone of religious organizations of all stripes.

Public-spirited society women and clubwomen experienced as activists sprang into the leadership of the General Federation, building a hierarchy on the national, state, and local levels, and shaping programs that stressed women's responsibilities in the public sector. Usually these leaders were in advance of the bulk of their membership, more progressive in their outlook. Policy was created by women like Mary I. Wood, a New Hampshire suffragist, who, besides her church work, served on the school board, tried to improve the working conditions of store clerks, and promoted public health nursing.[12] Club members time and again elected national presidents with broad interests and a vision of change, like the conservationist Sarah Sophia Decker of Colorado, who fought for irrigation and national parks as well as reform of the civil service. Keep away from discussion of religion and politics, such leaders told local club members, but involve yourselves in reform.

The leaders sent this message in one way after another. The GFWC and the various state federations welcomed clubs already engaged with civic projects: alumnae associations, reform clubs, health protective associations, the Women's Educational and Industrial Union network, and Mothers' Clubs.[13] Clubwomen from all over the country attended national conventions, where they heard the party line. At state and regional conventions and in their own chapter meetings they listened to the national leaders, who traveled widely at their own expense with messages like that of Mary Decker: "Dante is dead. He has been dead for several centuries, and I think it is time that we dropped the study of his *Inferno* and turned our attention to our own."[14] The GFWC Bureau of Information supplied members with books and data. As clubwomen grew too busy with public projects to write papers for club meetings, the bureau furnished them ready-made. Periodicals kept members informed about federation policies and the work of other clubs and highlighted stories of successful career women.

Two similar organizations paralleled the GFWC in purposes and work. In the 1890s Hannah G. Solomon of Chicago founded the National Council of Jewish

THE DAR INTERESTED ITSELF IN PUBLIC HOUSEKEEPING AND WOMAN SUFFRAGE—AND, WHEN WAR CAME, IN KNITTING FOR THE "BOYS" OVERSEAS. (NATIONAL ARCHIVES)

Women, to teach Jewish women their obligations to their religion *and* to the community. In the early years the council focused particularly on helping Jewish immigrants, but, as with the GFWC, it broadened its concerns and its efforts. Solomon, whose sense of humor balanced her social conscience, liked to describe a 1910 inspection tour of the city dumps that she conducted: She wore trailing white lace and carried an elegant parasol. For her the incident symbolized women's lack of preparation for their new obligations, but also their commitment and determination.

In the 1890s too the National Association of Colored Women (NACW) originated, with the pacifist and suffragist Mary Church Terrell as its first president. By 1916 it represented 50,000 women in more than 1,000 clubs. Like the almost entirely white GFWC, the NACW drew its membership from middle-class, educated Protestant women, who shared the white clubwomen's values of the central importance of the home and woman's influence in it. Like their white sisters, the black clubwomen set agendas of reform and aid to the poor. But, they deeply believed, their mission differed from that of the whites because their situation differed. They saw themselves as tied to the lowly, the illiterate, even the vicious by links of race and sex—and by the blanket condemnations of black women. So they adopted the motto "Lifting as We Climb." To an even greater degree than the white organization, the NACW consciously undertook to help women of the laboring class. As Fannie Barrier Williams saw it, "Among colored women the club is the effort of the few competent in behalf of the many incompetent. . . . Among white women the club is the onward movement of the already uplifted." [15]

Although women in the GFWC failed to welcome most Jewish and black women, they did know how to increase their strength by cooperating with other women's groups. They worked with the Association of Collegiate Alumnae (later the American Association of University Women) and the National Educational Association on educational reform; with the Daughters of the American Revolution on historic preservation; with the Women's Christian Temperance Union on temperance, the preservation of sexual purity, the age of consent for young women, and the elimination of white slavery; with the Women's Trade Union League on protective labor legislation; and with the National Household Economics Association on pure food and efficiency in the home.

New Business

In time, club members grew more sophisticated, more daring, and more willing to assume large responsibilities. Women's clubs inside and outside the federations enthusiastically undertook the tasks of improving their environments, both physical and social. In Buffalo the women of the Civic Club labored to make

THE FABLED FORTUNES OF BETTY AND NELL
A true tale - but a sad story

Betty and Nell were friends
They did the same kind of work. But–

Nell had to rush at 6 A.M. to be at the Factory at 7

Betty Snoozed until 6.30 her Job Started at 8.

When Saturday came Nell worked until 6 Just the Same

but Betty Quit at 12–then she Shopped or–only Mended

Nell made 100 Metal Parts an Hour–and Hated each one

Betty made 158 Metal Parts and Counted Them with Glee

On Sunday Nell made over her Old Clothes

While Betty's bunch Followed the Call of the Great Outdoors

Nell worked 10 hours– she Came Home 'all in'

Betty worked 8 hours– Evenings she was Full of Pep

Nell's pay looked sick and So Did She

What happened ?

Betty's Envelope Bulged and her Smile Didn't Come Off

Nell got Weary and Careless– she Mashed her Finger

Betty stopped at Five–She kept Well and never lost pay

MORAL:
Girls who work 44 hours a week are happier and actually do more work than girls who work 60 hours a week

CLUBWOMEN'S EFFORTS TO HELP WORKING WOMEN LED TO THE WOMEN'S BUREAU OF THE DEPARTMENT OF LABOR AND PROPAGANDA LIKE THIS. (NATIONAL ARCHIVES)

their city a congenial place to live. They improved its physical environment with their work for the lighting, cleaning, and beautification of city streets and their purchase of smokeless coal. But they also enhanced its social conditions by advocating outdoor relief rather than workhouses, founding a school for truants, and providing instruction in marketable skills and an employment bureau for working women. Their Protective Committee, staffed by the lawyer husbands of club members, between 1884 and 1916 recovered $35,000 in wages wrong-fully denied to seamstresses and domestics.

The history of the justly admired and much-imitated Boston Women's Educational and Industrial Union (WEIU) illuminates municipal housekeeping at its best: the broadening of interests, the undertaking of more and more diverse labors, and an increasing sense of responsibility for women of all classes and for the community as a whole. Founded in 1877 with 42 members, by 1915 the WEIU had enlisted 4,500. They committed numberless hours to a whole range of activities, including for years providing school lunches for the children of Boston—at one time 18,000 a day. Dr. Susan Kingsbury, installed in 1907 as director of research, set up a program of social fact-finding, gave $500 awards to women graduate students initiating fieldwork, and published studies on women and labor. This research led to legislation regulating installment buying, the sale of milk, old age pensions, factory inspections, factory sanitation, minimum wages, protection for seekers of small loans, and an early form of maternity leave.

Not only did clubwomen, black and white, engineer and lobby for reform legislation, but also after its passage they watched over its administration and helped to implement it. The Chicago Woman's Club, for example, worked for years to improve juvenile justice in Illinois. After the establishment there of the first juvenile court in the world, a committee headed by settlement worker Julia Lathrop hired and paid the salaries of the probation officers and maintained a detention home for children awaiting the court's judgment. Twenty-five years after its founding, Jane Addams commented ironically that every woman in Cook County except herself took personal credit for the juvenile court; true enough, said Lathrop, since the court would never have been established without the backing of thousands of women.[16]

What escaped many a man who chuckled condescendingly about his wife's club activities or denounced her for venturing into the public arena was that she and her sister clubwomen, without the power of the ballot, were effecting reform after reform that dramatically altered the quality of life in the United States. Pure food laws are often credited to Upton Sinclair's eye-opening novel *The Jungle*, but in fact the clubwomen pushed them through. Teddy Roosevelt is hailed as conservationist, but the clubwomen's hard, sustained work brought the results. Credit the great men, to be sure, but hail the "ordinary" women.

Fortunately for us all, committed clubwomen ignored the advice of men like Edward Bok, editor of the *Ladies' Home Journal*, who could tolerate the clubwoman "provided she joins merely one [club] and does not place its interests, in importance, before the higher duties of the home." "Friends, this is only the raging of the heathen," responded GFWC president Decker. "Let them keep on talking and we will keep on working." Mary E. Woolley, president of Mount Holyoke, clothed clubwomen's labors in the vestments of sanctity:

You have been worshipping just as thoroughly during these past meetings in efforts toward the betterment of humanity, in efforts toward civic righteousness, toward the saving of children from ignorance and suffering, toward helping women in better conditions for earning their own living, toward the preserving of the nation's forests — in all these ways you have been worshipping just as truly as you are here tonight [at a vesper service].[17]

Work they did. They put in an astounding number of hours at their volunteer labors. Some few even made such work into a full-time career, like Grace Hoadley Dodge, who forswore society life for full-time, *unpaid* labors with working girls' associations, the YWCA, Travelers Aid, and the Columbia Teachers College, limiting herself to a two-week vacation a year. But most women perforce had to restrict the number of hours they volunteered, like Caroline Bartlett Crane, a staggeringly competent woman, who organized a Women's Civic Improvement League and a Charity Organizations Board in

SOAP, SOUP, AND SALVATION! THE SALVATION ARMY TOOK AS ITS SPECIAL MISSION RELIEF AND RELIGION FOR THE POOR AND THE DERELICT. (NEW YORK PUBLIC LIBRARY PHOTO)

Kalamazoo, Michigan. The municipal "sanitary survey" she developed came into such demand in other cities that she finally had to impose a fee for her services, but she consistently refused to spend more than two months a year away from home—and the two children she and her husband adopted when she was 55.

An Organization for Every Purpose

The club members in the federations and in local groups took on all sorts of different interests and causes. But women were also attracted to one-issue organizations—though even these had a disconcerting way of spreading out in many directions. The Florence Crittenden Missions tried to assist "fallen women." The Junior Leagues worked "for the benefit of the poor and the betterment of the city."[18] The many woman suffrage organizations concentrated their energies on the ballot. The Young Women's Christian Association focused on helping and protecting women, especially working women, in a world that urbanization, industrialization, and finally a catastrophic war rapidly changed.

Women's professional organizations multiplied from 1910–20, as women solidified their positions in the working world: among many, the International Association of Policewomen, the Medical Women's National Association, the Federation of Teachers, the National Association of Deans of Women, the National Federation of Business and Professional Women's Clubs. These organizations, like trade unions, meant to protect their own members, establish professional standards, and improve their status. But, perhaps because so many women worked in the helping professions, they too undertook reforms that changed the quality of life for the general public.

Thousands of churchwomen of various denominations were cutting paths parallel to those of the GFWC.[19] The Methodist Woman's Home Missionary Society, for instance, undertaking to help in the westward expansion of the church, started by raising money for parsonages but soon moved on to establish city missions and houses for "women who had lost their virtue." By 1920 the Methodist women's growing social concern had expressed itself in more than 25 social settlements in mill towns, coalfields, and industrial centers; the advocacy of equal pay for women workers, protective legislation, elimination of child labor, and the right of labor to organize; and the beginnings of cooperation with black women.[20]

Among these organizations at least nominally dedicated to a particular cause was the Woman's Christian Temperance Union (WCTU). In the late 19th century the WCTU was the strongest, most powerful women's organization, boasting 150,000 dues-paying members at a time when the GFWC could claim only 20,000 and the National American Woman Suffrage Association only 13,000.[21] Moreover, the WCTU had developed a powerful network, reaching down into the small towns and the rural areas.

Under the strong leadership of Frances Willard, the WCTU broadened its interests, ultimately aiming to erase all man-made evils, "from prostitution to political corruption." It took on such causes as penal reform, sex education, planned parenthood, eradicating the double standard of sexual morality, and abolishing poverty. Yet work on all these fronts did not weaken the organization's campaign for temperance. Believing that education could prevent people from drinking, the WCTU "compelled the legislature of every state in the Union, after a campaign that lasted from 1880 to 1902, to enact so-called scientific instruction laws. These statutes provided for the compulsory teaching of the dangers of drinking in all American public schools."[22] WCTU members also shut down saloons and shepherded through several state legislatures laws providing for local option.

What enabled this remarkable display of power was the determination of the WCTU members. All too many women knew personally or through a friend or neighbor the afflictions of a family with a resident drunk. As Mary Austin wrote, the wheels of the Prohibition movement were "kept going by the daily exigencies of women whose fathers, brothers, sons, husbands, whose dearly beloved of every kin, set up in them, through drinking habits, the driving force of anguish."[23] Women had reason to detest the saloons, which had become centers of gambling and prostitution, as their owners resorted to whatever degenerate attraction lured men onto their premises. Many of the bartenders were pimps, and many bars housed prostitutes.

At the same time women were told over and over of their own responsibility for men's drinking. In her report on life among Pennsylvania steelworkers Margaret F. Byington commented: "The thoughtful women are especially conscious that part of the responsibility for keeping the men away from the saloons belongs to them. The heat and thirst due to mill work, combined with the lack of other amusements, make the brightness and festivity of bar-rooms very appealing, and intemperance is consequently a serious evil in the town. The wives feel that they must help to overcome this temptation."[24] The novelist Marion Harland went even farther: Men must be fed decently, or else. "I don't mind telling you," remarks a young husband, lolling in a comfortable chair watching his wife do the dishes, "that more men are driven to drink by bad cookery than by any other one thing."[25]

Propaganda like this helps to account for the formation of a special corps of WCTU members composed of young women pledged to marry only total abstainers. "Lips that touch liquor shall never touch mine."

In such circumstances, supported by the WCTU, Carry Nation began her "hachetation" in 1900, driven to it by her own poor health, which she attributed to her drunken forebears, and by the drunken husband of her first marriage. She moved around Kansas, undeterred by jail sentences, smashing saloons with her hatchet or whatever other weapon came to hand and gaining publicity for her cause. In Topeka, where she rampaged through several saloons, officials arrested her but dared not treat her too harshly lest they be forced to acknowledge the existence of an illegal liquor traffic in Kansas, officially a dry state. As she moved out into other parts of the country, reporters followed her. The attention she drew helped the cause. The brewers and distillers tried to turn this publicity to their advantage, sending "her telegrams and letters jocosely thanking her for advertising their products, and offering to finance further smashings; one brewer in Missouri offered her five hundred dollars if she would confine her destruction to kegs containing his beer. Saloonkeepers decorated their bars with hatchets and signs saying, 'All Nations Welcome but Carry,' while bartenders concocted special Carry Nation cocktails and highballs."[26] The papers reported all these gestures, and many considered them uproariously funny, but in the long run they harmed the liquor interests and increased the determination of the temperance workers.

Despite all this ardor, though, the WCTU after the death of Frances Willard in 1898 was undergoing something of a metamorphosis. First, the male-dominated Anti-Saloon League was taking over leadership of the temperance cause.[27] Second, the WCTU itself was shifting its emphasis from education to prohibition, a shift that did not sit well with everyone. People who had sympathized with its efforts to educate disliked its efforts to coerce.[28] Its new goal gave it a more conservative, interfering, busybody image that repelled some society women and college graduates.

More cosmopolitan women found other movements more challenging and more fulfilling. The WCTU had always drawn its membership largely from among churchgoing Protestants, and it continued to attract them, particularly those in the small towns and rural areas. But at the turn of the century, "suffrage took over from temperance work as the reform priority of the educated girl. . . . She tended to study social sciences rather than evangelism, and to be fired by statistics on poverty rather than the Sermon on the Mount."[29] The more adventurous and more highly educated and more progressive women left the WCTU to go elsewhere—and, as we have seen, there were greener pastures to go to. The woman suffragists' argument that if women could get the ballot, they could effect many reforms, not just temperance, persuaded some women to work with them rather than the WCTU.

Women had spearheaded the drive for temperance up until the turn of the century. Thousands of them continued to work for it heart and soul. In 1900 the WCTU persuaded the secretary of the navy to prohibit the use of alcohol by enlisted men. In 1903, by similar means, the WCTU abolished alcohol in army canteens and even got Congress to remove the bar in the Capitol. In 1905 the WCTU unveiled a bust of Frances Willard in Statuary Hall of the Capitol, the first woman so honored. "In the first decade of this century, the W.C.T.U. was delivering [through its propaganda in the public schools] by hundreds of thousands a year new voters in whose minds the temperance principle was . . . firmly implanted."[30] But in the final push for the prohibition amendment, the women temperance workers yielded the vanguard to their male cohorts.

The Settlement Movement

Late in the 19th century, some reformers who wanted to help the disadvantaged chose to live among them, in establishments they called settlement houses. From its earliest days, when in New York in 1889 the College Settlements Association opened one of the first, the American settlement movement grew rapidly. In the same year Jane Addams and Ellen Gates Starr founded Hull House in Chicago. And four years later Lillian Wald started New York's Henry Street Settlement. None of them realized that they were inventing the modern profession of social work.

By the turn of the century, more than 100 houses were operating, and by 1910 more than 400.[31] In 1911 they banded together into the National Settlement House League.

They served all sorts of people. By 1910 Jews were operating some 24 settlement houses. The White Rose Mission of Victoria Earle Matthews, a woman born into slavery, helped black women migrants from the South to find jobs in the North. Its workers met them at the docks in Norfolk and New York, offered them the benefits of an employment agency and a training center, and gave them courses in black history.

In the settlement houses, usually situated in the slums of America's mush-rooming urban centers, lived and learned and labored for a year or two or three a changing population of thousands of bright, socially concerned, college-educated women and, in lesser numbers, men—women not only outnumbered the men but also, on average, stayed longer. They chose to live there, Jane Addams wrote, out of "genuine preference for residence in an industrial quarter to any other part of the city, because it [was] interesting and [made] the human appeal; and . . . the conviction . . . that the things which make men alike are finer and better than the things that keep them apart."[32]

The hope for better things sustained both the settlement house residents and the population of their neighborhoods. This hope was justified partly because the settlement houses concentrated their attention on the most likely candidates for upward mobility, the working poor, rather than the despairingly unemployed. But also hope scented the atmosphere of the Progressive Era: "hope in all," wrote Mary Simkhovitch of New York's Greenwich House, "—in the mechanic, in the laborer, in the office and factory worker, in every element of the population—that differentiated the life of an American city neighborhood from similar sections in London or Paris or Vienna."[33]

Ideally, the settlement house residents came not as Ladies (or Sirs) Bountiful, but as students eager to learn from their neighbors. They had to learn to listen to what those neighbors wanted, rather than what the residents felt was good for them. They came to work not *for* but *with* the people who lived in the communities of the settlement houses. Working with their neighbors taught them the potential of community action. In New Orleans, for instance, struck in 1905 by an outbreak of yellow fever, each member of the Kingsley House settlement women's club pledged to oil her own cistern, street gutter, and privy to prevent mosquitoes from breeding and to canvass house-to-house the block in which she lived and persuade her neighbors to do likewise.

The residents supported themselves, often by full-time work, but they also expected to help run the settlement house and volunteer in the community. That might mean cooking or washing dishes for the other residents or planning a street carnival. It might mean teaching Plato or managing a community loan fund.

It certainly meant discerning problems and improvising solutions. It meant calling on one's neighbors and receiving their calls, with special provisions for entertaining their children. It meant acting as negotiating agent between the institutions of the city and the people for whose benefit these institutions existed but who lacked the language or the information to claim the services they needed.

Residency meant living and working with brilliant women selflessly dedicated to the welfare of their neighborhoods, women experienced in the politics of change. At Hull House in Chicago, for instance, the young college graduate encountered a dazzling constellation—among others:

- *Jane Addams*, a founding mother of the settlement movement in the United States;
- *Florence Kelley*, later the director of the National Consumers' League, who while living at Hull House investigated the sweating system of manufacture in Chicago with its concomitant of child labor, then lobbied through the first factory law of Illinois, regulating the sanitary conditions of sweatshops and fixing 14 as the minimum age for employment;
- *Dr. Alice Hamilton*, the future pioneer of the field of industrial medicine and Harvard's first woman professor, but in her Hull House years spending her working days as bacteriologist at the Memorial Institute for Infectious Disease and her "spare time" teaching evening classes, taking children on outings, investigating a neighborhood typhoid epidemic, and fighting the cocaine traffic;
- *Julia Lathrop*, who during her 20-year residency at Hull House helped to reform the state's county farms and almshouses, instituting separate facilities for delinquent children and the insane, and launched a school to train social workers;
- *Ellen Gates Starr*, who moved from genteel encouragment of the arts and crafts to flaming advocacy of striking textile workers, but whose appearance, demeanor, and speech remained so delicate and proper as to convince a jury of her innocence when she was arrested for interfering with a police officer in the discharge of his duty;
- *Dr. Sophonisba Breckinridge,* dean of one of the first schools for social workers, whose research on children gave social workers the raw materials of their discipline; and
- *Alzina Parsons Stevens,* who worked her way up from laborer in a cotton mill (where at the age of 13 she lost her right index finger) by learning typesetting, working successively as proofreader, compositor, correspondent, and editor, joining the typographical union, presiding over a

women's labor group, attaining a high position in the Knights of Labor and then in the American Federation of Labor, and in her Hull House years becoming assistant factory inspector to Florence Kelley and the first probation officer of the new Cook County juvenile court.

To work with such women, to help them change the society, was heady stuff. It taught young residents lessons in courage, taught them the importance of research before reformation, and gave them experience in confronting the powers-that-be. Alice Hamilton's study of the relationship between typhoid and various systems of plumbing (or the absence thereof) ultimately caused the firing of 11 out of 24 employees in the Sanitary Bureau, a result that made local politicians actively unhappy, as well as the plumbers in whose unions the residents uncovered graft.

But their mentors in the settlement houses also taught the young residents the inappropriateness of knee-jerk sentimentality—as when Mrs. Stevens astringently reprimanded a young resident defending a corrupt labor leader: It was, she said, "the worst kind of snobbishness to assume that you must not have the same standards of honor for working people as you have for the well-to-do."[34] Real respect for their immigrant neighbors, the young residents learned, included a value for their differences and a delight in the multiethnic cultures they brought to America—an attitude that defied the pervasive nativism of the era.

Residents were introduced into the network of people working for social reform, among whom their settlement-house mentors were moving spirits. Their professors had taught them that education entailed an obligation. In the settlement houses they found ways to meet that obligation—and a purpose for their lives.

MRS. FLORENCE KELLEY. SETTLEMENT HOUSE RESIDENT, EXECUTIVE SECRETARY OF THE CONSUMER'S LEAGUE. (NATIONAL ARCHIVES)

Almost all of them were trying to figure out their relationship to the world's problems, which the pulpit, the press, the lecture platform, and the educational establishment were forcing on their attention. Religious principles impelled some, especially from the more liberal Protestant denominations. Budding writers sought material. Some saw the experience as a foundation for their careers. Some used it for growing time. Others wanted a cheap place to live. Still others found the settlement environment intellectually stimulating, for "radicals, intellectuals, and socialists of all stripes held forth in the settlement house atmosphere that encouraged new ways of thinking and acting."[35] Above all, the settlement house offered idealistic young people the sense of helping to change the world in surroundings vastly different from the middle-class environments in which most of them had grown up—though after 1900, children of immigrants began to return to the slums as settlement residents. All in all the settlement world was, as Arthur Bullard termed it, a kind of "ethical Bohemia." And, of course, with all those like-minded young people working together, the settlements served as marriage bureaus for young workers.

The impact of the settlement movement reverberated throughout the Progressive Era, directly affecting the lives of hundreds of thousands of women, and indirectly those of millions. Settlement leaders across the country relied on each other. They also knew the leaders of the women's clubs, the pacifist organizations, the professional women's associations, the women's labor unions, and the temperance and suffrage movements. Together they formed a national power structure that could rally the efforts of literally millions of American women.

It was those millions of women, under such leadership, who changed the quality of life for their generations and for Americans today. In the process they also, however inadvertently, changed themselves.

Woman after woman testified to the increased self-confidence and the new insights to which her first timid or reluctant steps into the public sphere had led her. The society matron Vira B. Whitehouse started her work with the New York State Woman Suffrage Association convinced that all she could offer was an ability to dance and to act as hostess at dinner. Yet during World War I, President Wilson, at the behest of a man who had seen her operate in her suffrage work, appointed her the American representative to the foreign press in Switzerland, a position in which she battled the U.S. State Department to a standstill. Of course she could do it, she said, because those men knew that if necessary she could call on the support of all those women in the suffrage movement. Even the accomplishments of the amazing Eleanor Roosevelt become more explicable when we understand that she received her earliest education in reform and public affairs from settlement-house work, from Florence Kelley's Consumers' League, and from the New York Women's Civic Club.

Source Notes

1. "The Woman's Part in a Man's Business," *The Voice of the Negro* (November 1904):543, quoted in Paula Giddings, *When and Where I Enter: The Impact of Black Women on Race and Sex in America* (New York: Bantam Books, 1984), p. 96.

2. Maud Nathan, *The Story of an Epoch-Making Movement* (Garden City, N.Y.: Doubleday, Page and Co., 1926), p. 19.

3. Mary R. Beard, *Women's Work in Municipalities* (New York: 1915), p. 221, quoted by Paula Baker, "The Domestication of Politics: Women and American Political Society, 1780–1920," in Ellen Carol DuBois and Vicki L. Ruiz, eds., *Unequal Sisters: A Multicultural Reader in U.S. Women's History* (New York: Routledge, 1990), p. 78.

4. Karen J. Blair, *The Clubwoman as Feminist: True Womanhood Redefined, 1868–1914* (New York: Holmes and Meier, 1980), p. 7.

5. Ellen Duvall, "A Point of Honor," *Atlantic Monthly* 88 (1901):53.

6. Helen M. Winslow, *The President of Quex: A Woman's Club Story* (Boston: Lothrop, Lee and Shepard, 1906), pp. 281, 283, 185–86.

7. Jane Addams, *Twenty Years at Hull House, with Autobiographical Notes* (1910; reprint, New York: Macmillan, 1924), p. 70.

8. Quoted in Rheta Childe Dorr, *What Eight Million Women Want* (1910; reprint, New York: Kraus Reprint Co., 1971), pp. 143–44.

9. Addams, *Twenty Years at Hull House*, pp. 357–58.

10. Blair, p. 100.

11. Ibid., p. 76.

12. H. H. Metcalf, "Mary I. Wood," *Granite Monthly* 42 (March 1910), quoted in Blair, p. 97, note 24.

13. These Mothers' Clubs were not gossipy little aggregations of mothers chatting about their babies, but activists who fought for legislation to give mothers equal guardianship with fathers over children, the establishment of kindergartens and playgrounds, legislation for dependent and deviant children, foster homes, widows' pensions, and juvenile courts. Founded in 1897, the National Congress of Mothers by 1920 had chapters in 36 states with 190,000 members. Sheila M. Rothman, *Woman's Proper Place; A History of Changing Ideals and Practices, 1870 to the Present* (New York: Basic Books, 1978), p. 96.

14. Quoted in William L. O'Neill, *Everyone Was Brave: The Decline and Fall of Feminism in America* (Chicago: Quadrangle Books, 1969), p. 150.

15. Quoted in Giddings, p. 98. White women, on the other hand, would counter that they too tried to help their less fortunate sisters.

16. Jane Addams, *My Friend, Julia Lathrop* (New York: Macmillan, 1935), p. 143.
17. Quoted in Blair, pp. 105, 106.
18. Stephen Birmingham, *The Grandes Dames* (New York: Simon and Schuster, 1982), p. 238.
19. "More women belonged to local church associations or groups [than to the WCTU or to the suffrage organizations], but each of these was more or less independent until 1877, when the International Conference of Women's Christian Associations was organized, the forerunner to the modern YWCA." Vern L. Bullough and Bonnie Bullough, *The Care of the Sick: The Emergence of Modern Nursing* (New York: Prodist [a division of Neale Watson Academic Publications], 1978), p. 135.
20. For a discussion of women's changing status within the Methodist church, see Jacquelyn Dowd Hall, *Revolt Against Chivalry: Jessie Daniel Ames and the Women's Campaign Against Lynching* (New York: Columbia Univ. Press, 1979), pp. 77ff. See also Mrs. R. W. Macdonell, *Belle Harris Bennett: Her Life Work* (1928; reprint, New York: Garland, 1987).
21. Ruth Bordin, *Woman and Temperance; The Quest for Power and Liberty, 1873–1900* (Philadelphia: Temple Univ. Press, 1981), pp. 3–4.
22. Herbert Asbury, *The Great Illusion: An Informal History of Prohibition* (Garden City, N.Y.: Doubleday, 1950), p. 87.
23. Mary Austin, *Earth Horizon* (Boston: Houghton Mifflin, 1932), p. 147. Austin comments on the common belief of the period that a drunken father could genetically mar the fetus. See also Bordin, p. 162: "Nothing was as destructive to a powerless woman's existence as a drunken husband. . . . The wife and mother has no legal remedies. She has no political remedies."
24. Margaret F. Byington, *Homestead, the Households of a Mill Town* (1910; reprint, The University Center for International Studies, Univ. of Pittsburgh, 1974), p. 109.
25. Marion Harland, *The Distractions of Martha* (New York: Scribner's, 1906), pp. 100–01.
26. Asbury, p. 119.
27. In a sense the WCTU surrendered its leadership in the temperance movement. "The WCTU moved from rejection of the Anti-Saloon League toward cooperation with it. In 1895 the League founders had invited WCTU representation at their first national convention, but the white-ribbon executive committee had politely refused, explaining that 'in the past' antisaloon movements had served more in the interest of the major parties than of prohibition. After Frances Willard's death in 1898, however, the WCTU ceased to adopt resolutions of support for the Prohibition party and moved toward friendlier relations with its rival organization." Jack S. Blocker, Jr., *Retreat from Reform: The Prohibition Movement in the United States, 1890–1913* (Westport, Conn.: Greenwood Press, 1976), p. 138.

The quarrel within the temperance movement resembled that within the suffrage movement particularly in the debate over the "good man theory," the idea that a movement should support the politician who aids its cause, regardless of party, a position adopted by the Anti-Saloon League and the National American Woman Suffrage Association but opposed by the Prohibition Party and the National Woman's Party.

28. Thrusting responsibility for family morality on women led inevitably to women's trying to control male behavior. "Since drinking had been largely a male activity, the concern of the woman for Temperance was itself an act of controlling the relations between the sexes." Joseph R. Gusfield, *Symbolic Crusade: Status Politics and the American Temperance Movement* (1963; reprint, Westport, Conn.: Greenwood Press, 1980), p. 89.

29. Andrew Sinclair, *The Emancipation of American Women* (New York: Harper Torchbooks, 1965), p. 226.

30. Inez Haynes Irwin, *Angels and Amazons: A Hundred Years of American Women* (1933; reprint, New York: Arno Press, 1974), p. 329.

31. Allen F. Davis, *Spearheads for Reform: The Social Settlements and the Progressive Movement, 1890–1914* (New York: Oxford Univ. Press, 1967), p. 12.

32. Addams, *Twenty Years at Hull House*, pp. 111–12.

33. Mary K. Simkhovitch, *Neighborhood: My Story of Greenwich House* (New York: Norton, 1938), p. 144.

34. Quoted in Alice Hamilton, *Exploring the Dangerous Trades: The Autobiography of Alice Hamilton, M.D.* (1943; reprint, Boston: Northeastern Univ. Press, 1985), p. 62.

35. Sara M. Evans, *Born for Liberty: A History of Women in America* (New York: Free Press, 1989), p. 149.

CHAPTER 5

Black Women on the Move

During the Progressive Era, black women were moving in several senses of the word. Physically numbers of them were pulling up stakes and moving, from the country to the city, from the Southeast to the North and to middle America. Workwise they were moving from agriculture toward factory jobs and domestic service. Socially they were expanding the ideal of the extended family into community service.

Did their experiences really differ from those of white women, many of whom also were going to the cities, taking on new jobs, entering new professions, and discovering new social responsibilities? Yes. Flatly, yes. For the obstacle of racial prejudice and a different racial history influenced, or maybe dominated, the daily life, the ambitions, the possibilities open to black women.

What They Faced

It's hard today to comprehend the universality of the barefaced, conscienceless bigotry that surged like a systemic but unrecognized poison through the daily life of Americans before and during World War I. "Nice" white people didn't feel guilty about being racist; they didn't even know they *were* racists. They condescended; they told racist jokes; they used racist terms—whether or not they feared or hated black people. These practices simply went, uncriticized, with the territory. Their unthinking cruelty would evoke gasps from today's most forthright racist.

The General Federation of Women's Clubs, as well as even the most liberal suffragist groups, repudiated black women who sought to forward their causes. Unions didn't want them as members. Poor white cotton factory workers struck not for higher wages and better conditions, but to keep blacks from working on the machines.[1] So thoroughly did racism imbue the white population that "the

New Orleans *Blue Book*, a guide to bordellos published from 1897 to 1915, printed first an alphabetical list of white prostitutes, then octoroon, then colored; the unconscious listings in all minds seemed to follow this kind of order."[2] In short, in the Progressive Era the attitudes of white Americans toward black Americans showed little progress.

Denied education and job opportunity, most black people, especially in the South, faced inevitable defeat. A resurgent South steadily gnawed away the gains blacks had made after the Civil War. The work ethic held out no hope for them: Life beat them, stymied their best efforts, proved not worth living. "What the colored women need," observed one of them during World War I, "is an opportunity to make money. As it is, they have to take what employment they can get, live in old tumbled down houses or resort to street walking, and I think a woman ought to think more of her blood than to do that. What occupation is open to us where we can make really good wages? We are not employed as clerks, we cannot all be school teachers, and so we cannot see any use in working our parents to death to get educated."[3] Black women had little choice but to take the jobs that white women left or refused. The years 1900–30, for instance, saw the number of native-born white women domestics fall by 40 percent, while the number of black household workers increased 43 percent.[4]

Sexual harassment is too mild a term for the tortures inflicted on black women. The press assaulted them as immoral scourges: "Like White women, one writer said, 'Black women had the brains of a child, the passions of a woman,' but unlike Whites, Black women were 'steeped in centuries of ignorance and savagery, and wrapped about with immoral vices.'. . . 'I sometimes hear of a virtuous Negro woman,' wrote a commentator for *The Independent* in 1902, 'but the idea is absolutely inconceivable to me.'"[5]

Elements in both black and white society conspired against the chastity of black women. Black parents feared to allow their daughters to become nurses, since only a few could get hospital jobs, and white men would make private nursing impossible. Many southern white males considered black women their natural prey; men in households—North or South—where black women labored as domestic servants demanded sexual favors as a condition of employment. Desperate white wives descended to soliciting black women to become their husbands' mistresses, in preference to seeing their husbands consort with other white women. Black men also threatened black women. "Thousands of women," wrote educator Nannie Helen Burroughs, "are . . . in the clutches of men of our race who are not worth the cost of their existence. They can dress well, and live on the earnings of servant girls."[6] Shady employment bureaus signed up southern black women for what the women believed were respectable jobs as domestic servants, lent them money for the fare north, and forced them to prostitute themselves to repay the loan.

In no section of the United States, except in the one or two all-black towns like the one where novelist-to-be Zora Neale Hurston was growing up, could black people escape daily manifestations of prejudice. But the quality of life and their educational and job opportunities were lowest of all in the Southeast. There they could not use public libraries or visit public museums. They could not attend lectures because city ordinances prohibited the mingling of the races. Most towns of fewer than 25,000 people offered them no hospital facilities at all. Their children had to attend the worst of public schools, or none. State and local governments imposed more and more segregation laws, and the Ku Klux Klan rode again.

All these assaults evoked self-hatred in some black women. Americans, said the white educator Lura Beam, had no sense of African beauty; only the Armory Show of 1913 opened her own eyes to its loveliness. Most white Americans, even those who dedicated their lives to the service of black people, called them ugly, a judgment difficult for black women to resist: "I have known Negro women who said they minded their looks more than any other burden they bore."[7] Black people built a caste system on skin color—the lighter the better. Nannie Burroughs charged, "There are men right in our own race, and they are legion, who would rather marry a woman for her color than for her character. . . . The white man who crosses the line and leaves an heir is doing a favor for some Black man who would marry the most debased woman, whose only stock in trade is her color, in preference to the most royal queen in ebony."[8] And black parents resisted Beam's efforts to replace their white teachers with black teachers: "My child shall not go to school to a nigger."[9]

Beam, who spent a dozen years in the South sharing the obloquy and ostracism of her black students, said that they called the first two decades of the 20th century a period of Lost Hope. She believed that this deprivation of hope contributed to the early deaths of her students and black co-workers. "I have a long list of those I knew who died young before 1920," she wrote. "Going back to the same schools year after year, I used to miss both young children and young teachers. When I asked, I was told they were out in the cemetery on the hillside. The living with whom one was trying to make an engagement always put themselves in the shadow of death. They said they would come, 'If I live and nothing happen.'"[10]

Attitudes toward black people changed little during the Progressive Era. In those years white Americans lynched two or three black men and women a week. The war years brought race riots, which broke out violently again in 1919. The public conscience hardly fluttered.

Taking Charge

But thousands and thousands of black women refused to accept the status of victim. Somehow they found the strength to change the direction of their lives—sometimes by getting an education, sometimes by seeking fresh opportunities in new places.

As Deborah Gray White has pointed out, black women gained strength from one another. "Strength had to be cultivated. It came no more naturally to them than to anyone. If they seemed exceptionally strong it was partly because they often functioned in groups and derived strength from numbers."[11]

Perhaps too they drew their self-reliance and independence in part from their long experience as workers, often alongside men. Many more of them worked for pay than did other American women. In 1900, when only 16 percent of white women over 10 were in the work force, it included 40.7 percent of black women. By 1920 the gap between the two groups had narrowed a bit: 19.5 percent of white women and 38.9 percent of black women.[12]

Black women fortunate enough to gain an education exercised influence far beyond their numbers. They could hardly escape a sense of obligation. Janie Porter Barrett remembered that when she was a student at Hampton Institute longing for fun and pretty things she tired of hearing about her duty to her race: "Why, on Sundays I used to wake up and say to myself, 'Today I don't have to do a single thing for my race.'"[13] Their social activism stood on two legs: one, the inherited tradition of interdependence among black folk, of community responsibility; the other, the can-do, go-ahead attitude of the self-reliant black woman.

The necessity to think and act politically was thrust upon black teachers. They could count on only a modicum of support. For their pay they had to rely on hostile white administrators or poor black parents. They taught more children than their white colleagues, in smaller schools, with less equipment, and for 45 percent of the white teachers' salaries. Yet they were expected to lead in community improvement.

Take, for example, a black teacher in Alabama in 1912. She was asked to work eight months of the year for $290, out of which she also paid "three teachers and two extra teachers." The state supported only three months of schooling. It was up to her to raise other funds and to try to pay for the construction of a school building. Like other rural teachers, she was expected to establish a School Improvement League of parents and friends to better not only her school but also community life generally.[14]

Or consider Mamie Garvin Fields. Born into the black aristocracy of Charleston, South Carolina, and a graduate of Claflin University, she worked as a dressmaker and later as an elementary school teacher, even during her marriage to Robert Fields, a bricklayer. Though she had to fritter away her energies negotiating with her school board for basic supplies, she found time and strength to involve herself with the City Federation of Colored Women's Clubs, trying to improve the living conditions of the poor, concentrating particularly on the problems of homeless young girls.[15]

WORK DOMINATED THE LIVES OF BLACK WOMEN IN THE RURAL SOUTH.
(NATIONAL ARCHIVES)

But most black women were either agricultural workers or domestic servants. In 1900, when black people constituted about 11 percent of the population, 440,000 black women labored in the fields, as compared with 290,000 white women. From 1900 to 1920, the number of white women in agricultural labor grew, but that of black women declined slightly, what with hard times on the tobacco and cotton farms of the Southeast, the black migration cityward, and the new job opportunities that World War I offered.[16]

Although black tenant farmer husbands and fathers tried to use the field labor of women and children only at planting and harvesting, plantations owners employed riders to force all hands into the fields. A sharecropper's wife usually rose about 4:00 A.M. to get breakfast over an open fire. Often she had to spend a 12-hour day in the fields. When she came home, she collected firewood, fetched water, milked the cow, cooked, and stayed up at night to cope with the rest of the housework.

Confronted with the lifelong prospect of such labor, blacks began to move into the small towns and then into the cities of the South. There many women patched together piecemeal existences: washing and ironing; cooking for special occasions; working part-time on farms; selling vegetables, chickens, eggs, milk,

BLACK WOMEN ALSO TOILED IN THE CRANBERRY FIELDS OF MASSACHUSETTS.
(NATIONAL ARCHIVES)

and butter. Others hired themselves out as domestic servants. In southern towns and cities, and later on as they moved northward and westward, most black women found their first jobs—jobs of last opportunity—as domestic servants. In 1900, 43.5 percent of black women in the labor force worked in private household service, and that ratio moved upward during the Progressive Era, even as the percentage of white women domestic workers declined.[17]

In the homes where they worked, black maids waged a series of battles with their white mistresses. The white women, of course, held most of the power. They demanded long hours and paid low wages. But, disconcertingly, the servants found ways to fight back. They insisted on day service rather than live-in jobs, so that they could go home at night to their own children, whom they often had been forced to leave alone all day; and when they went home, they carried "service pans" of leftovers. They arrived late and left early. They took time off without notice. Employers complained that the servants did nothing unless specifically told, that they stole, that they seized every opportunity to irritate. If a mistress established a reputation for being too finicky, domestics might blacklist her. Sometimes, of course, employer and employee established happier, long-term relationships. But often they scuffled and skirmished, unable to get along with or without each other.

In a market where the demand for domestic service outran the supply, working women learned that if they controlled nothing else, they could at least control the quality of their own labor and its very supply. They even formed organizations like the Association of Women Wage-Earners to promote self-reliance, teach domestic science, provide job placement, and negotiate with their employers.

No matter how many small victories they won, though, black women shared white women's distaste for domestic service. By preference they turned to industry, accepting the meanest, dirtiest, worst tasks in laundries and sugar and tobacco factories, shucking oysters in oyster-processing plants, taking janitorial jobs when nothing better offered. But during the Progressive Era the industrial work force never really assimilated them; they constituted at best an emergency pool, to be tapped in times of strikes or of war or to do work that everyone else rejected. Low wages, seasonal work, and the absence of any chance to advance delivered their own clear message: It was pointless for black workers to arrive punctually, to come regularly, to work at their best pitch. Most black women learned to find their emotional satisfactions, to define themselves, not by job status but by motherhood.

The Northward Migration

In the North a domestic servant could earn $1.50–$2 a day, plus carfare and meals—just under what she could earn for a week in urban Mississippi. She might earn in a northern factory six times what she received picking cotton on a southern farm.[18] And she hoped to diminish the sexual abuse heaped upon her and hers: "There is no sacrifice I would not make, no hardship I would not undergo, rather than allow my daughters to go in service where they would be thrown constantly in contact with Southern white men, for they consider the colored girl their special prey."[19]

So between 1890 and 1910 "around 200,000 black Southerners fled to the North; and between 1910 and 1920 another 300,000 to 1,000,000 followed. The Department of Labor reported that in eighteen months of 1916–17 the migration was variously estimated at 200,000 to 700,000. . . . Whatever the exact figures, 1916 and the two war years that followed brought the northward Negro movement to its peak."[20] Women spearheaded the migration, moving in greater numbers.

All kinds of black women went. One woman wrote to the *Defender*, a black newspaper that encouraged migration, "I am a poor woman and have a husband and five children living and three dead. . . . This is my native home but it is not fit to live in. . . . Will you please let me know where the cars is going to stop?"[21] Some of the migrants were little girls 10 or 11 years old, whose families sent them north to Washington, D.C. Naomi Yates remembered, "By four you'd do field work; by six you'd be doing small pieces in a tub every washday and bring all the clear water for rinsing the clothes. By eight, you'd be able to mind children, do cooking, and wash. By ten you'd be trained up. . . . No play, 'cause they told you: life was to be hardest on you—always."[22] The brightest black women students, said Lura Beam, left the South.

The exodus appalled southern whites, who dragged blacks off trains heading north and even went so far as to improve working conditions and raise wages. Yet between 1900 and 1920, hundreds of thousands of blacks fled north, escaping sharecropping, disfranchisement, Jim Crow laws, and a plague of boll weevils to establish themselves in a flawed promised land, where racist, nativist employers still preferred white foreign-born immigrants to black native-born Americans, "despite their favorable levels of educational attainment compared to European peasants."[23]

Often, at least partly because many black women were better educated and more employable than black men, the women preceded their menfolk in the northward hegira. Their lot was not an easy one. But black women were used to fending for themselves. They helped one another, and many individuals and organizations helped them.

The "Old Black Elite" of prosperous blacks and long-time northern blacks, the National Urban League, the National League for the Protection of Colored Women, the National Association of Colored Women, and black-run settlement houses joined with the YWCAs to help them, organizing social clubs, employment services, recreational facilities, and day nurseries. These groups housed young black women traveling north and defended them against pimps and procurers. They funded homes for working women and for the elderly. They taught courses in nutrition and hygiene and northern standards of household maintenance.

In this migration black women were moving, as it were, from the fire into the frying pan. They could give their children better educations. They lessened somewhat their daughters' vulnerability to sexual harassment. They earned more money. They could use some public facilities.

But they continued to suffer discrimination and insults. The ranks of white labor unions and of clerical work were almost always closed to them. Before World War I, seldom could they get jobs in industry. During the war, factory owners who had always shut them out eagerly hired them—but only for as long as the war emergency lasted and usually only for jobs they couldn't persuade anyone else to take. Even then black women were usually given the machines hardest to operate and relegated to the darkest and worst-ventilated work positions and the smallest and dirtiest restrooms. At piecework, they received a lower rate than whites. Government offices would hire only the most light skinned and segregated even those. Black women could work in department stores as stock girls, elevator operators, cafeteria waitresses, and scrubwomen but not as sales clerks.[24]

Yet most black women, married or not, continued to have to work throughout their lifetimes. Underemployed and intermittently unemployed husbands simply couldn't earn enough to support their families. The women could almost always find relatively steady work in domestic service, so that annually they outearned their husbands, even though they received much lower daily or weekly wages. A Philadelphia study of 1899 showed one black family where the husband earned $150 a year as a hod carrier and day laborer; the wife earned $180 a year as a laundress; the son earned

UNCLE SAM NEEDED THEM—TEMPORARILY. WEIGHING WIRE COILS IN ONE OF THE NEW WARTIME JOBS. (NATIONAL ARCHIVES)

$125 a year, plus meals, as a building porter; they rented out three of their seven rooms. That family was well-off compared with another family of three who lived in one room and rented out two others; the wife as a domestic servant earned $100 or more of their $125–$150 yearly income.[25]

Black migrants, as their numbers increased, encountered severe housing shortages, exorbitant rents, and dreadful conditions in the cities, where most of them settled. Blacks, wrote Florette Henri,

> were charged higher rent than whites for the same accommodations. When a Chicago paper advertised 'seven rooms, $25.00' and 'seven rooms for colored people, $37.50,' it is a safe bet that the apartment labeled 'colored' was not worth $12.50 more than the other. . . . Chicago surveys in 1909 and 1919 showed blacks paying 100 per cent more. The situation prevailed in every big city except Washington.[26]

Housekeeping was harder in the North, especially as many women had to take in boarders. City life weakened marriages and strained women's relations with their children. A good many of the women who moved north were widowed or separated. Even if they lived with their husbands, though, many black women, as primary wage earners, could not stay home—unlike immigrant mothers, most of whom did not leave their homes for full-time work. Black working children tended to use their earnings for themselves rather than contributing them to the family coffers. Daughters were apt to find their pleasures in cafes, department stores, theaters, and "pay dances" rather than join their mothers in church services, benevolent society meetings, and front stoop sitting. In short, most black working-class women who migrated gradually lost their traditional life-styles and much of their influence.

Lifting as They Climbed

Despite all the roadblocks in their way, though, black women, in the North and South, were organizing around national and community interests—both those they shared with white Americans and those specific to black Americans.

Although they had earlier used it in other ways, they were old hands at collective action for the common good. What's more, their lives and those of their foremothers had not imposed upon them the strict separation of the public and private spheres that in the 19th century had restricted white women—so many black women had always worked outside their homes. Those who founded the Woman's Union, a female insurance company, chose as its motto "The Hand that Rocks the Cradle Rules the World." But to *them* that motto meant that women could *both* rock the cradle and found corporations. Women like these took it for granted that they could and should do public housekeeping.

Resistance against the terrible practice of lynching initiated the black women's club movement, thanks to that courageous woman Ida B. Wells-Barnett.[27] The daughter of a slave mother and an Indian father, Wells in 1891 at the age of 29 lost her teaching job because she publicly criticized the schools for black children. Thereupon she bought an interest in the *Memphis Free Speech*: As editor she not only denounced a local lynching but hacked at the very roots of lynching by charging that its basis was not chivalry but economics. The mob, she said, was not defending outraged white womanhood; rather, white business-men were out to destroy the black competition.

This analysis stripped away the respectability with which self-righteous whites had tried to cloak murder and torture. Doubtless many dark motives drove the lynch mobs: lust for unbridled power, sadism, jealousy at the mere idea that a white woman could love a black man, a determination to keep blacks "in their place." Certainly Wells in the many investigations of lynchings that she conducted throughout her lifetime found ample evidence of white greed. Lura Beam came upon a lynching in Albany, Georgia, that grew out of a tawdry quarrel: A white man paid a black gambler's debt of $30; the work the gambler did in return failed to satisfy. The white man beat the black, who resisted and killed the white man. In searching for him, a mob lynched nine blacks, including a pregnant woman who insisted too loudly that her husband had nothing to do with the killing. They hanged her head downward "as more convenient for the disembowelling."[28] In many lynchings sexual activity was not even alleged. Yet for decades the white public had cherished the myth that lynchings were knightly feats to protect their womenfolk.

Her white Memphis townsmen took umbrage when Wells advanced a much more likely cause, and their rage grew when she successfully urged black people to move out of the town that so abused them. While she was away, a mob destroyed her newspaper office, and she was warned not to return on pain of death.

Instead she launched a campaign against lynching and the killing of innocent black Americans that she conducted bravely throughout her life, with whatever help she could muster or alone. In 1917, for instance, black soldiers in Houston were accused of running amok and shooting up the town. Twelve of them were hanged, and Wells sought in vain for a black church in which to hold a funeral service for them. Her distribution of buttons memorializing them attracted the attentions of Secret Service men. Yes indeed, Wells told them, she *had* criticized the government: It had done a dastardly thing.

If it is treason for me to think and say so, then you will have to make the most of it. . . . I would consider it an honor to spend whatever years are necessary in prison as the one member of the race who protested, rather than to be with all the 11,999,999 Negroes who didn't have to go to prison because they kept their mouths shut. Lay on, Macduff, and damn'd be him that first cries 'Hold, enough!'"[29]

As she traveled the country lecturing, Wells helped found black women's clubs on the model of those she had seen in England. In the Southeast as in the North and Midwest, black women eagerly banded together in clubs that not only took up the same causes as the white women's clubs, but also addressed the problems unique to black Americans.

Besides, they desperately wanted to refute the charges of ignorance and immorality constantly being hurled at black women: ". . . to be a colored woman," wrote Fannie Barrier Williams, "is to be discredited, mistrusted and often meanly hated."[30] In the name of sheer self-preservation Mary Church Terrell called on middle-class black women to help "the lowly, illiterate and even vicious, to whom [they were] bound by ties of race and sex."[31] When in 1896 black clubwomen joined together in the National Association of Colored Women (NACW) under Terrell's leadership, they chose the motto "Lifting as We Climb." So they set out to help their neighbors and to improve their neighborhoods, which over the years they defined in broader and broader terms. In the process they trained new leadership within the black community.

In Atlanta, for instance, Lugenia Burns Hope, wife of the president of Morehouse College, founded a Neighborhood Union which became a model for black women's clubs all over the South. "Our method of relief in the neighborhood," said Hope, "is to have each neighbor feel the responsibility of his [read *her*] next door neighbor."[32] This highly structured organization divided Atlanta into zones, each supervised by a chairwoman, and the zones into districts, each operated under presiding officers and corps of neighborhood workers. The arrangement guaranteed a thoroughgoing knowledge of the needs of people everywhere in Atlanta. It also demanded the absolute commitment of the clubwomen. And it worked.

The Neighborhood Union, seeing the solution to black problems in mass education and knowing how the white society had deprived black children, investigated every black school in Atlanta and publicized its findings. Its members improved school facilities; they abolished double sessions; they raised teachers' salaries; they fought to prevent the elimination for black children of grades seven and eight. They demanded special classes for retarded youngsters. They successfully protested a law that required white teachers to teach only white children, black teachers to teach only black children—not because they didn't want black teachers but because the schools couldn't get enough black teachers to teach all the black children.

They supplemented the training black children received in schools by providing nursery schools, kindergartens, playgrounds, clubs, and neighborhood centers for them. They operated vacation schools. They taught the children's mothers cooking and home nursing.

In all these ways and many others, black clubwomen tried to meet the special needs of their race, like those created by the great migration. Determined to save young black women from prostitution, the clubwomen tried to provide them with economic alternatives. They taught young women domestic skills in Nannie Burroughs's National Training School (called the School of Three B's for the importance it placed on Bible, bath, and broom). They opened boardinghouses for them, like the Phillis Wheatley Homes. They supported hospitals and nursing training schools.

Often they were doing just the same sort of thing as white clubwomen. But the black women's habit of taking responsibility for other women, for the extended family, and for the black community as an extension of the family perhaps gave their activities a warmer, more personal cast.

Separate and Unequal

Black Americans also interested themselves in the issues foremost in the minds of white women, like woman suffrage. Tragically, the hands that black women held out to their white sisters were commonly ignored or slapped away. Almost all of the white women's organizations refused to admit black members, either out of fear of losing white members or out of sheer racism. The New England Woman's Club did admit the black leader Josephine Ruffin but "also hired a newly freed slave as the clubhouse domestic worker rather than permit her to join."[33] The General Federation of (white) Women's Clubs repudiated Ruffin's appeals to unite with black clubs. At their 1900 convention, which she attended as a delegate of both the predominantly white New England Federation of Women's Clubs and the black Woman's New Era Club, they would seat her only to represent the white club.

That convention also refused Mary Church Terrell permission to bring greetings from the National Association of Colored Women, though she did succeed that year in speaking to the National American Woman Suffrage Association (NAWSA). But at its 1903 meeting the NAWSA board endorsed a states' rights position for the organization, tantamount in many states to endorsing the exclusion of black women. When the National Association for Colored Women applied for membership, NAWSA asked the black women to hold the application until after the Senate vote on a national woman suffrage amendment, and the black women complied. The Woman's Party, the radical wing of the suffrage movement, professed sympathy for black woman's suffrage, but before their 1913 parade (in which 41 black women participated), leaders asked Ida B. Wells not to march with the mostly white Chicago delegation of which she was a part.[34] (Wells outwitted them, though; she stood among the spectators watching the parade until the Chicago dele-

CLUBWOMAN MARY CHURCH TERRELL PORTRAYED BY AFRICAN-AMERICAN BETSY G. REYNEAU. (NATIONAL ARCHIVES)

gation came by, when she stepped into line with them and they closed ranks around her and marched triumphantly ahead.) Even in 1920 with the 19th Amendment passed and ratified, Woman's Party leader Alice Paul deemed the time still not ripe to fight for the voting rights of black women.[35]

Black women worked for suffrage in their own ways and own groups—by the early 1900s they had established black suffrage clubs all over the country— but it's no wonder that Mary Church Terrell believed that if white suffragists could get the vote without enfranchising black women, they would. The temperance movement compiled an equally dismal record, maintaining separate organizations for blacks and whites, despite the effective black temperance crusade conducted even after the passage of the prohibition amendment as black women worked with individuals to prevent backsliding.[36]

Black clubwomen suffered equally dispiriting treatment from black male-dominated organizations. Consider, for instance, the Tuskegee Woman's Club headed by Booker T. Washington's third wife, Margaret Murray Washington. By 1910 the club had been functioning effectively for 15 years: It had established the Russell Plantation, on which students ran a farm and learned household and industrial arts; it had also started and staffed a public library. Yet the Tuskegee Negro Conference of that year excluded women—a rejection that apparently spurred the women to even more impressive achievements. The biracial National League on Urban Conditions, an outgrowth of efforts to protect black women migrating north, reserved its leadership posts for men and white women, though its principal workers were black clubwomen.

This kind of treatment, the persecution leveled everywhere in America at blacks, and the repression exercised against women sharpened the insurgent edge on black clubwomen's efforts. While they understood Booker T. Washington's emphasis on industrial education, they wanted more than that for black children. Mary Church Terrell was, after all, a Greek scholar; Anna Julia Cooper, who at 67 earned a Ph.D. from the Sorbonne, risked her job in the Washington, D. C., school system to channel black students into America's best universities. Clubwomen appreciated Mr. Washington's political clout and fund-raising skills, but they wanted the equal political and social rights that he was willing to sacrifice. They, not he, fought the prohibition of interracial marriage.[37]

Their differences are encapsulated in Ida B. Wells's response to the philanthropist Julius Rosenwald, to whom she was appealing for money, when he repeated a story derogatory to black women that Washington had told him:

> *We have very great respect for Mr. Washington's ability to reach the influential people of this country and interest them in his theories of industrial education and secure their help for the same. We don't all agree entirely with his program. As to his being our leader, I will answer your question by asking one. Rabbi Hirsch is your leading Jew in Chicago. . . .*

I am wondering if you Jews would acclaim him so highly if every time he appeared before a gentile audience he would amuse them by telling stories about Jews burning down their stores to get their insurance?[38]

". . . the women of the NACW," writes Paula Giddings, "had defended the race when no one else had. They had defended themselves when their men had not."[39] Black clubwomen exercised a strength fired by adversity, a courage tempered by hardship, a daring honed by affliction.

"We Specialize in the Wholly Impossible"[40]

A striking number of black Americans set out on their own to better the lot of others. Carrie Steele, herself an orphan, founded an orphan home and school with funds she earned by working as a laborer in a railroad station, selling copies of her autobiography, selling her own home—whatever she could think of. After her death, her work was carried on by her husband's second wife.[41] Ada Harris of Indianapolis reclaimed a poor all-black settlement infested with crap games and prostitution rings, where she had taught school since the late 1880s. By 1909 the principal of the local school, she took heavy personal risks to save the community, like buying a $1,500 property with a $35 down payment, so it could be put to use as a boys' club.[42]

At Mt. Meigs, Alabama, Georgia Washington enabled a new life-style for whole families when she founded the People's Village School, around which black people could buy land. By 1910, 50 families had purchased some 3,000 acres. Amelia Perry Pride with funds from the North and the support of Lynchburg, Virginia, women built an old folks' home while at the same time she functioned as a full-time teacher and homemaker.[43]

Women like these lit not just candles but torches to illumine the paths of their children and grandchildren. One woman inspired another. Lucy Craft Haney through the liberal arts curriculum she founded at her Normal and Industrial Institute educated a whole cadre of high achieving women. Haney's student Mary McLeod Bethune founded Bethune-Cookman Institute, the National Council of Negro Women, and the Southeastern Federation of Colored Women's Clubs. Another, Janie Porter Barrett, organized the first settlement house in Virginia and established a school for black women, financially supported by black women's clubs. And yet another, Charlotte Hawkins Brown, built the Palmer Memorial Institute from a run-down country grammar school into a thriving secondary school and junior college (whilst, incidentally, raising some seven orphaned young relatives).[44]

Equally creative and daring were the black women who pioneered in new professions and undertakings, trampling out paths for others to follow through

MARY MCLEOD BETHUNE, BY AFRICAN-AMERICAN
SCULPTOR SELMA BURKE.   (NATIONAL ARCHIVES)

the wilderness of gender and racial discrimination. Phi Beta Kappa Jessie Fauset, midwife of the Harlem Renaissance of the 1920s, moved from teaching to literary editing to writing novels about middle-class blacks.[45] Maggie Lena Walker, first American woman bank president, acted as Grand Worthy Secretary of one of the larger and more successful of the many black American mutual benefit societies, which combined insurance functions with economic development and social and political activities. No queen bee, she always sought out other women to work with her. [46] Lillian Harris fitted out an old baby carriage with a boiler out of which she sold southern food like pigs' feet, hog maws, and chitterlings on Harlem streets. She grew rich on the proceeds and invested in real estate, transforming herself from "Pig Foot Mary" into a business executive. [47] Twenty-two black women opened a department store in Richmond, Virginia, to give black women jobs and business experience and black customers the chance to buy quality goods at affordable prices.[48]

Better known are the entertainers. At the turn of the century, some black women found employment singing in the bars, saloons, and brothels of New Orleans, Memphis, Kansas City, St. Louis, and Chicago. Other young, beautiful, talented black women entered the world of road shows.

In either case, it was a tough life of whiskey, two-timing men, and nostalgia, a life reflected in their songs. One of its earliest denizens was Gertrude Pridgett "Ma" Rainey, who began her career by winning a local talent show in Columbus, Georgia, called "Bunch of Blackberries." She and "Pa" for many years traveled in minstrel troupes with a song-and-dance act. But, possibly by 1902, this "Mother of the Blues," a "squat, heavy-featured woman, with her flamboyant dress, flaring hair, and necklace and ear pendants of gold coins," and her penchant for jewelry and young men, sang the blues.[49] Sometimes she wrote her own lyrics. Starring in the Rabbit Foot Minstrels (among other shows), she made the vaudeville circuit in the segregated world of the Theatre Owners Booking Agency—also known as TOBA: Tough on Black Artists. In the Rabbit Foot Minstrels she was joined by Bessie Smith, who had begun as a street singer, and Ida Cox, who later formed her own "Raisin' Cain" company.[50]

Across the Boundaries

All along, of course, despite separatism and bitter racial antagonism, everywhere at some level a few white women and black women had been communicating. The Mississippi Signature Quilt Top attests to this kind of relationship. Made at the turn of the century by neighbors, friends, and former slaves of Dixie Plantation, the quilt in the writing between the blocks shows the names of the makers, with such identifying phrases as "1st Manager's Wife," "Landlady of St. James Hotel," and, poignantly, "'Joe Wanderer.' Born in cotton field—and her mother threw her away. Found and cared for by Mrs. S. A. Mayhall."[51] Here and there from Reconstruction times onward white women had tried to help blacks. Several northern white women gave generously and courageously of their fortunes and their lives, and northern churchwomen sent aid to struggling black schools.

In 1899 Southern Methodist women established for black people the Bureau of Social Service, superintended by Mrs. J. D. Hammond, daughter of a slaveowner, who denounced her own race for hypocrisy and insensitivity and castigated them for permitting black slums, sending youngsters to jail, allowing inequities in law courts, accepting stinking Jim Crow cars, and failing to educate black talent.[52] In 1911 Mary De Bardeleben overcame the resistance of her family and her bishop to become the first southern white woman in mission service to black Americans.[53] Step by small step, southern white churchwomen began financial support for a black settlement house, cooperated with the Urban League and Fisk University to train black professional workers, and experimented with biracial boards.

Meanwhile the YWCA had been advancing just as hesitantly, with one setback after another as whites insulted black workers, and blacks accused the Y of discrimination. The Y founded its first black branch in 1899. Yet even in 1915 the sole black representative to attend the national convention alleged that "the 'Y' was a spiritual farce, rather than a spiritual force."[54]

But from these tentative efforts in the YWCA and in the women's missionary societies came finally in 1920 a move for genuine cooperation among black and white women. It manifested itself particularly in the Association of Southern Women for the Prevention of Lynching and the Woman's Committee of the Commission on Interracial Cooperation (CIC). In an all-too-familiar pattern, the male CIC, which had developed in part out of YMCA war experience, hesitated to invite women to participate in their work. The women had to insist. Convinced, like Nannie Burroughs, that "the men might as well hang their harps on a willow tree, as to try to settle the race problem in the South without the aid of the Southern white woman," white churchwomen made their way onto the CIC.[54]

In 1919 Lugenia Hope of the black Atlanta Neighborhood Union, frustrated in her attempts to integrate black women into the YWCA, turned to other channels of cooperation between blacks and whites. At the same time Belle Bennett of the Methodist Woman's Missionary Council called on southern white women to cooperate with black women on local and regional levels. At Hope's invitation, the whites Sara Estelle Haskin and Carrie Parks Johnson, both advocates of women's laity rights within the Methodist church and one a YWCA worker, attended the biennial conference of the National Association of Colored Women. Haskin and Johnson experienced an epiphany: The black women they met and heard were intelligent, serious, high achieving. "While we have thought we were doing the best we could," Johnson reported, "a race has grown up in our very midst that we do not know. We know the cook in the kitchen, we know the maid in the house, we know the man in the yard, we know the criminal in the daily papers, we know the worst there is to know—but the masses of the best people of my race do not know the best of the Negro race."[56]

In October 1920 the CIC's newly formed Woman's Committee sponsored a South-wide conference of 91 white women representing the major Protestant denominations, women's clubs, and the YWCA, at which three black women spoke. All of them impressed their listeners, but Charlotte Hawkins Brown reached their hearts and consciences: She described how, on her way to the conference, she had been expelled from her Pullman car by a menacing crowd of white men, without objection from southern white women bound for that very meeting, and how, crushed and humiliated, she had struggled to respond with the forgiveness for which no one had asked. She confided in them the shame virtuous black women suffered as a result of the myth of their promiscuity. She challenged them to confront the evil of lynching. Above all, she reminded them of their own responsibility for the sufferings of black Americans: "The Negro women of the South," she said, "lay everything that happens to the members of their race at the door of the Southern white woman."[57]

In an emotional outpouring, the delegates sang a hymn of fellowship—and, more to the point, laid plans to work together. At the end of the Progressive Era, black and white women of conscience seemed poised to step together onto a new path of mutual respect and cooperation. It proved, alas, a rocky road.

Source Notes

1. Barbara Meyer Wertheimer, *We Were There: The Story of Working Women in America* (New York: Pantheon Books, 1977), p. 228.
2. Lura Beam, *He Called Them by the Lightning: A Teacher's Odyssey in the Negro South, 1908–1919* (New York: Bobbs-Merrill, 1967), p. 89.
3. Quoted in Maurine Weiner: Greenwald, *Women, War, and Work: The Impact of World War I on Women Workers in the United States* (Westport, Conn.: Greenwood Press, 1980), p. 27.
4. Elizabeth Clark-Lewis, "'This Work Had a End': African-American Domestic Workers in Washington, D.C., 1910–1940," in Carol Groneman and Mary Beth Norton, eds., *"To Toil the Livelong Day": America's Women at Work, 1780–1980* (Ithaca, N.Y.: Cornell Univ. Press, 1987), p. 197.
5. Paula Giddings, *When and Where I Enter: The Impact of Black Women on Race and Sex in America* (New York: Bantam Books, 1984), p. 82.
6. Nannie H. Burroughs, "Not Color But Character," *The Voice of the Negro* (July 1904), p. 108, quoted in Giddings, p. 114.
7. Beam, p. 212.
8. Burroughs, "Not Color But Character," p. 277, quoted by Giddings, p. 115.
9. Beam, p. 150. As European-Americans trying to understand African-American history, we advance the hypothesis of self-hatred with some reluctance and uncertainty, particularly with Lucille Clifton's poem exulting in black beauty echoing in our ears.
10. Bearm, p. 182.
11. Deborah Gray White, *Ar'n't I a Woman? Female Slaves in the Plantation South* (New York: Norton, 1984), pp. 119–41.
12. Teresa L. Amott and Julie A. Matthaei, *Race, Gender, and Work: A Multicultural Economic History of Women in the United States* (Boston: South End Press, 1991), p. 403.
13. Florence Lattimore, *A Place of Delight: The Locust Street Social Settlement for Negroes at Hampton, Virginia* (Hampton, Va.: The Press of the Hampton Normal and Agricultural Institute, 1915), p. 6, quoted by Cynthia Neverdon-Morton, *Afro-American Women of the South and the Advancement of the Race, 1895–1925* (Knoxville: Univ. of Tennessee Press, 1989), p. 105.
14. Neverdon-Morton, p. 79.
15. Jacqueline Jones, *Labor of Love, Labor of Sorrow: Black Women, Work, and the Family from Slavery to the Present* (New York: Basic Books, 1985), p. 146.

16. Carl N. Degler, *At Odds: Women and the Family in America from the Revolution to the Present* (New York: Oxford Univ. Press, 1980), p. 405, and Jones, pp. 80–90, passim.

17. Amott and Matthaei, pp. 158, 125.

18. Giddings, p. 141.

19. "Southern Colored Woman, The Race Problem—An Autobiography," *Independent* 56 (March 17, 1904):587, quoted by David M. Katzman in *Seven Days a Week: Women and Domestic Service in Industrializing America* (New York: Oxford Univ. Press, 1978), pp. 26–27.

20. Florette Henri, *Black Migration: Movement North, 1900–1920* (Garden City, N.Y.: Anchor Press/Doubleday, 1975), p. 51.

21. This letter responded to a plan announced in the *Defender* for special railroad cars to transport African-American people to the North. Henri, p. 65.

22. Quoted by Clark-Lewis in Groneman and Norton, pp. 199–200. For a description of one little black girl sent out to work at eight in St. Louis, see Phyllis Rose, *Jazz Cleopatra: Josephine Baker in Her Time* (New York: Vintage, 1991), p. 12.

23. Jones, p. 153.

24. But cf. Giddings, p. 143, and Greenwald, pp. 22–45.

25. Wertheimer, p. 229.

26. Henri, pp. 102, 103.

27. The number of lynchings peaked in the 1880s and 1890s, declining thereafter from an average of 188 a year during the 1880s to 93 a year in the first decade of the 20th century. But from 1905–14 there were always two or three a week. During the summer of 1919 they again increased; thereafter mob violence against black people occurred less frequently— but did not stop. Jacquelyn Dowd Hall, *Revolt Against Chivalry: Jessie Daniel Ames and the Women's Campaign Against Lynching* (New York: Columbia Univ. Press, 1979), p. 133.

28. Beam, p. 172.

29. Ida B. Wells, *Crusade for Justice: The Autobiography of Ida B. Wells*, ed. Alfreda M. Duster (Chicago: Univ. of Chicago Press, 1970), p. 370.

30. *Independent*, July 14, 1904, pp. 91–92, quoted in *Notable American Women, 1607–1950: A Biographical Dictionary* (Cambridge: Harvard Univ. Press, 1971), vol. 3, 620.

31. Quoted by Sara M. Evans, *Born for Liberty: A History of Women in America* (New York: Free Press, 1989), p. 152.

32. Quoted in Neverdon-Morton, p. 152.

33. Karen J. Blair, *The Clubwoman as Feminist: True Womanhood Redefined, 1868–1914* (New York: Holmes and Meier, 1980), p. 108.

34. Neverdon-Morton, pp. 203–04.

35. June Sochen, *Herstory: A Woman's View of American History* (New York: Alfred, 1974), p. 279. Even in 1921, after the passage of the woman suffrage amendment, Alice Paul refused to tell Mary Church Terrell whether or not she endorsed it for all women, or just for white women. In the Resolutions Committee of the Woman's Party, Terrell argued, "Colored women need the ballot to protect themselves because their men cannot protect them since the Fourteenth and Fifteenth amendments are null and void. They are lynched and are victims of the Jim Crow laws and other evils." In support of her argument she told the story of a black woman seven months pregnant whose baby was torn from her body; a committee member asked what the pregnant woman had done to precipitate the lynching. Dorothy Sterling, *Black Foremothers, Three Lives* (Old Westbury, N.Y.: Feminist Press, 1979), p. 147.
36. Neverdon–Morton, p. 207.
37. On clubwomen's attitudes toward Booker T. Washington, see Giddings, pp. 102–8. Note especially her report of Washington's retaliation against both Mary Church Terrell and Ida B. Wells, pp. 107–8. Note too that these differences between black clubwomen and Washington foreshadow the differences between black women and black clergymen in the civil rights movement.
38. Wells, p. 331.
39. Giddings, p. 134.
40. Motto of the National Training School founded by Nannie Burroughs.
41. Neverdon-Morton, pp. 143–44.
42. Darlene Clark Hine, "'We Specialize in the Wholly Impossible': The Philanthropic Work of Black Women," in Kathleen D. McCarthy, ed., *Lady Bountiful Revisited: Women, Philanthropy, and Power* (New Brunswick, N.J.: Rutgers Univ. Press, 1990), p. 72.
43. Neverdon-Morton, p. 109.
44. Hall, pp. 81–82, 92.
45. Barbara Christian, *Black Women Novelists: The Development of a Tradition, 1892–1976* (Westport, Conn.: Greenwood Press, 1980), p. 43. See also the entry on Fauset in *Notable American Women: The Modern Period*.
46. Elsa Barkley Brown, "Maggie Lena Walker and the Independent Order of St. Luke," in Ellen Carol DuBois and Vicki L. Ruiz, eds., *Unequal Sisters: A Multicultural Reader in U.S. Women's History* (New York: Routledge, 1990), p. 210.
47. Henri, p. 162.
48. Brown, "Maggie Lena Walker and the Independent Order of St. Luke," in Ellen DuBois and Ruiz, p. 214.
49. *Notable American Women, 1607–1950*, vol. 3, pp. 110–11.
50. For information on these fascinating women, see Daphne Duval Harrison, "Black Women in the Blues Tradition," in Sharon Harley and Rosalyn

Terborg-Penn, eds., *The Afro-American Woman: Struggles and Images* (Port Washington, N.Y.: Kennikot Press, 1978).
51. This quilt top is now owned by the New England Quilt Museum, 256 Market St., Lowell, MA 01852-1856.
52. Anne Firor Scott, *The Southern Lady: From Pedestal to Politics, 1830–1930* (Chicago: Univ. of Chicago Press, 1972), pp. 195ff.
53. Hall, p. 72.
54. Ibid., p. 83.
55. For a description of churchwomen's struggle for power within their own institutions, see Hall, pp. 77–89.
56. Quoted in Hall, p. 89.
57. Ibid., p. 93.

CHAPTER 6

How Are You
Going to Keep 'Em Down?
A Sexual Revolution

The clock had struck "Sex O'Clock in America," announced *Current Opinion* in 1913. Its editorial writer was stunned by the use of words like *prostitute* in polite conversation. Although rigid standards still limited the sexual activity of American women, and the birth of a baby out of wedlock still damned and doomed the mother, many Americans were changing their minds about woman's sexual nature and reexamining their ideas about men's and women's relationships.

Late in the 19th century, some American women, as a part of a widespread effort to clean up society, joined crusades for "social purity" and "social hygiene." Women who could not bring themselves to work for such a radical cause as woman suffrage felt quite comfortable in trying to modify sexual behavior: insisting on the necessity for sex education, censuring pornography, arguing for women's right to refuse marital sex, trying to hold men to the same standards of sexual conduct as women, and campaigning to abolish prostitution. They were fighting to protect themselves and their children against venereal disease, and their marriages against men's license, drunkenness, and brutality. Many of them also felt a good bit of sympathy for their sisters in the oldest profession—particularly when they recognized their own vulnerability in their economic dependence on men.

The Oldest Profession

Most of the women who tried to help them saw prostitutes as victims of men's lust and greed. During the first years of the 20th century, terror of the "white slave trade" mounted—with how much reason, it's hard to say. Clearly, this trade in seducing or forcing women into prostitution and holding them against their will did exist, and it was far-flung, crossing international boundaries. Authorities convoked international conferences on the problem. Between June 1910 and January 1915, 1,057 men were convicted of white slavery in the United States.[1]

But individuals or loosely allied groups conducted this trade, not one giant conspiracy. The importers of European or Asian women had no connection with the boys in New York City who built small businesses by "ruining" young girls and then introducing them to madams after the girls' families had thrown them out, or with the phony employment bureaus that misled applicants about the nature of the jobs for which they were interviewing.

Though the popular image portrayed its victims as white and rural, in fact white slavery most endangered single immigrant women traveling to America and in their early days here, black women moving from the South to the North, and young working women when they looked for boardinghouses or frequented dance halls and other cheap amusements—or even just tried to survive on their minuscule earnings. More than half of young women workers interviewed in contemporary studies alleged that they had been solicited while looking for jobs.[2]

Middle-class women's organizations undertook to protect potential victims. Concerned Chicago women got lists from Ellis Island of unaccompanied immigrant girls taking the train for Chicago so they could protect them; in 1908 Julia Lathrop organized these guardians into the Illinois Immigrants' Protective League. The Council of Jewish Women, led by Sadie American, knitted together a network of protection. Their Department of Immigrant Aid in 1904 placed a full-time Yiddish-speaking worker, Mrs. Meirowitz, on Ellis Island to record the names of all unaccompanied Jewish females from 12 to 30 and to intercede in their behalf when deportation threatened, and in 250 American cities Jewish ladies visited the homes of the thousands of young women immigrants logged by Mrs. Meirowitz. The Boston Women's Trade Union League undertook to guard the meeting halls of working women against white slavers.

Once captured, the victim of white slavery almost never escaped. The madam or pimp who controlled her took away her clothes and her money, only returning them after she was too demoralized to escape. Theoretically she could buy her way out, but in fact the necessity to pay back her purchase price; her receipt of no more than half of what she earned; and the inflated prices she had to pay for clothing, jewelry, and room and board frustrated her. Some pimps and madams threatened her with razor slashing or shooting. All of them imposed on her a self-hatred and guilt that usually immobilized her.

Most prostitutes, of course, entered the trade not by entrapment but by chance or choice. The economic system far outdid white slavers in victimizing women. Women faced with the impossibility of supporting themselves, let alone their dependents, on the pittance they might earn in factories or department stores supplemented their incomes as best they could or elected prostitution as their best option. For from 1900–1915 prostitutes in American cities earned on average $50 to $400 a week. "From a variety of grim alternatives," writes Ruth Rosen, "women chose their means of survival. . . . Some came to 'the life' out of sheer destitution. Many came out of rising expectations, or through a search for companionship. Others drifted into prostitution after 'giving it away free for years' and 'getting wizened [wised] up.'"[3]

A few comparatively fortunate prostitutes spent the best years of their short working lives in one of the upper-class brothels that wealthy men used as clubs, under the rough-and-ready protection of a madam who satisfied herself with a less-than-extortionate share of the take. There they serviced four or five men a night, for a fee of $5 to $10 each. Brothels for the middle class, charging their customers $1, emphasized efficiency. In the dirty, stinking cribs, where the charge was $0.50, men waited in line for prostitutes expected to cope with 13 to 30 men a night. Among the most miserable were the prostitutes imported from China: starved, beaten, subjected to humiliating physical examinations by prospective purchasers, chased down by the tongs (Chinese associations) if they ran away, locked in small cells; the brothel owners gave customers keys and kept the money.

Social Purity

American women's organizations struggled to eradicate prostitution, or at least limit it, by all sorts of methods. In this effort suffragist organizations, the Women's Christian Temperance Union, the General Federation of Women's Clubs, and Mothers' Congresses joined with the Anti-Saloon League, the Sunday School Association, and local civic leagues. Some tried to regulate men's conduct by devices like requiring a certificate of freedom from venereal disease to obtain a marriage license. Others tried to raise the age of consent—in some states at that time men could rape 10-year-old girls without punishment. Groups founded shelters for women who wanted to leave prostitution. Organizations like the YWCA and the National Council of Jewish Women exposed procurers masquerading as employment agencies and themselves helped women find lodging and work. Others offered aid to women travelers. When the Denver political machine tried to force prostitutes to register so that their votes could be exchanged for police protection, middle-class women opposed the scheme. Some women involved themselves directly: Rose Livingston, the "Angel of Chinatown," herself a drug addict and former white slave, suffered many beatings in her efforts to rescue captive prostitutes. In World War I some women joined in the military propaganda campaigns to persuade soldiers to abstain from sex.[4]

But whatever tack they took, women who fought against prostitution or for prostitutes faced formidable odds. All sorts of men and quite a few women had an interest in perpetuating the trade. Doctors sold prostitutes certificates of health. Police and politicians sold them protection. Businessmen held investments in brothels. Bartenders, waiters, chauffeurs, and cabdrivers steered customers to prostitutes. Breweries forced saloonkeepers to establish prostitutes on their premises to attract business. Landlords charged madams double and triple rents.

Besides, the women who tried to help them often failed to look at the situation from the prostitutes' point of view. After all, the prostitute and her would-be rescuer often came from different races, different ethnic backgrounds, different classes. Many prostitutes thought women stupid to sweat and slave in factories or domestic service when they could earn more money with less time and effort in the brothel. The rescuers, on the other hand, assumed that *anything* was better than a life of prostitution and held out as an alternative the prospect of seven-day-a-week domestic service for board and $2 or $3 a week. Women missionaries tried to convert prostitutes to their own form of salvation.

Prostitutes and rescuers just didn't speak the same language. When her financial backers wanted to name her shelter for prostitutes "The Montreal Mission for Friendless Girls," ex-prostitute Maimie Pinzer protested: "I thank God you are not friendless, but if you were—and were 18 years old—you would no more admit it than any girl does. The kind of girl—the human jelly fish—that is willing to be classed as 'friendless' I haven't much time for."[5]

Even the most sympathetic and insightful would-be rescuers often lost out in the face of public belief that a woman could no more recover her respectability than she could her virginity. Judges, parents, and the general public refused her a second chance. Parents disowned their "erring" daughters. At Hull House Jane Addams dared not admit into a social club two girls who had been decoyed into a brothel when they were looking for a place to live because the parents of the other members would have risen in protest. A pamphlet distributed in foreign ports by the Council of Jewish Women warned, ". . . any immigrant girl coming to America who is found not to be virtuous, or who allows herself to be misled after coming, will be sent back where she came from."[6] Not surprisingly, most rescue efforts failed.

The explosive reform campaign detonated by the social purity movement also failed, as the authorities substituted punishing prostitutes for prevention and rehabilitation. Women's efforts to prevent prostitution through minimum wage laws, sex education, wholesome recreation facilities, and sanctions against pimps had all focused on helping "victimized" women. The federal Mann Act of 1910, which forbade taking women across state lines for immoral purposes, was directed against the white slave trade. But the rising panic about white slavery and prostitution that crested about 1916 turned state and local governments toward repressing the most visible evidence of commercialized vice and away from preventing it or helping its victims.

In a pattern now all too familiar, authorities closed down the red-light districts that earlier had flourished and openly advertised. By 1917, 31 states had enacted laws to this purpose. The storm of activity struck prostitutes disastrously, driving them from their "houses." It forced them into even more dangerous work as call girls, streetwalkers, and masseuses. It transferred control from prostitutes and madams to pimps. For the first time in the United States, it made prostitution a crime, thereby integrating prostitutes into the criminal underworld.

Worst of all, the "American Plan," a nefarious anti-VD provision of the World War I years, authorized the military to arrest any woman within five miles of a military cantonment and suspend her civil rights. If she was found to be infected, she could be sentenced either to a hospital or to a "farm colony."[7] In the doughboy-worshiping hysteria of World War I America, it took real courage to oppose this flagrant abrogation of women's civil rights—as some clubwomen bravely did.

In the end Progressive Era governments chose to punish prostitutes, not to change the system that produced prostitution.

Sex and the New Woman

Ironically enough, at the very time prostitutes were being criminalized and imprisoned, other women were claiming more sexual freedom and more control

"WHAT ARE WE COMING TO?" (NEW YORK PUBLIC LIBRARY PHOTO FILES)

over their own bodies. Younger women were more frequently indulging in premarital and extramarital sex than their foremothers.[8]

Intellectuals, inspired by Sigmund Freud and Havelock Ellis, were openly discussing the nature of female sexuality. Radicals argued in the name of gender equality that women should share men's sexual freedom. Like the social purists they urged the adoption of a single standard—but the men's standard. Some of the young sophisticates of Greenwich Village and bohemias in other large cities, safely away from the small towns in which most of them had been born, put these ideas into practice in affairs not only pleasurable but also sanctioned in their own circles.

Upper-class women were drawn to the new cabarets, where unchaperoned men and women could disport themselves publicly and informally together. By such behavior 19-year-old banker's daughter Eugenia Kelly so distressed her mother that she petitioned to have Eugenia declared incorrigible: "'Why, if I didn't go to at least six cabarets a night,' Mrs. Kelly quoted her daughter, 'I would lose my social standing.'"[9] In the cabarets, alleged Mrs. Kelly, Eugenia had learned to smoke and drink. In this era of rampant nativism and class snobbery, the cabarets provided intimate, sexy settings, where the likes of Sophie Tucker sang songs replete with double entendres and rich customers drank and mingled freely with immigrant entertainers and chorus girls. Worse still, in 1912 the cabarets introduced tango teas, welcoming unescorted women and furnishing gigolos for them to dance with. A woman purportedly out shopping could drop in for a tango in the arms of some "swarthy lower-class Italian or Jew" and her father or husband be none the wiser. "Where Is Your Daughter This Afternoon?" asked *Harper's Weekly* in January 1914.

Just Say No

The new openness about sex affected middle-class women somewhat differently. They could now remedy their acknowledged ignorance about human reproduction by reading newly available textbooks, and they advocated sex education for others. Even more important, they tried to seize control over male sexuality, both outside and inside marriage.[10]

In the late 19th century the voluntary-motherhood campaign championed women's right to decide when or when not to have babies. Because advocates of voluntary motherhood also rejected the use of contraception, their arguments necessarily implied women's right to decide when or when not to have sex. What a neat turning of the tables! For decades men had been allocating responsibility for morality to women, attributing to women a purely feminine instinct for what was virtuous. Yet at the same time husbands had been claiming property rights over their wives' bodies. Surely a woman who as mother would bear unique responsibility for the soul of her child should decide when to birth that child. Now, instead of pleading a headache, a reluctant wife could refuse sex secure in the knowledge that she was doing her bit for social purity and voluntary motherhood.

Mary Austin, novelist and social critic, argued persuasively that if men had initiated an effective *men's* temperance campaign, women might never have tried to assume control over sexuality.

> *Practically all these matters stemmed from the situation of women married to hard-drinking husbands; the relation of amorousness to alcohol, of degeneracy to drink and venereal disease, and the problems these gave rise to as affecting divorce from the Christian standpoint—they led on to the whole study of eugenics . . . , and to the pathologies of sex.*[11]

Women terrified by the then-current belief that drunken husbands could genetically harm a fetus, she said, came to see their only salvation in controlling sexuality.

Women also trembled for themselves and their children over the prevalence of venereal disease. Although no reliable figures for its incidence exist, it was apparently rampant. Husbands infected innocent wives and their babies, and doctors conspired with husbands to keep the women ignorant of venereal disease in their husbands or even in themselves. "Seventy-five per cent of all operations peculiar to women," Katharine Houghton Hepburn wrote in 1910, "are necessary because the husband has infected the wife with one of the diseases which are spread through all ranks of society by means of the social evil [VD]." [12] Pediatricians believed that 25 percent to 50 percent of adult blindness was due to gonococcal infection at birth. The Children's Bureau estimated that syphilis caused 73,000 infant deaths in 1916.[13] Genuine fears about the health of their children as well as a wish to limit the size of their families prompted women to try to control male sexuality.

In any case, whether because of the voluntary-motherhood campaign or for other reasons, married couples were apparently not having sex as often as their progenitors. Median frequencies of coitus in married couples dropped from 3.2 per week for women born before 1900 to 2.6 per week among those born after 1900.[14]

By implication, the voluntary-motherhood campaign acknowledged female sexuality, if only as a maternal instinct within marriage. Sooner or later, that is, woman's longing for a child would lead her to desire physical union with her husband.

But was motherhood all there was to sex for women? Reality broke through. For one thing, young middle-class women's health was improving, as they discarded corsets and other constricting clothing and exercised more—swimming, golfing, bicycling, playing tennis. For another, with the new openness, middle-class women's knowledge about sex was growing. It was both a sign of the times and a prophecy of the future that, about 1900, genuinely passionate ladies began to appear in American fiction. Kate Chopin published in 1899 her novel *The Awakening*, which came close to asserting that a woman could be her own person only by the free exercise of her sexuality.

But as late as 1908 the remarkable gynecologist Robert Latou Dickinson still had to urge other doctors to tell women patients that they need not be alarmed if they enjoyed intercourse. The 47 women in a turn-of-the-century study by Clelia Duel Mosher ranged from naive to ignorant in their premarital information about sex; three or four excepted, they knew at best something of female physiology but little to nothing of male physiology and the act of sex. Yet most of them liked sex and wished they and their husbands could enjoy more of it. Sixty-one percent of them thought that a true purpose of intercourse was pleasure to both sexes.[15]

The changes occurring in sexual behavior were intimately interwoven with the idea that women have a right to control their own bodies. It was right for them to enjoy sex. It was right for them to decide when to have and when not to have sex, and when to have and when not to have babies.

What Price Virtue?

Working-class women too were modifying their sexual habits. On their jobs these women, mostly young, single, and marriage bound, most either natives of foreign countries or the daughters of immigrants, faced conditions their parents never imagined. In factories, laundries, restaurants, and department stores their co-workers talked openly of their romances and their sexuality, exchanging risque jokes, smutty cards, and sexual advice. Their workplaces afforded little or no privacy. The sexual aspersions and invitations of their male co-workers constantly belittled them. Their bosses—whether foremen or floorwalkers— often demanded sexual favors as the price of promotion or indeed of just keeping their jobs. Male customers at restaurants often left their cards, and waitresses knew that responding brought good tips. Low wages forced working women to some form of supplementing their wardrobes or their income.

Working women's social clubs, like The Lady Flashers, might afford opportunity for pickups and sexual experimentation. As one working girl reported (who knows with what delight in shocking a settlement-house investigator?): ". . . in all [clubs] they have kissing all through pleasure time, and use slang language."[16] Tenement streets did not blink at kissing, hugging, and fondling in doorways or on street corners.

Young women from the country and small towns were moving into the cities, away from their families and from curious neighbors. Young immigrant working women, even if they continued to live at home, were questioning their parents' standards of behavior. After all, who knew better how to adapt to America—their Old World parents, who often spoke no English and didn't even know where their daughters worked, or they themselves, who daily faced the brutalities of sexual harassment from their bosses? The standards they developed differed not only from their parents' but also from those of the middle class, perforce allowing more liberties.

These working women could not take their young men home to the crowded tenements in which their families lived, so they met them on the streets. Or they met them at titillating music hall performances; or on Coney Island excursions, where strangers involved each other in practical jokes; or in the cheap dance halls, where they executed suggestively "tough dances" like the grizzly bear and Charlie Chaplin wiggle with animal imitations, wild spinning, slow shimmies, and pelvic gyrations.

The women, earning a fraction of men's wages, could barely afford the price of admission to such amusement places. If they wanted "treats" like food and drink, the men they met must provide them. Some women entered the competition for male attention with low decolletages, gauze stockings, high-heeled shoes, extravagantly decorated hats, and "rats" or "puffs" in their hair. As every woman knows, and sweatshop employee Sadie Frowne observed, "If you want to get any notion took of you, you gotta have some style about you."[17] In accepting treats, women tacitly agreed to some degree of intimacy, from mild flirtation to intercourse. "Don't yeh know there ain't no feller goin' t'spend coin on yeh fer nothin'? Yeh gotta be a good Indian, Kid — we all gotta!" [18]

Not that the working classes valued chastity less than people with more money: They just defined it a bit differently. Some working women thought premarital sex acceptable when the man was a "steady," especially when it was the only way to keep him.[19] A hatmaker accompanied early dates with the warning that there would be "nothing doing," inveighing against the "charity girls" who engaged in intercourse on the first meeting. And charity girls prided themselves on never taking money in exchange for their favors, only presents and pleasure.[20] But, if only out of self-protection, one and all scorned and avoided the woman who had a baby out of wedlock.

Hi-Diddle-E-Dee, The Married Life for Me

Amidst all these changes in women's sexual habits, marriage still loomed as the destiny—or the only economically viable choice—of most American women. In fact, they were marrying younger: in 1900 the median age at first marriage was 21.9; in 1910, 21.6, in 1920, 21.1.[21]

But these weren't always such marriages as their mothers had known. As Sidney Ditzion has observed, "A wholesale revolt against marriage led by disaffected womanhood was under way."[22] Partly because some of their mothers had altered the institution, mostly because of the impact of the industrial revolution and urbanization, marriage wasn't what it used to be.

For one thing, divorce was proliferating. And marriage undertaken with knowledge of a possible way out differs drastically from marriage that is a lifetime's emotional security or a life sentence. The increase in the divorce rate begun in the 19th century, low though the rate was, continued in the Progressive Era. From 1900 to 1920 it doubled, from four per 100 married couples in 1900 to eight in 1920—where it stabilized for some time. Longer life expectancy, the availability of other choices for women, and heightened expectations of marriage all led women to acknowledge their own discontent with the institution and to decide to act on it. The emphasis of the social purity movement on women's right, even women's responsibility, not to have sex with their husbands if they thought it injurious to their families altered their conceptions of a wife's role. In 1912 the Unitarian minister Anna Garlin Spencer was writing: "In so far as greater freedom in divorce is one effect of the refusal of women to sustain marital relations with unfit men . . . it is a movement for the benefit and not for the injury of the family."[23]

All the same, a divorce rate of 8 percent hardly makes a ripple. In 1906 Margaret Deland could, without straining the credulity of her readers, publish a novel in which a character declared that he had never seen a divorced person in his life. Deland simply reflected the belief of many of her readers that women, however wronged, owed it to society not to weaken its fabric by resorting to divorce, for, Deland said and many believed, "the whole vast fabric of society" would be rent were women to break their marriage vows, no matter what the provocation—even infanticide. And society stigmatized divorced women— even high society. Mrs. O. H. P. Belmont told about the treatment she received after divorcing William Vanderbilt in 1895:

> *I was one of the first women in America to dare to get a divorce from an influential man. Up to that time divorce had been the prerogative solely of actresses. Rich men could marry women, treat them in any way they chose, and ignore them. . . . I have gone down the aisle of the church when women I had known since childhood drew back in their pews and refused to speak to me. I have been the guest at parties where the hostess was the only woman in the room who talked to me. Why? Because I had dared to criticize openly an influential man's behavior.*[24]

What perhaps mattered more than the possibility of divorce in changing societal attitudes was that some women no longer thought of marriage as their inevitable destiny. And marriage freely chosen differs from marriage necessitated by economic helplessness. Some professional women, convinced that marriage and career didn't go together, chose careers. Ida Tarbell argued that the single state protected women against the "inferiority and servitude" inflicted by marriage. "I know that something perhaps, humanly speaking, supremely precious has passed me by," wrote Wellesley professor Vida Scudder of marriage, "but had it come to me how much it would have excluded!"[25] Frustrated at the difficulty of combining a job and children, another career woman argued, "I think it would be a fearful thing to die and have done nothing for the race but to have babies,—a rat or a cow could do as much."[26]

Some opted for alternative living arrangements with other women. Many a college-educated woman fashioned a satisfying life for herself outside conventional marriage—some by resorting to so-called Boston marriages, in which they made their homes and built their lives in partnership with other professional women. Some working-class women too, by extraordinary ability and energy, good fortune, or passion for a cause, managed to make their own economic way—women like unionists Leonora O'Reilly and Rosa Schneiderman. Sheer zest for adventure made homesteader Eleanor Stewart reluctant to marry.

Women like these at long last brought into question the assumption that any woman would marry if she could. Their self-sufficiency, their preference for the company of women rather than of men, their ability to support themselves economically, and their freedom to choose an alternative rattled the bars of marriage. The "old maid" remained a butt of jokes among the vulgar for decades more, but those who could read the handwriting on the wall knew that at least some women had a genuine choice about whether or not to marry.

Companionate Marriage

Most women, of course, went right on getting married and having children—just not as many as their mothers had borne. But they had new ideas about their marriages and their families.

As, with industrialization and urbanization, their husbands' jobs took them away from their birthplaces and into the cities, women interacted less with their extended families and more within their nuclear families. And most families (except on farms and among recent immigrants) no longer functioned as economic units. Without shared work and without the buffers provided by extended families, relationships within nuclear families intensified, producing emotional stresses and strains. No longer was an aunt on hand to relieve a tired mother of a colicky baby, or a grandfather to laugh off the grievances of a commonplace marital tiff. The father went off for the day to earn the family living, and the mother was left to cope with cross children and household emergencies as best she could.

But women and men alike were working out a new concept of marriage, an ideal often called "companionate marriage"—that is, a relationship in which husband and wife perceived each other as equals, sharing joys and responsibil-

Copyright 1910 by The Fairman © N.Y.

STILL IN THE GAME.

LOVE AND MARRIAGE. IN THE PROGRESSIVE ERA, AS NOW, AMERICAN SOCIETY PUSHED YOUNG WOMEN TOWARD DOMESTICITY. (POSTCARD OF 1911, COLLECTION OF BETTY PIERSON)

ities in a partnership. This ideal may well have asked men to change more than women, for it redefined masculine roles. A husband could no longer fulfill his duty by merely being a good provider and leaving responsibility for child rearing and family morality up to his wife. "The home is man's affair as much as woman's. . . . When God created homemakers, male and female created he them," wrote Martha and Robert Bruere in 1912.[27]

Yet at the same time, men were expecting more of women. The idea of the New Woman provided advanced young men with the image of a woman companion, bright, athletic, undaunted, well-informed, ready to share in fun and work—and the pleasures of marital sex. Married women were expected to keep themselves attractive. One woman commented in 1907, "In the old days a married woman was supposed to be a frump and a bore and a physical wreck. Now you are supposed to keep up intellectually, to look young and well and be fresh and bright and entertaining."[28] A novel of the period spelled out the New Woman's responsibility: "Living in a man's house and spending his money and even bearing and raising his children, isn't an honest partnership with him unless there's more in it for him than he could possibly get elsewhere for the same money and effort and devotion. . . . Children are desired, now, for the happiness they only can create. And wives likewise!"[29]

Although expectations like these flourished mostly among the prosperous, they were waveringly reflected even in poor immigrant households, where their Yankee-influenced husbands and children pestered women to discard the ways of dressing that they had learned as the very bases of their modesty and good repute: Jewish mothers, for instance, heard advice to take off their wigs, which they had put on at marriage and thought never to discard.

These pressures to adopt new standards of conduct, to develop new kinds of relationships between husband and wife, influenced particularly the young families who were moving to the suburbs. No doubt most of them thought of themselves as fortunate and modern. They

Beauty draws more than horses. You've got the pull all right!

LOVE AND MARRIAGE. (POSTCARD OF 1910, COLLECTION OF BETTY PIERSON)

looked forward to a rising standard of living, in which they wanted their children to share. They wanted to be able to provide more goodies for fewer children. One reason for moving away from where the husband worked was to get the children out of the thronged, disease-ridden city and to provide them with the kind of rural landscape that their parents either remembered from their own childhood or wished they had known. In the suburbs these nuclear families could find privacy, exclusivity, homogeneity. They could live and send their children to school with people like themselves.

After the stresses of the business day in the city, the suburban idyll said, the father would restore his soul with gardening, woodworking, or whatever other activity he associated with rural virtue. The mother, safely away from urban noise and dirt, nonetheless could take the train in to lunch and shop in the glamorous department stores. Husband and wife would center their lives in new homes specially designed for more togetherness—fewer sewing rooms and dens dedicated to privacy and individual pursuits, larger common spaces for shared family activities. Evenings and weekends mother and father together would share parenting, household chores, and recreation with their offspring.[30]

What exactly made the new models of companionate marriage and family togetherness so attractive? Perhaps men accepted their new duties out of a sense of justice or a belief that they would benefit their children. Perhaps they assumed them as a necessary concession. After all, feminists were proclaiming women's rights to individuality; nativists were panicking over the declining birthrate of white Protestant women; politicians were viewing the divorce rate with more than their customary alarm. A new marital life-style might be a small price to pay to keep women in the home. Or perhaps men just found the prospect of family fun with a New Woman and a couple of nice kids more appealing than lodge meetings and male bonding.

At any rate many a young suburban husband plunged into muscular domesticity, cheered on by bodybuilder Bernarr Macfadden, who advocated that

MIDDLE-CLASS DOMESTICITY IN MONTANA. (NATIONAL ARCHIVES)

fathers should participate as much as possible in rearing their children, beginning by being present during birth. Fathers dried dishes and put up wallpaper and took their offspring camping. The family that bicycled together also participated together in community life, church work, and club work. Together husband and wife joined debating societies, natural science clubs, Granges, and literary societies.

Like all daydreams realized, companionate marriage imposed new stresses and strains. It was hard for people to stop following the models of conduct of their parents, observed in childhood. It was hard to give up patriarchal authority. It was hard to change. And they had yet to learn of the tensions produced by all that togetherness, which heightened emotions within their nuclear families. But companionate marriage, whether or not made in heaven, suited the New Woman—woman as free spirit and equal companion, not as subordinate saint.

All in all, what with changing family life-styles, changing relationships between women and men, and the more open concern about sexuality, people were living in interesting times. Nice middle-class ladies no longer pursed their lips at mention of sex—how could they, when they were crusading to stamp out prostitution, calling for sex education for women, struggling for control over male sexuality inside and outside marriage, trying to protect against venereal disease, and trying to limit the size of their families?

Children: To Be or Not to Be?

Even for contented couples, marriage was changing. Few husbands worked at home anymore. Among the working class and in the shrinking farm population, families remained an economic unit, with many contributing members. But elsewhere, the burden of support was thrust more and more upon the father, now more apt to be an employee than an entrepreneur. Increasingly children didn't earn—they cost. As reformers succeeded in passing laws against child labor, childhood was prolonged. So was education, which was extended at the lower end by kindergartens and at the upper by college, even for girls. Servants were departing for more inviting jobs. More wives and mothers found themselves alone in the house or apartment for greater portions of the day.

What's more, the number of years that white, middle-class women had to devote to their families dropped with the declining birthrate, which went from 32.3 per 1,000 in 1900 to 27.7 in 1920 and was still falling. Pundits offered a variety of explanations. Urbanization and industrialization had reduced the need for children to help work the farm. With the drop in the infant mortality rate from 141 deaths per 1,000 births in 1900 to 79 in 1920, couples worried less about ensuring the survival of the family by a multitude of births.[31] The cost of living was rising, and with it the cost of supporting children. Couples were deliberately limiting their families, to give fewer children more privileges. And—the most popular hypothesis of all—women just didn't want so many children.

Politicians, doctors, and other regulators of public morality, of course, were in a tizzy. The physicians responsible for the popular *Household Physician* deplored women who didn't want children, and offered only an (erroneous) rhythm method of contraception: ". . . if there is no coition for ten days after the courses [menses], or three days before, the chances of pregnancy are much diminished." They mentioned condoms only as protection for men against infections from women.[32] The media wrung their hands over the declining birthrate, their worries exacerbated by nativism and racism, for immigrant and black Americans were still producing lots of babies, while upper-middle- and upper-class white couples weren't. "Race suicide," yelled the boisterous Teddy Roosevelt, whose first wife had died in childbirth and whose second suffered ill health as she bore him five children. Some writers "even compared the obligation of women to bear children with the duty of military service for men. . . . [The noted psychologist G. Stanley Hall] claimed [in 1904] that any person who interfered with either of these duties should be regarded as a traitor."[33]

Not every woman agreed. Ida Husted Harper wrote that some marriages ought to remain childless. "A Childless Wife" asserted her greater usefulness to society as a professional woman than as a mother.[34] Lydia Commander tartly shifted the blame: "When we make such social arrangements that women may have work without forgoing motherhood, we may expect such a birthrate as will maintain and rationally increase our nation. To bring about such conditions is our national task. Until it is accomplished we will not find any growth in our birthrate. 'Race suicide' is a social question, and upon society rests the burden of finding its solution."[35]

A New York City woman also laid the problem at society's door. In a 1907 article in the *Independent* she attributed the baby shortage to the cost of living and capitalist exploitation, alleging that she had been forced to go to work to supplement her husband's earnings:

> *Now, gentlemen, You Who Rule Us, we are your "wage slaves." . . . You Who Do Rule Us may take our savings and go to Europe with them, or do sleight of hand tricks in insurance and railroading with them, so that we will not know where they are. You may raise our rent and the prices of our food steadily, as you have been doing for years back, without raising our wages to correspond. You can refuse us any certainty of work, wages, or provision for old age. We cannot help ourselves. But there is one thing you cannot do. You cannot ask me to breed for your factories.[36]*

Yes, they could. Most of the advocates of a higher birthrate directed their diatribes against women. More and more Harvard and Yale graduates, to be sure, were staying single, and those who married were having fewer children. But Wellesley women got the blame, not Ivy League men. "Those women" must be possessed of a spirit of feminism, or a contrary spirit of individualism. They were worshiping, accused Anna A. Rogers, "the brazen calf of Self."[37]

Other "experts" more generously blamed not women themselves but their education. G. Stanley Hall, for instance: "From the available data it seems, however," he wrote in 1908, "that the more scholastic the education of women, the fewer children and the harder, more dangerous, and more dreaded is parturition, and the less the ability to nurse children. Not intelligence but education by present man-made ways is inversely as fecundity."[38]

Left to Their Own Devices

More and more upper- and middle-class women were indeed using birth control devices. They simply demanded them from their physicians, even after the distribution of contraception was criminalized in the 1870s. Of Clelia Duel Mosher's subjects, for instance, 83 percent were using some form—or, more commonly, forms—of contraception: in descending order of popularity: douches, the rhythm method, withdrawal, condoms, or pessaries (a form of diaphragm).

But both their practice of using more than one kind of birth control and their words reveal the worries of these women about the available methods and the depth of their concern about controlling the size of their families. A Cornell graduate wrote, "My husband and I . . . believe in intercourse for its own sake—we wish it for ourselves and spiritually miss it, rather than physically, when it does not occur, because it is the highest, most sacred expression of our oneness. On the other hand there are sometimes long periods when we are not willing to incur even a slight risk of pregnancy, and then we deny ourselves the intercourse, feeling all the time that we are losing that which keeps us closest to each other."[39] Another woman said that during the first 10 years of their marriage she and her husband had sometimes gone two to three years at a stretch with no intercourse, adding that she would never repeat such a deprivation.

Prostitutes, with less clout with doctors than middle-class women, and even greater reasons for concern, resorted to the less reliable methods of birth control, like sponges and douching, and ultimately relied on (illegal) abortion.

Poor women worried, tried to abort themselves, and died in the attempt. Sometimes they eked out payments to a back-street abortionist in weekly installments. They passed around whatever information—or old wives' tales— they could lay their hands on. As miner's wife May Wing of Cripple Creek, Colorado, reminisced,

I know, when I was married, the older women, they used Vaseline a lot. They said a greased egg wouldn't hatch. . . . I never did use the rock salt. Because we were told that it wasn't a good thing to use—it affected the mind. . . . And then, of course, we were more or less a little bit careful. I suppose the Catholics called it the rhythm, you know, and we were taught on that. Well, of course, we were always told as long as you nursed a baby, you wouldn't conceive. . . . They was a lady that come through one time. . . . She took cocoa butter, and you took a shoebox, with the top on it, and then you put holes in it. Then you put this melted cocoa butter in it. Then there was something else she used to put in it . . . Boric acid. So much boric acid with so much cocoa butter. And you made these—they'd be a little cone, like, and you'd use those. . . . Yes, it worked. And in later years, in the magazine, you saw where there was a rubber kind of thing, that you would insert in your vagina. Like a diaphragm.[40]

But "most women lived in continual dread of conception; the great mass of married women submitted helplessly and when they found themselves pregnant, their alarm and worry would result in the determination to get rid of their expected offspring; it was incredible what fantastic methods despair could invent; jumping off tables, rolling on the floor, massaging the stomach, drinking nauseating concoctions, and using blunt instruments."[41]

"Tell Jake to Sleep on the Roof"

In such a climate, the rise of the birth control movement was inevitable. The country was divided on both abortion and the use of contraceptive devices. Abortion had been criminalized only in the latter part of the 19th century, and then not so much by popular demand as by the machinations of doctors.[42] The nation was rapidly discovering the unanticipated effects of having yielded in the 1870s to the pleas of blue-nosed old Anthony Comstock and his Society for the Suppression of Vice, which had panicked Congress into prohibiting mailing, transporting, or importing "obscene, lewd, or lascivious articles"—that is, birth control devices and information.[43] Additionally, 22 states had enacted "little Comstock laws," the most extreme Connecticut's absolute ban on the *use* of birth control devices.

These laws, for obvious reasons, never won complete public support. Many upper- and middle-class women evaded them. Almost every middle-class family among his clients, said a doctor in 1906, expected him to implement their desire to prevent conception.[44] But the authorities also often honored the laws in the breach rather than in the enforcement. They overlooked the circulation of scientific publications describing contraception. Juries often refused to convict abortionists. Emma Goldman distributed contraceptive information at public meetings for a decade, with only intermittent interference from officialdom.

Throughout the Progressive Era more and more voices rose in advocacy of birth control. Many Americans supported smaller families not only as a matter of personal choice and as desirable social policy. Some wanted not only to curb but also to control births: Supporters of the eugenics movement advocated allowing only parents of "superior" physique and intellect to conceive. Others argued that only people who could afford them should have babies.

Sometimes people who argued in this vein were expressing genuine concern for the welfare of the poor; sometimes, alas, a nativist fear of alien contamination. But in 1907 Lydia Commander, while certainly demonstrating her share of nativist hysteria, asserted that immigrant Americans wanted to limit their families quite as much as the native born. The impulse came, she insisted, from being American, not from being rich or poor, female or male. "The small family appears to be an American ideal which immigrants accept as they do other American ideals. Just as they learn to prize free schools, manhood suffrage, free speech, and good wages, they adopt methods for limiting reproduction. It is a part of the process of naturalization. The rapidity with which they do this appears to vary, as with Americans, according to the grade of intelligence."[45]

Unlike rich and middle-class women, though, poor immigrants lacked access to birth control information. They appealed for help to the visiting nurses—who, like doctors, recommended abstinence and refused to break the law by giving contraceptive information to these poor patients. Margaret Sanger, herself a visiting nurse, wrote movingly of Sadie Sachs, her life threatened by yet another pregnancy, who could extract from the doctor nothing more helpful than the advice: "Tell Jake to sleep on the roof." It was Sadie's subsequent death, Sanger wrote, that inspired her birth control crusade.

She was fired also by her discovery of the abysmal ignorance of poor women about their own bodies and by the theories of social reform advocated by her friends in Greenwich Village. These young radicals saw family planning as a means of working-class uplift. They denounced as unjust denying to the poor information that although illegal was still available to the middle and upper classes. The right to know, they argued, was a basic human right. So was the right to free sexual expression.

They came up against some formidable opposition. They confronted not only church, state, and tradition, but also businessmen eager to maintain endless supplies of cheap labor.

Sanger began by writing a series of articles called "What Every Girl Should Know" for the labor paper *The Call*. Although she dealt there not with birth control but with venereal disease and feminine hygiene, the U.S. Post Office in 1912 banned *The Call* from the mails. The editor retaliated by printing the headline "What Every Girl Should Know" and under it the words: "NOTHING! By order of the Post Office Department."[46] In 1914 Sanger went on to found her own paper, *The Woman Rebel*, in which she scattered her shots, damning the Rockefellers, religion, and marriage. Although she advocated *birth control*—a term that she coined, she did not print birth control information. Her arrest on obscenity charges placed her in a dilemma: She might have enjoyed facing trial on the charge of publishing contraceptive information, but she saw no point in going to jail for obscenity. Instead she fled to Europe, to study European methods of birth control distribution and to learn from Havelock Ellis, who gave her advice for her own course of behavior—more caution and more prudence!

Sanger left behind her in the United States a pamphlet, *Family Limitation*, in which she not only praised intercourse as tonic and beautifying to women but also recommended birth control devices—douches, condoms, suppositories, and cervical cap pessaries. She won no friends among doctors by recommending that women teach each other the use of the pessary. Her support came instead from radicals, like the members of the International Workers of the World who distributed the pamphlets for her.

In 1915, while Sanger was still in Europe, Mary Ware Dennett led middle-class women in reorganizing the National Birth Control League founded by Sanger in 1914. Dennett was a different woman than the flamboyant Sanger, who had a lot to learn about organizing efficiently and keeping her eye on the goal. Of forebears whom she herself described as "deadly respectable," Dennett had interested herself not in radical theory but in a handicraft shop and interior decoration before taking up the cause of woman suffrage. With the political sophistication she gained in the suffrage movement, she organized middle-class women into a law-abiding campaign to repeal the Comstock laws. Those laws, she argued, violated the right to free speech by forbidding the transmission of birth control information.

Sanger, back from Europe and a bit put out by the takeover of "her" campaign, was nonetheless pleased when she disembarked on October 10, 1915, to see on the cover of the highly respectable ladies' magazine *Pictorial Review* a headline with her own term, *birth control*. She took off on a speaking tour to the West Coast that attracted both supporters and publicity. A year later, Sanger, her sister Ethel Byrne (also a nurse), and Fania Mindell distributed a flier in English, Yiddish, and Italian advertising a birth control clinic they were opening in Brooklyn:

> *Mothers! Can you afford to have a large family?*
> *Do you want any more children?*
> *If not, why do you have them?*
> *Do not kill, do not take life, but prevent.*
> *Safe, harmless information can be obtained of trained*
>   *nurses. . . . Tell your friends and neighbors. All*
>   *mothers welcome. A registration fee of 10 cents*
>   *entitles mothers to this information.*[47]

Neighborhood women flocked in. The police came, confiscated condoms and pessaries. The district attorney brought suit against Sanger, Byrne, and Mindell. Supporters rallied. Mrs. Amos Pinchot organized a "Committee of 100" women to help in the legal battle. On the day of Byrne's trial, 50 women, many of them socially prominent, took her to breakfast at the Vanderbilt Hotel and escorted her to the courtroom. Jailed, she began a hunger strike. When the authorities force-fed her with milk, brandy, and eggs, the news jostled World War I on front pages for four days. "It will be hard," the *New York Tribune* editorialized, "to make the youth of 1967 believe that in 1917 a woman was imprisoned for doing what Mrs. Byrne did."[48] Sanger emerged from her own prison term as the injured innocent, greeted by comrades singing the "Marseillaise." Her picture behind bars ended a movie entitled *Birth Control*, in which she was featured working in the slums and opening her clinic—a movie that the ads called an "Illuminating Drama for the Ages" and "A Cheerup Photoplay for the Universe."

Despite such militant displays, Sanger was beginning to rethink her strategies and to part company with her radical friends. Recognizing her need for money and influence, she turned to the group who had them—wealthy women. She didn't want to join Dennett, but she began to adopt Dennett's techniques. When in 1919 Dennett replaced the National Birth Control League with the Voluntary Parenthood League, Sanger set up the rival American Birth Control League, financed by the likes of Mrs. George Rublee, Mrs. Paul D. Cravath, and Mrs. Dwight Morrow. The end of the Progressive Era left the situation unresolved, with Dennett still trying to repeal the Comstock laws and Sanger struggling to amend those laws to allow dissemination of contraceptive information by the medical profession only. But in ever-increasing numbers, American women were claiming the right to control their own fertility.

Brought to Bed

They were also rethinking the birthing process. The advertisements that began to appear in 1904 for maternity clothes signaled a shift in attitudes, as women involved in the public sphere discarded the "confinements" that had kept pregnancy modestly hidden at home.

Many women still shuddered, with good reason, at the danger and pain they faced in childbirth. After all, even in 1915, 61 American women died for every 10,000 live babies born, over against two per 10,000 in the 1970s.[49] And many a woman endured terrible pain without either breathing exercises or anesthetics. "My birthday!" wrote Magnolia Le Guin on February 18, 1904, "35 years old, and have been a mother 5 times and will be one again, if nothing prevents, *quite soon*. May be before another day. (The torture is so great I shrink with all my nature from the trying ordeal.)"[50]

Women with a choice were changing birthing. More of them were hiring doctors rather than midwives, particularly women doctors. More of them were having their babies in hospitals rather than at home. And more of them were demanding relief from pain.

All these decisions had side effects. Employing a doctor did not always mean surrendering control. Many a doctor had never officiated in a birth during her or his training, and the knowledgeable women, themselves mothers several times over, whom pregnant women called to stay with them during delivery could overawe the physician. But doctors with their forceps and their cesareans intervened more than midwives, sometimes unnecessarily, out of impatience or sheer ignorance.

The extravagant precautions against infection in some hospitals aggravated the patients' discomfort:

> *In 1900 each patient at Sloane [Maternity Hospital] received an enema immediately upon admission and then a vaginal douche with bichloride of mercury, the favored antiseptic. Nurses then washed the woman's head with kerosene, ether, and ammonia, her nipples and umbilicus with ether; they shaved the pubic hair of charity patients, assuming that poor people harbored more germs, and clipped it for private patients. They gave women in labor an enema every twelve hours and continued to douche the vagina during and after labor with saline solutions to which whisky or bichloride of mercury was added. The zeal against infection led to more douching than was really necessary or safe, for the solutions were ineffective against the germs and served to spread any infection that was already present.*[51]

Ether and chloroform were already available in 1900 to ease the pain, but they couldn't be used until late in the birthing because they relaxed the muscles and interfered with labor. They also put the child at risk and nauseated the mother. For a long time American doctors rejected the "twilight sleep" developed in Germany. Under this system women received morphine at the beginning of labor, then a dose of the memory-destroying scopolamine, followed by ether or chloroform when the fetus was in the birth canal. During the births women writhed in pain, but they woke up feeling fine, with no memory of suffering.

Finally women like Mrs. John Jacob Astor who could afford it crossed the submarine-infested Atlantic of World War I to give birth in Germany. Their enthusiastic reports started a demand in the United States, which grew into a successful campaign. Women who had once experienced twilight sleep, wrote Marguerite Tracy and Constance Leupp in a 1914 article in *McClure's* magazine, would "walk all the way from California [to Germany]" to deliver under its influence.[52] Physicians like Dr. Bertha Van Hoosen advocated this "greatest boon the Twentieth Century could give to women."[53]

The National Twilight Sleep Association claimed that the system abolished the need for forceps, shortened labor, reduced the time of convalescence and the danger of hemorrhage, and helped the milk flow. By this time American women were experts in organization and propaganda. Led by prominent physicians like Dr. Eliza Taylor Ransom and laywomen like Mrs. Julian Heath of the National Housewife's League, author Rheta Childe Dorr of the Committee on the Industrial Conditions of Women and Children, and Mary Ware Dennett of the National Suffrage Association, they sponsored rallies to tell women about the new possibility and pressure doctors to use it. Women who had experienced it gave testimonials, holding their healthy babies in their arms. They held meetings in department stores. The subject was a natural for press attention.

Quite proper concerns about the safety of this anesthetic and mixed reviews in the medical journals held some physicians back. But, although medical experts continued to debate the dangers and benefits of twilight sleep, the laywomen who advocated it had made their point, motivating a serious scientific search for safe ways of easing the pain of childbirth.

During the Progressive Era women giving birth both gained and lost. The process was safer in 1920 than it had been in 1900 for both mother and child. More women received some relief from pain. But as doctors took over from midwives and hospitals from home births, women lost the comfort of being surrounded by loving friends and relatives, the control they had exercised, and their very humanity. Sterility and expertise exacted their price.

With whatever amusement, alarm, or approval women today may react to the burning sexual issues of the years 1900–20, they must credit their foremothers who brought these issues into the open. By the voluntary-motherhood campaign and the birth control campaign they insisted on control: control over whether or not to have sex with their husbands, control over whether or not to bear children—in short, control over their own bodies. In companionate marriage they moved away from the patriarchal model toward a relationship between equals. Only in the birthing process did they lose some degree of the control they had formerly exercised—in return for greater safety and less pain. Many of the problems for which they failed to find solutions, like standards of sexual conduct, prostitution, birth control, abortion, and the use of midwives and anesthetics in birthing, still trouble Americans today. But given the choice, most women of the 1990s would opt to live in the world as those women of the Progressive Era changed it, rather than the world as they found it.

Source Notes

1. Ruth Rosen, *The Lost Sisterhood: Prostitution in America, 1900–1918* (Baltimore: Johns Hopkins Univ. Press, 1982), chap. 7.

2. Robert A. Woods and Albert J. Kennedy, *The Settlement Horizon* (New York: Russell Sage Foundation, 1922; New York: Arno Press, 1970), p. 17.

3. Ruth Rosen and Sue Davidson, eds., *The Maimie Papers* (Old Westbury, N.Y.: Feminist Press with the Schlesinger Library of Radcliffe College, 1977), pp. xxvii, xxviii, xxv. Hereafter cited as *The Maimie Papers*.

4. These efforts evoked a predictable lack of success. More practical was the army's distribution of condoms and copies of Margaret Sanger's pamphlet "What Every Young Girl Should Know"—for the distribution of which to civilians her husband had been jailed.

5. *The Maimie Papers*, pp. xxxiv–xxxv.

6. Quoted in Edward J. Bristow, *Prostitution and Prejudice: The Jewish Fight Against White Slavery, 1870–1939* (New York: Schocken Books, 1983), p. 269.

7. Rosen, chap. 2. For an extended description of the American plan, see below, pp 221–22.

8. Steven Mintz and Susan Kellogg, *Domestic Revolutions; A Social History of American Family Life* (New York: Free Press, 1988), p. 112.

9. Lewis A. Erenberg, *Steppin' Out: New York Nightlife and the Transformation of American Culture, 1889–1930* (Chicago: Univ. of Chicago Press, 1981), p. 78, quoting from a *New York Times* story of May 23, 1915.

10. Women were being told that it was their duty to control male sexuality. In the words of a popular novelist railing against women, "You leave him to his two gross temptations,—Power and Lust. Man is given you to protect, and you drive him into the market-place, where he fights for your ease, and then relaxes in the refined sensualities you offer him as the reward for his toil. With the fall of man into the beast's trough must come the degradation of women." Robert Herrick, *Together* (1908; reprint, Greenwich, Conn.: Fawcett, 1962), p. 389.

11. Mary Austin, *A Woman of Genius* (1912; reprint, Old Westbury, N.Y.: Feminist Press, 1985), p. 149.

12. Quoted in Mark Thomas Connelly, "Prostitution, Venereal Disease, and American Medicine," in Judith Walzer Leavitt, ed., *Women and Health in America: Historical Readings* (Madison: Univ. of Wisconsin Press, 1984), p. 201.

13. Richard W. Wertz and Dorothy C. Wertz, *Lying-In: A History of Childbirth in America* (New York: Free Press, 1977), p. 140. At least one household medical compendium insisted that *women* who overindulged in sex created gonorrhea. Herbert E. Buffum, Ira Warren, William Thorndike, A. T. Lovering, A. E. Small, J. Heber Smith, and Charles P. Lyman, *The Household Physician: A Twentieth Century Medica* (Boston: Woodruff, 1905, 1919), p. 405. Hereafter cited as *Household Physician.*

14. Alfred Kinsey's figures, noted in Carl N. Degler, *At Odds: Women and the Family in America from the Revolution to the Present* (New York: Oxford Univ. Press, 1980), p. 296. For a contemporary study see that of Clelia Duel Mosher, summarized in Barbara Kuhn Campbell, *The "Liberated" Woman of 1914: Prominent Women in the Progressive Era* (Ann Arbor: Univ. of Michigan Research Press, 1979), pp. 82–91.

15. Study by Clelia Duel Mosher, summarized in Campbell, pp. 82–91.

16. Quoted in Kathy Peiss, *Cheap Amusements: Working Women and Leisure in Turn-of-the-Century New York* (Philadelphia: Temple Univ. Press, 1986), p. 62.

17. Ibid., p. 64.

18. Peiss, "'Charity Girls,'" in Ann Snitow, Christine Stansell, and Sharon Thompson, eds., *Powers of Desire: The Politics of Sexuality* (New York: Monthly Review Press, 1983), p. 84.

19. Peiss, "'Charity Girls,'" in Snitow, Stansell, and Thompson, pp. 87, 85.

20. Peiss, "Dance Madness: New York City Dance Halls and Working-Class Sexuality, 1900–1920," in Charles Stephenson and Robert Asher, eds., *Life and Labor: Dimensions of American Working-Class History* (Albany: State Univ. of New York Press, 1986), p. 187.

21. Elyce J. Rotella, *From Home to Office: U.S. Women at Work, 1870–1930* (Ann Arbor: Univ. of Michigan Research Press, 1981). This decline was part of a long-term trend. "In 1890, the median age of first marriage for women was 22 years; by 1955, the median age was 20.2 years." Lynn Y. Weiner, *From Working Girl to Working Mother: The Female Labor Force in the United States, 1820–1980* (Chapel Hill: Univ. of North Carolina Press, 1985), p. 23.

22. Sidney Ditzion, *Marriage, Morals and Sex in America: A History of Ideas* (New York: Octagon Books, 1969), p. 367.

23. Anna Garlin Spencer, *Woman's Share in Social Culture* (New York: Mitchell Kennerley, 1912), pp. 259–60, quoted in Campbell, p. 75.

24. Mrs. O. H. P. Belmont, "Women as Dictators," *Ladies' Home Journal* (September 1922), quoted by Campbell, pp. 95–96.

25. Quoted in Degler, p. 164. Some educated women actually blushed over revealing their decisions to marry to their friends. When Lucy Sprague Mitchell wrote her Radcliffe classmate about her marriage, she said she was a bit "embarrassed either to defend [her] conduct this last year or to

ignore the blight that has been cast with Cassandra-like cheer upon [her] future." Joyce Antler, *Lucy Sprague Mitchell: The Making of a Modern Woman* (New Haven: Yale Univ. Press, 1987), p. 201.

26. Lydia Kingsmill Commander, *The American Idea* (1907; reprint, New York: Arno Press, 1972), p. 272.

27. Quoted in Margaret Marsh, *Suburban Lives* (New Brunswick, N.J.: Rutgers Univ. Press, 1990), p. 67.

28. Quoted in David M. Kennedy, *Birth Control in America: The Career of Margaret Sanger* (New Haven: Yale Univ. Press, 1970), p. 140.

29. Clara E. Laughlin, *The Keys of Heaven* (New York: George H. Doran, 1918), pp. 184–85.

30. More conservative rural folks too were being sent the same message; see Martha Foote Crow, *The American Country Girl* (1915; reprint, New York, Arno Press, 1974), pp. 138–39.

31. Degler, pp. 181, 72-73.

32. *Household Physician*, pp. 409, 466.

33. Vern L. Bullough, *The Subordinate Sex: A History of Attitudes Toward Women* (Urbana: Univ. of Illinois Press, 1973), pp. 311–12.

34. Linda Gordon, *Woman's Body, Woman's Right: A Social History of Birth Control in America* (New York: Penguin Books, 1977), p. 147.

35. Commander, p. 284.

36. Quoted in Richard Hofstadter, *The Age of Reform from Bryan to F.D.R.* (New York: Vintage, 1955), pp. 171–72.

37. Anna A. Rogers, "Why American Marriages Fail," *Atlantic Monthly* 100 (September 1907):292.

38. Stanley Hall, *Adolescence*, vol. 2 (New York: Appleton, 1908), p. 635, quoted in Campbell, pp. 29–30.

39. Campbell, p. 89.

40. Quoted in Elizabeth Jameson, "Women as Workers, Women as Civilizers: True Womanhood in the American West," in Susan Armitage and Elizabeth Jameson, eds., *The Women's West* (Enid: Univ. of Oklahoma Press, 1987), p. 153.

41. Elizabeth Ewen, *Immigrant Women in the Land of Dollars: Life and Culture on the Lower East Side, 1890–1925* (New York: Monthly Review Press, 1985), p. 133.

42. Physicians considered illogical the quickening standard widely accepted as marking the beginning of life. They thought themselves the supreme champions of life. Some were nativistic and antifeminist. Some recognized in anti-abortion statutes a way to deploy the powers of the state against their irregular rivals in the medical field, like midwives. James C. Mohr, "Patterns of Abortion and the Response of American Physicians, 1790–1930," in Leavitt, *Women and Health*, passim.

43. Kennedy, p. 24.

44. Ibid., p. 45.
45. Commander, p. 18.
46. Kennedy, p. 77.
47. Ibid., p. 83.
48. Quoted in Kennedy, p. 86. The clouded crystal ball—at least it's not so hard to believe in 1992.
49. Barbara Ehrenreich and Deirdre English, *Complaints and Disorders: The Sexual Politics of Sickness* (Old Westbury, N.Y.: Feminist Press, 1973), p. 19. By 1918 the United States ranked 17th among 20 nations in maternal mortality. In that year, 23,000 women died in childbirth, up from 16,000 in 1916. Wertz and Wertz, p. 155.
50. Charles A. Le Guin, ed., *A Home-Concealed Woman: The Diaries of Magnolia Wynn Le Guin, 1901–1913* (Athens: Univ. of Georgia Press, 1990), p. 113.
51. Wertz and Wertz, p. 138.
52. Judith Walzer Leavitt, *Brought to Bed: Childbearing in America, 1750 to 1950* (New York: Oxford Univ. Press, 1986), p. 130.
53. Quoted in Leavitt, *Brought to Bed*, p. 128.

Chapter 7

Votes for Women

Woman suffrage did not come easily or cheaply to the United States. From 1848, when Elizabeth Cady Stanton first demanded votes for women, until the ratification of the 19th Amendment in 1920, women paid the price of complete commitment: enormous effort sustained for years; painful and repeated defeats; jeers and assaults by hoodlums; the humiliation and physical suffering of jails, workhouses, beatings, and forced feeding. Although some gallant men fought for and with them, in the main women wrested the prize of suffrage from the unwilling grasp of the president of the United States, midwestern brewers, eastern industrialists, racist southerners, and political machines all over the country.

The Red Rose

Why did it take American suffragists so long to win the vote? Considering the forces arrayed against them, maybe we should ask instead, how did they manage to win the vote at all?

Of course the rank and file of men didn't want to surrender this evidence of their superior power and intelligence. Who willingly gives up superior status? Besides, among men, commented Inez Irwin, "there worked the instinctive sense of sex-superiority and that primitive feeling . . . that whenever a woman tried to do anything which men had hitherto done exclusively, she was funny."[1] Or worse—for by seeking the vote, they said, she was sapping the strength of the country. As the president of the Aero Club of America testified before a congressional committee, votes for women meant "the dilution with the qualities of the cow of the qualities of the bull upon which all the herd's safety must depend."[2]

Of course the political machines didn't want impractical women with ideas about fairness and honesty tampering with their smooth functioning. Of course southern gentlemen—and southern ladies—abhorred the very thought of black women in the voting booth. Of course northeastern urbanites deplored the mere hint of extending the vote to Irish women—bad enough that Irish men exercised it. Of course the alcohol interests specifically and corporate America generally (especially the oil industry and the railroads) feared the crusading might of voting women. Who knew to what lengths they might go? To the legislation of fair labor practices? To the prohibition of the sale of alcoholic beverages?[3]

Economic and social interests like these swayed not only men but also women to oppose woman suffrage. Many a loyal corporate wife, many a spouse of a local barkeeper were persuaded by just such arguments.

Other antisuffrage women genuinely feared losing shelter, losing the protection that chivalry was supposed to afford womanhood. A few men are always quick to point out that if women want "men's rights," then women must be prepared to engage in the scuffles and hurly-burly of "a man's world." Some women quailed at the prospect, retreating behind the wall of male approval as they protested their happiness with the status quo.

Some activist women believed with the militant labor organizer Mother Jones that "you don't need a vote to raise hell." As far as she was concerned, the plutocrats were manipulating women, keeping them busy with suffrage, prohibition, and charity, to divert them from the real, that is, the economic issues.

Most persuasive to conservative women of all the arguments against enfranchisement were fears of contamination from the dirty business of politics and the threat to the idea of separate roles for the two sexes. Men and women, they felt, had different duties. Men voted both for themselves and for their families: Why then thrust the "burden" of voting on women? If women were to trail their skirts through the filthy alleys of politics, what would become of the American family, the American home, and, indeed, of the protections traditionally afforded ladies? When, if ever, women edged their way into the public sphere, it should be for philanthropic purposes, not to assume the burdens of political responsibility.

"There never was a moment when the possession of a vote would not have been a hindrance and a burden to me," proclaimed Molly Elliot Seawell, self-described as an author, a householder, a property-owner, a taxpayer, and the employer of five persons.

I had no claim on any man whatever to help me fight my way to the polls; after I had voted I could not enforce my vote. I should have become involved in controversies that might have impaired my earning capacity; and there would have been the temptation, ever present to the weaker individual, of voting to please my employers. . . . These considerations, great in any woman's case, would have been enormously increased in the case of the wife and the mother of a family, with all the sacrifice of property privileges and confusion of political and family relationships which would have resulted. I admit that I should peculiarly dislike being divorced by a husband for non- support. . . . I believe woman suffrage to be an unmixed evil.[4]

So some women wore the red rose of the anti-suffragists, convinced that they were defending the sanctity of home and hearth. They deeply believed that they were fighting for the rights of "true women"—women, that is, who recognized their duty and privilege to rule the world by rocking the cradle; who wanted to remain feminine, not to risk picking up the bad habits of corrupt men. They were genuinely horrified at the tactics of the more radical suffragists, denouncing the women who picketed the White House as fanatics, freaks, spoiled children.

Some of them believed that votes for women wouldn't make any difference anyway. As voters, they argued, women wouldn't improve society, for, like men, women would spread their votes all over the political spectrum. And voting wouldn't improve the status of women, who really needed economic rather than political power. Still others, like "Grandmother Brown," just followed their innate conservatism: "I never wanted to vote, would rather not. I thought that if there was anything the men could do by themselves we'd better let them do it. I have always felt this way, that it is a woman's duty to make a happy home and teach her children to vote the Republican ticket."[5]

But active women antisuffragists always constituted a small minority. They included virtually no black women. Antisuffragism was never a mass movement, and its activities were sporadic. It did spawn 25 state organizations and the National Association Opposed to Woman Suffrage, composed mostly of clubwomen. Its Massachusetts organization, largest of the state groups, built a membership of 12,500, but in some states only a committee or auxiliary represented antisuffragist sentiment. Some state associations had no permanent headquarters; some were active only in the cities.[6]

Yet some impressive women opposed woman suffrage, the muckraking journalist Ida Tarbell among them. Some feminists who devoted their lives to reform nonetheless opposed the extension of the vote to women. In truth, despite the vicious, hard-nosed, slanderous campaigns that antisuffrage interests conducted, many women antisuffragists were sisters under the skin to the women fighting for the vote. One such, bested in argument at a suffrage hearing by the politically adept Harriot Stanton Blatch, remarked: "I have been given today much to think about. I am not convinced, but I am silenced."[7] Another, a congressional wife, burst into sympathetic tears when she saw the suffragists picketing the White House.

And Minnie Bronson, general secretary of the National Association Opposed to Woman Suffrage, generously apologized to Alice Paul of the National Woman's Party for questioning Paul's prediction that Wilson would finally declare for the suffrage amendment: ". . . that the President of the United States would under cover assist a proposition which he had publicly and unqualifiedly repudiated, seemed to us unworthy of his high office. . . . However, the President's subsequent public support of the Federal Suffrage Amendment . . . indicates the truth of your original assertion, and we therefore deem it incumbent upon ourselves to apologize"—with copies to the president and to members of Congress.[8] Relations weren't always so harmonious, though, as the anti-suffragists tried to stem the tide of the group they called, after the color of the suffragists' sashes, "The Yellow Peril."[9]

Who Needs the Vote?

At the turn of the century, American society was warming into an environment favorable to woman suffrage. Governments at the local, state, and federal levels were concerning themselves with social welfare and cleaning up politics. Women by virtue of their traditional roles qualified for these new undertakings—maybe better than men. "The instant . . . the State took upon itself any form of educative, charitable, or personally helpful work," preached the Reverend Anna Garlin Spencer, "it entered the area of distinctive feminine training and power, and therefore became in need of the service of women."[10]

All along men had assigned charitable tasks to women. Now women were beginning to feel that to accomplish these tasks they needed political power, embodied in the vote. Suffragists, abandoning their former emphasis on the rights issue, were saying that women had an actual duty to vote. A duty! That was more like it. Women raised to the ideal of doing their duty responded to the call.

How else could they regulate or abolish child labor? How else could they get pure food? How else could they improve neighborhood health? How else could they protect women who worked in factories or women being tricked into prostitution? The journalist Will Irwin encapsulated this reasoning with his story of interviewing a Tammany leader soon after the catastrophic Triangle Shirtwaist fire. Why, asked Irwin, did women in garment factories receive no fire protection? "'That's easy,' replied the practical politician, 'they ain't got no votes!'"[11] In Sacramento, the chair of the Committee of Public Morals laughed contemptuously at the pleas (for measures to protect young women against prostitution) of women representing 50,000 other Californians: "Well, you are no more than fifty thousand mice! How many votes can you deliver?"[12]

In the states that had granted full voting rights, beginning with Wyoming in 1890, women had proof positive of the ballot's clout. In Illinois, where women could vote in municipal elections, when a state senator who had killed a bill for an eight-hour day for women workers ran for a judgeship, the Women's Trade

Union League asked women voters to oust him. He lost. "The morning after the election," wrote labor leader Agnes Nestor, "in he stormed berating us for defeating him. He got our *deepest* sympathy."[13]

Above all, in the silence of their hearts many women still felt shame that no matter what their education, maturity, or wisdom, they were not judged worthy to help govern themselves and their own country. Belle Kearney bitterly depicts a brother, riding off to vote,

> *lifting his hat in mock courtesy [to say]: "Good morning, sister. You taught us and trained us in the way we should go. You gave us money from your hard earnings, and helped us to get a start in the world. You are interested infinitely more in good government and understand politics a thousand times better than we, but it is election day and we leave you at home with the idiots and Indians, incapables, paupers, lunatics, criminals and the other women that the authorities in this nation do not deem it proper to trust with the ballot; while we, lordly men, march to the polls and express our opinions in a way that counts."*[14]

From a small, radical group concerned about justice and women's rights, supporters of woman suffrage during the first two decades of the 20th century mobilized their forces into a middle-of-the-road mass movement. Jane Addams, writing about the Chicago effort to secure the municipal vote for women, observed, "During the campaign when I acted as chairman of the federation of a hundred women's organizations, nothing impressed me so forcibly as the fact that the response came from bodies of women representing the most varied traditions."[15]

Woman suffragists had in common only their desire for the vote. Their motives differed as much as their traditions. Church societies of Swedish-American women joined in because Scandinavian women had exercised the municipal franchise since the 17th century. Organizations of working women wanted the vote to secure rudimentary sanitation and safety precautions in their workplaces. Mothers' Clubs needed to legislate public kindergartens and clean milk. Property-owning women were protesting taxation without representation. Organizations of professional women, associations of college students and alumnae, and women's clubs were working for municipal reforms. Russian-American women wanted covered markets to keep grime off their food. Italian-Americans wanted public washhouses. "Go home and work for the vote," Mary Cassatt told the distinguished art collector Louisine Havemeyer at the beginning of World War I. "If the world is to be saved, it will be the women who save it."[16]

By the second decade of the 20th century, joining in the woman suffrage movement brought with it no fear of ostracism. It was thoroughly respectable, and in the large cities smart, fashionable. By 1916 the United Daughters of the Confederacy and the Daughters of the American Revolution were openly working for it.

WOMAN SUFFRAGE ATTRACTED THE SUPPORT OF ALL KINDS OF WOMEN, INCLUDING THESE WARTIME DELEGATES SENT BY THOUSANDS OF MUNITION WORKERS TO URGE WILSON TO ENDORSE THE FEDERAL AMENDMENT. (NATIONAL ARCHIVES)

With the endorsement of woman suffrage by such centrist groups as the General Federation of Women's Clubs, membership in the National American Woman Suffrage Association surged in 1917 to 2 million. Even the left wing of the movement, Alice Paul's Woman's Party, which recruited only active workers, boasted rolls of 50,000. Pro-suffrage sentiment spread so widely that it infected the most unlikely women: According to Inez Irwin, in the 1917 New York State suffrage campaign, "so many wives, mothers and daughters of Tammany men—and especially of the leaders—had become ardent converts" that Tammany Hall, the notorious New York City political machine, threw in the sponge and ceased to oppose it.[17]

All through the suffrage campaign, numbers of men braved derision to help the women. Their efforts were apt to be discounted or overlooked by the press. "Even when the Men's League occupied five blocks, four abreast, marching solid in the suffrage parade up Fifth Avenue," wrote Max Eastman, "the press could see only a grudging thousand of them."[18] Many a woman suffragist's husband supported her financially and emotionally. Others, even men married to antisuffragists, perceived the question as one of simple justice. "They were very willing to go to a Suffrage meeting," Mabel Vernon reported on Nevada men's reactions, "particularly in the mining camps, where to advertise that a woman is going to speak is almost enough to cause them to close down the mines in order that they might hear her. . . . There was one mining camp . . . where the men said, 'We will give you ninety per cent, ladies, there is not a bit of doubt about it.' When the returns came in from that camp, there were eleven votes against it [woman suffrage], and one hundred and one for it."[19]

For the final vote in the House of Representatives on the 19th Amendment, four devoted congressmen came from sickbeds:

> *Sims of Tennessee, with a broken arm and shoulder, which he refused to have set for fear he would be incapacitated from attending, and who, despite excruciating pain, stayed till the end trying to influence uncertain colleagues; Republican House Leader Mann of Illinois, who had been in a Baltimore hospital for six months and who appeared, pale as a ghost and hardly able to stand upright; Crosser of Ohio; and Barnhart of Indiana, the latter carried in on a stretcher on the very last roll call. Representative Hicks of New York kept faith with his wife, an ardent suffragist, who had just passed away; he left her death-bed to come to Washington for the roll call, and then went home to attend her funeral.[20]*

For the most part, though, women did the work of the movement, controlled it, and directed its course. It touched the lives of all sorts of women all over the United States. Like most reforms, it drew most of its workers from the middle class, but factory girls and society women, students and grandmothers spoke for it, contributed time and money to it, and marched side by side for it. What Inez Irwin wrote of the Woman's Party applied to suffragists generally. They "were of all kinds and descriptions; they emerged from all ranks and classes: they came from all over the United States." The movement did not belong exclusively to women of great wealth and social position, nor to working women, nor to women of the arts or the professions, nor to women of the home, but to all of these. "It was an all-woman movement. Indeed, often women who on every other possible opinion were as far apart as the two poles, worked together for the furtherance of the Federal Amendment. . . . It was as though, among an archipelago of differing intellectual interests and social convictions, [suffragists] had found one little island on which they could stand in an absolute unanimity."[21]

Pulling Together—and Apart: NAWSA

The many existing organizations for women formed a network for the rapid spread of suffragist news and views. A woman who only stepped outside her home to attend the Ladies' Aid meeting at her church might hear a suffragist speak there. The massive General Federation of Women's Clubs, the even larger Women's Christian Temperance Union, the Young Women's Christian Association, the Daughters of the American Revolution, and some trade unions all provided forums for suffragist propaganda. And the leaders of both the National Woman Suffrage Association (NAWSA) and the National Woman's Party (WP) brilliantly publicized their activities with one attention-getting ploy after another.

From 1900–20, two great women headed NAWSA: Anna Howard Shaw presided from 1904 to 1915, and Carrie Chapman Catt from 1900 to 1904 and again from 1915 to 1920. The older of these, Anna Howard Shaw, born in 1847, at 12 years of age had to assume responsibility for the survival of her family in a crude log cabin on a Michigan homestead, an experience that left her with a low estimate of men and a burning ambition to succeed in a man's world. This ambition propelled her to qualify herself as a Methodist preacher. Ordained by the Methodist Protestant church, she served two churches simultaneously for seven years. But at 36, discontented and perhaps a bit bored, she enrolled in Boston University's medical school, filling in her spare time by lecturing on temperance and woman suffrage. By the time she received her M.D. three years

later, she had decided that neither the ministry nor medicine could meet women's basic problems, but only "the removal of the stigma of disenfranchisement."[22]

The Reverend Dr. Shaw had the defects of her virtues. The strength of body, mind, and will that enabled her to educate herself as both a minister and a doctor in an era when these professions hardly welcomed women empowered her to endure the travel that the presidency of a national organization required. Her sparkling oratory won many to her cause. But her very determination

DR. ANNA HOWARD SHAW. (NATIONAL ARCHIVES)

made it hard for her to compromise. She antagonized men and didn't get along well with her people in NAWSA. Jealously guarding her power, she discouraged initiative among her co-workers. She completely lacked organizational skills. Under her presidency, NAWSA staggered and stumbled. By 1915, it was a shambles, with no structure, no national headquarters, no office help. Some states had no organizations, and no one knew the names of all the state officers. The national board rarely met. Business was conducted—or neglected—by correspondence. Only the grass roots lived on: Active suffragists during Shaw's tenure at NAWSA concentrated on state campaigns.

Her presidency was a good act to follow, and Carrie Chapman Catt knew just how. Born in 1859, she grew up on midwestern farms, active, self-reliant, and defiant of conventions that thrust inferiority on women. Earning her way through Iowa State College, she developed a faith in evolution that lasted all her life. Always, when things went wrong, she consoled herself and strengthened others with the assurance that they would eventually come right—they had to, for it was the nature of the universe to evolve toward ever higher forms. But she firmly believed also in helping evolution along.

In 1885 Catt interrupted a promising career in the public schools to marry Leo Chapman and become assistant editor of his newspaper. When he died soon thereafter, she moved from newspaper work to lecturing and to volunteer work for NAWSA. Before she remarried in 1890, she and George William Catt signed a remarkable prenuptial contract, guaranteeing her four months a year for suffrage work. Encouraging her to do the reforming for them both while he earned the living, he more than honored their contract. So did she. Her work for NAWSA so impressed its president Susan B. Anthony that she nominated Catt as her successor. Her husband's fatal illness cut short Catt's first term as president: She resigned in 1904 to take care of him, but in her four-year tenure she had built a nationwide organization, a treasury, and an effective system of administrative procedurest—which Shaw destroyed by neglect.

The admirable Mr. Catt left his wife well provided for. For a few years after his death she devoted herself first to the international suffrage movement and then to the New York State campaign. By the time she was called back to the presidency of NAWSA in 1915, she was well prepared. Her first term had taught her the importance of going into office with her own people and on her own terms. NAWSA desperately needed Catt's proven organizational skills. Moreover, Catt had at her own disposal $1 million that Mrs. Frank Leslie had willed to her to use for woman suffrage as she saw fit. Under these circumstances NAWSA willingly agreed to Catt's demand for a centralized, hierarchical, almost military organization in which she herself held the power.

It was a good bargain for Catt and for NAWSA. Catt thoroughly understood the difficulties, in an era before air travel, radio, or the fax machine, of holding together a far-flung organization whose members shared only one common belief: They wanted the vote. Her charisma attracted and sustained the loyalty

MRS. CARRIE CHAPMAN CATT. (NATIONAL ARCHIVES)

of workers. Her "pulse-feeling," as she called it, calmed quarrels within the ranks and built a good staff. NAWSA's smooth functioning, its careful training of its workers, and its minutely detailed records reassured members that they had behind them a solid organization on which they could count for support and guidance and that would make the most of their every accomplishment. Many of them knew "Mother Catt" personally, for she visited almost every state. Then, with a flourish, Catt produced her "Winning Plan."

The plan prophesied victory in six years. It triumphed in four. Catt based it on the consecration of her members, some of whom signed pledges to devote themselves exclusively to NAWSA until the federal amendment passed. As the plan required, state associations entered compacts to get the amendment submitted to Congress and then ratified by their own legislatures. At the same time a few more states, notably New York, won full suffrage for women. NAWSA members kept the suffrage issue constantly before the public. They built suffrage planks into both the Democratic and the Republican party platforms. By coaxing, public questioning, and the exercise of infinite patience and tact, they eventually maneuvered President Wilson into active support of the federal amendment. In the words of the *New York Times*, "The foxes have holes, and birds of the air have nests, but the politician has no hiding place when the suffragists get after him."[23]

Even after America entered World War I these women didn't let up a whit but simply piled war work on top of their suffrage work. They ran themselves ragged. But they had fun as well as aching hearts and feet to show for it.

For Catt, with all her other expertise, was a born advertising genius, and she fostered publicity skills in her workers. They concocted all sorts of attention-getting stunts. In those days before reliable cars or passable roads, let alone road maps, for instance, NAWSA women drove the 3,000 miles across the United States to carry a petition with 500,000 signatures from California to Washington, their car festooned with suffragist banners, stopping frequently for well-attended and well-reported rallies.[24]

All over the country suffragist women in NAWSA and in smaller suffrage organizations chose their own ways of contributing to the cause. Some, like Sylvie Thygeson, preferred the parlor. A well-off young matron, she had little afternoon gatherings of six or eight women. Thygeson recalled,

> *You had a cup of tea. A little social gathering. While we were drinking tea, I gave a little talk and they asked questions about what was going on . . . usually quite intelligent questions as to what was being done, who was doing it, who was prominent at the time, things like that. . . . It was a lot better, I thought at the time, than to have a lecture. Because a lot of them wouldn't go to a lecture. And it was what I could do.*[25]

NAWSA workers in California owed their narrow margin of victory to women like Thygeson. While the liquor interests were funneling huge sums of money into antisuffrage propaganda in California's cities, woman suffragists all over the state were persuading friends in their homes and in small meetings at Granges, in churches, and in schools.

More feisty women took to the streets, soapboxes in hand. Miriam Allen deFord held down jobs in Boston as a journalist, publicist, and editor of house organs.

> *In those days every evening in every city the downtown street corners were all occupied by soapboxes. . . . You'd talk for maybe fifteen or twenty minutes and then you'd ask for questions and try to answer them. . . . The audiences would be people going along the street. . . . We got jeers and catcalls. In those days you didn't use four-letter words, but we'd be interrupted, of course, and heckled. That was all part of it. You expected and learned how to handle it.*[26]

Other soapbox suffragists suffered sticks and stones as well as names hurled at them. "Sometimes," Laura Ellsworth Seiler remembered, "depending on the neighborhood, those soapboxes on which we stood were rather dangerous little things. Things would be thrown down from the roofs. Sometimes stones would be thrown into the crowd."[27]

At these speeches the soapboxers passed around petitions for whatever bills they were currently trying to push through the legislature. They had to weed out numbers of facetious phony names, but they always got some actual voters. "Soapboxing" was not for everyone. DeFord's landlady, for instance, wouldn't have dreamed of speaking in public—but she did try to register to vote:

"Different women would go down when it was time to register and try to register, and be turned down and get some publicity for the cause."[28]

Campaigning State by State

Suffragist leaders planned two complementary lines of attack: to pass a federal amendment but meanwhile to win full suffrage (not just the right to vote in municipal and/or state elections) in as many states as they could. Like all good politicians, they accepted compromise when they had to. If they could win the right to vote only in municipal elections, they accepted the advance and bided their time. Organizers like Catt believed that each small victory moved them toward their ultimate objective, the federal amendment.

The western states led the way to full suffrage. In Wyoming Territory women had exercised the right since 1869, and when Wyoming entered the Union in 1890 the women carried the right with them. Colorado women voted in all elections beginning in 1893, and Idaho and Utah women beginning in 1896.

The women of the state of Washington won their campaign in 1910 with the diversity of approaches and inventiveness characteristic of the suffrage movement. They carried their message to unions and Grange meetings. Not only did they advertise on billboards "Give the women a Square Deal," but they also saw to it that editorials and sermons dwelt on that theme. At every state fair, at every county fair, at every Chautauqua they ran a woman's day, offering prizes to other women's organizations for symbolic floats and distributing propaganda from a suffrage booth. They maintained a permanent suffrage exhibit at the Great Alaska-Yukon-Pacific Exposition of 1909 in Seattle. The dirigible balloon featured at the exposition carried a large silken banner inscribed "Votes for Women." And Dr. Cora Smith King carried a pennant with that motto to the summit of Mount Rainier, planting its staff in the highest snows.[29]

Most suffrage states were won through just such imaginative and sustained efforts. Each time, victory brought joy, as to Kansan Martha Farnsworth. She had worked devotedly for state "sufferage." On the morning after the critical election she wrote, "There is sunshine in my heart, for while I went to bed last night a *slave*, I awoke this morning a *free woman*."[30]

Victories in several western and midwestern states underlined the denial of the franchise to women in the East. Not only the women concerned but also the strategists at NAWSA badly wanted to win New York, both as a symbol and as a means of increasing pressure on Congress for the federal amendment. In one sense the campaign there began early in the 20th century when Harriot Stanton Blatch, daughter of Elizabeth Cady Stanton, returned from a stint with the militant British suffragists, took a disgusted look at what was going on, and commented that the suffrage movement in New York "bored its adherents and repelled its opponents."[31]

Blatch set about educating herself and other women politically. They needed it. One suffragist had earnestly told a politician that she didn't want anyone to vote for suffrage unless he was convinced that it was a good and worthy cause. Another had told Teddy Roosevelt during his campaign that she wouldn't bother him until after the election. Now suffragists began taking literature to the polls on election day, campaigning against unfriendly candidates, acting as poll watchers, lobbying legislators, and attending hearings at the capitol. They stationed "Silent Sentinels" outside the doors of the Judiciary Committee sessions, "typifying the patient waiting that women had done" for suffrage.[32] Inspired by Blatch's conviction that women factory workers and suffragists needed each other, suffragists visited factories to invite workers to their meetings and addressed trade unions and night schools. And they took glove makers and telephone operators and shirtwaist makers to Albany to tell the legislators of their need for the vote to protect themselves on their jobs.

Women all over the state came to life to work for the cause, especially after Blatch and Maude Malone conducted a trolley-car campaign from Seneca Falls to Syracuse and then down the Hudson to Poughkeepsie, stopping for open-air meetings in towns along the way. They sold the *Votes for Women Broadside* on the streets. At Vassar a student, Inez Milholland, forbidden by the college president to hold a gathering on campus, assembled 40 students in an adjoining cemetery to listen to the feminist theorist Charlotte Perkins Gilman and the cap maker and labor organizer Rosa Schneiderman. Mrs. Clarence Mackay formed the Equal Franchise Society, with both women and men members. Ethel Barrymore raised money for the cause by acting in three plays presented by Beatrice Forbes-Robertson, in a theater donated for the performance by Maxine Elliott. Mrs. H. O. Havemeyer exhibited for the first time in the United States the pictures of her friend Mary Cassatt, stipulating that the profits go to suffrage.

Suffragists dramatically paraded, showing the public their strength: In 1912, 20,000 marched in New York City. They introduced "Voiceless Speeches," turning cards on an easel in a shop window and attracting such crowds that the police tried to intervene, only to be overridden by the public and press. (The Voiceless Speeches succeeded particularly well when given by a beautiful girl, who attracted passers-by into the store.)

They danced:

> We learned over and over again as we toiled in our campaign that sermons
> and logic never convince, that human beings move because they feel, not
> because they think. For that reason we began to dance about our cause
> at great balls, instead of sitting in corners and arguing. Men's idea was
> different. They could not ask for the vote for village constables without

*getting into a brawl over it. . . . Women conquered in peace and quiet,
with some fun, right off their own bat.*[33]

At the 1913 Votes-for-Women Ball, the *New York Times* reported, "There were
tired, shabby little cash girls, waltzing in shirt waists. There were boys in worn,
well-brushed sack coats; and there were Mrs. Herbert Carpenter and Mrs. James
Lees Laidlaw in glittering ball gowns and their husbands in correct evening
dress."[34]

The suffragists may not have argued, but they certainly exercised all their
persuasive powers as they set out to educate the male voters.

> *The appeal to the firemen took the form of an automobile demonstration,
> open air speaking along the line of march of their annual parade and a
> ten dollar gold piece given to one of their number who made a daring
> rescue of a yellow-sashed dummy—a suffrage lady. A circular letter was
> sent to 800 firemen requesting their help for all suffragists. "Barbers'
> Day" produced ten columns of copy in leading New York dailies. Letters
> were sent in advance to 400 barbers informing them that on a certain day
> the suffragists would call upon them. The visits were made in autos
> decorated with barbers' poles and laden with maps and posters to hang
> up in the shops and the open air meetings were held out in front. Street
> cleaners on the day of the "White Wings" parade were given souvenirs
> of tiny brooms and suffrage leaflets. . . . Workers in the subway excava-
> tions were visited with Irish banners and shamrock fliers.*[35]

The women propagandized laborers in ethnic restaurants, on the docks, and at
public markets and went after other male immigrant votes with torchlight rallies,
street dances on the lower East Side and Irish, Syrian, Italian, and Polish block
parties.

Upstate, young women organizers roamed from city to town, organizing
sympathetic women as they went and giving street speeches. "We would rent a
car and put an enormous white, green and purple banner across the back,"
remembered Laura Ellsworth Seiler.

> *The white was for purity, of course; the green was for courage; and the
> purple was for justice. . . . I would stand up on the back seat to make the
> speech. . . . the most popular corner of the street was the one that held the
> bar. I always directed the chauffeur to stop just outside the bar. My
> mother, who was small and charming and utterly Victorian and convinced
> that all good things started with the favor of the male, would go through
> the swinging doors, and say, "Gentlemen, my daughter is going to talk
> about suffrage outside, and I think you would be interested. I hope you'll
> come out." And just like the Pied Piper, they would all dump their drinks
> on the bar and come out and make the nucleus of the crowd. I was always
> embarrassed to have to take up a collection. . . . But Mother had no such*

qualms. She would circulate about giving out the pamphlets and holding out a basket and saying, "I'm sure you want to help the cause," and the folding money would come in.[36]

Sometimes these street meetings had other outcomes. Watertown's Senator Brown had said that only a dozen women in his district believed in woman suffrage. Helen Todd, arriving in town in a prairie schooner drawn by oxen, made an appointment with the senator, held a big open-air meeting just before it, and invited all pro-suffragists to accompany her to his office. The whole crowd followed, curiosity no doubt playing its part, burst into the senator's office and filled the streets outside. "As Miss Todd reached the pale, half-frightened Brown as he stood behind his desk near a window, she gasped, 'Honestly, Mr. Senator, I had no idea when I invited believers in suffrage to follow me here from the street rally that your estimate of suffrage sentiment in your district was so completely wrong.'"[37]

Labor leader Rosa Schneiderman described how she devastated another state senator fearful that the ballot would strip women of their charm by pointing out, "not too gently I hope, that women were working in the foundries, stripped to the waist because of the heat, but he said nothing about their losing their charm. Nor had he mentioned the women in laundries who stood for thirteen and fourteen hours a day in terrible heat and steam with their hands in hot starch. I asked him if he thought they would lose more of their beauty and charm by putting a ballot in the ballot box than standing around all day in foundries or laundries."[38]

Such women of New York, undaunted by defeat in 1915, won their right to vote in 1917.

Pulling Together—and Apart: The National Woman's Party

Alice Paul appeared on the national scene in 1912 with impressive qualifications. A Quaker, a Ph.D. from the University of Pennsylvania, a settlement worker with experience in both the United States and Great Britain, and a veteran of the British suffrage movement, she volunteered to go to Washington at her own expense to work for the federal amendment. The offer must have seemed too good to be true. In any case, the NAWSA board, on the recommendation of Jane Addams, accepted. The board appointed to assist her the radical feminist lawyer Crystal Eastman and Lucy Burns, educated at Vassar, Yale, the University of Berlin, and the University of Bonn, with three years as a suffrage organizer in Scotland—Young Turks, the lot of them, on collision course with the NAWSA establishment.

Paul shared many qualities with Carrie Chapman Catt. She rejected violence. She was utterly dedicated to the cause. She was gifted in management, in public relations, and in inspired leadership. But Paul differed from NAWSA's president on two critically important strategies. Where Catt advocated a multipronged approach, Paul insisted on concentrating solely on the federal amendment. Where Catt advocated gentility, persuasion, and tact, Paul opted for confrontation and pressure politics. She insisted on holding the party in power responsible for not passing the federal suffrage amendment. If that meant opposing pro-suffrage Democratic congressmen, so be it. If that meant embarrassment to the Democratic president, so much the worse—for him.

In the not-so-very-long run, the same organization could contain neither two such strong leaders as Catt and Paul nor two such different philosophies. In late 1913 Paul moved out into her own Congressional Union, which in 1916 became the National Woman's Party.

Paul started off her work for NAWSA with a spectacular parade in Washington on the eve of Wilson's first inauguration, a parade organized, astonishingly enough, in only three weeks. Yet when Wilson arrived in town on March 3, 1913, he asked where everyone was, only to be told that "everyone" was at the suffrage parade. For the first time the Great Demand banner floated over the suffragists' heads: "We demand an amendment to the constitution of the United States enfranchising the women of the country." Eight thousand women marched, despite the absence of police protection, despite harassment so severe that Secretary of War Stimson finally had to call out the army cavalry. "Women were spat upon, slapped in the face, tripped up, pelted with burning cigar stubs, and insulted by jeers and obscene language. . . . Rowdies seized and insulted young girls."[39] Forced into single file by the pressures from the mob, every woman yet finished her march. The women's fortitude roused the admiration of bystanders and reporters.

That parade sounded the theme of Paul's work: dramatically conceived, quickly accomplished, impactful. Only a woman of her dedication and persuasiveness could have made it work.

For Paul was so single-minded, so focused on the passage of the federal amendment, that she allowed herself no time off, no recreation, and no other interests: She lived in a cold room so that she would not be tempted to read. One colleague said that she had worked with Paul for months before she saw her without a hat on. On the picket line she dictated to a stenographer to avoid "wasting" time.

Paul expected almost as much of others. If a visitor to Washington dropped into headquarters, Paul sent her to lobby her own congressmen and senators. At her request bewildered women found themselves accomplishing things they could never have anticipated. Amid the hasty preparations for the March 1913 parade, Paul spied Mrs. Gilson Gardner and sighed with relief: "There's Mrs. Gardner! She'll attend to it. The trappings for the horses have been ruined. Will you order some more? They must be delivered tomorrow night."[40] Puzzling over how to proceed, Gardner walked around the block several times before she found a tailor; she kept shop for him while he went to Paul's headquarters for measurements. And he delivered the trappings on time.

Paul accosted pretty young Margery Ross, visiting in Washington for a social winter, with: "Miss Ross, will you go to Wyoming on Saturday, and organize a State Convention there within three weeks?" In Wyoming Ross found only eight members of the Congressional Union, but three weeks later she ran a state convention with 120 delegates.

Again, Paul asked Nina Allender to go to Ohio the next day to campaign for the Woman's Party. No, said Allender, she couldn't. She was redecorating her home and had to select the wallpaper. "Oh, that's all right," said Paul blithely, "I'll send a girl right up there. *She'll pick your paper for you and see that it's put on.*" Paul's staff understood perfectly when an elderly woman explained why she was futilely picking at a typewriter keyboard with a stiff forefinger: "Because Alice Paul told me to."

Clearly it was not Paul's gracious manner that persuaded so many to do what she wanted. Most of the time she neglected to thank her workers. Nor, according to her close co-worker Lucy Burns, was she charismatic. But she was firmly convinced that people would honor her requests because of course they would want to help the cause along—so convinced that when headquarters lacked volunteers, she sent staff members out on streets to ask strangers for help. (Some women, it was said, learned to give Paul's headquarters a wide berth, for fear of being shanghaied.) Often what she asked her helpers to do was challenging and exciting: Her belief in their ability to accomplish the assigned task complimented them. As Mabel Vernon remarked: "She believed we could do it and so she made us believe it."

Paul also saw to it that they could do it. Before they went off into the blue, she briefed her workers carefully, going over their route, anticipating problems they might encounter, and discussing possible solutions with them. She kept in close telegraphic communication with her organizers but left them free to make big decisions, to change tactics suddenly. By shifting them from task to task, she not only piqued their interest but educated them. When her young women returned from the hinterlands, Paul sent them to lobby the appropriate congressmen, who welcomed fresh news from their home states; when they set out again, people in North Dakota and Missouri—especially editors— listened fascinated to women fresh from roaming the marble halls of the Capitol.

What's more, Paul was willing to take chances on people, testing them by the results they achieved. If a woman failed in one undertaking, Paul gave her a different one. She assigned one lamentably inept person to five different kinds of work before she gave her up. In accordance with this personnel philosophy, she entrusted responsibilities to younger and younger women, preferring youth and enthusiasm to expertise.

Paul's insistence on holding the Democratic Party responsible for the Congress's failure to pass the federal suffrage amendment frightened and irritated politicians and embarrassed her NAWSA sisters. She never wavered, despite Catt's repudiation of her tactics, despite the anger of citizens at accusations against the president in wartime, despite the horrors of beatings and force-feeding.

The Woman's Party (WP) opposed the Democrats in two ways: by picketing the Congress and the White House and by campaigning against Democratic candidates. They campaigned particularly in the suffrage states, appealing to enfranchised women to vote against Democrats. Harriot Stanton Blatch on the stage of the Blackstone Theatre in Chicago placed long-distance phone calls to 12 mass meetings in suffrage states, asking the women to vote against Wilson.

In these campaigns WP representatives spoke anywhere and everywhere: in drawing rooms, at prayer meetings, at quilting bees, in the public schools, in the public library, in union halls and railroad shops, and lumber and mining camps. "We intend to make a canvass of the stores and meet the clerks personally," wrote Jessie Hardy Stubbs, "and to get into all the factories, as far as possible, where women are employed, and urge these western women voters to stand by the working women of the East." From Wyoming Gertrude Hunter reported: "We had the thirty-five mile drive to make to a neighboring town for another meeting and we did it every mile through a high wind and torrents of rain, that flooded the trail with water, as we went over prairie and plowed fields. We did it, however, with only one blow-out, and two very narrow escapes from being completely turned over. . . . the voters came from miles and miles to attend, at least one hundred and fifty of them, on horseback, in wagons, buggies, and autos."

And a Mrs. Latimer boasted:

> After we had talked with the associate editor [of the Kansas City Star] and told him . . . that we intended to send a daily bulletin to the eight hundred and eight papers in the State of Kansas, that we were going to every one of the large towns in the State of Kansas, and have just as many meetings as possible, and that we would distribute fifty thousand pieces of literature, he looked at us and said, "Do you realize that this will take eight men and eighteen stenographers?" I said, "Possibly, but two women are going to do it."[41]

For the first time an interview with a woman appeared on the editorial page of the Star.

In the tangled web of political cause and effect, it's difficult to discern just how much the WP campaigners actually affected election results. But to Paul's satisfaction, their efforts worried the politicians. As she said to one congressman who alleged that they hadn't defeated a single Democratic candidate in a suffrage state, "Why, then, are you so stirred up over our campaign?"[42]

After the 1916 presidential campaign WP activity shifted gears. Having sent one futile deputation after another to a condescending President Wilson, the WP decided in January 1917, to send him a perpetual delegation in the form of a picket line. In their view, they were making him an offer he could not refuse. It took him a long time to recognize inevitability.

For the next year and a half suffragists picketed the White House or Congress. Always carrying brilliantly colored and highly photogenic banners, in rain, snow, and cold, in Washington's torpid heat, they stood at their posts or marched. Women in their teens and women in their eighties picketed. Women fainted, recovered, and returned to their posts. The personnel and the messages on their banners changed with the occasion. One day college women marched; on another, professional women; on Labor Day Sunday, factory workers. On Wilson's second Inauguration Day, 1,000 women, marching by states, circled the White House in the pouring rain, under a banner with Inez Milholland's words: "Mr. President, how long must women wait for liberty?" The White House gates locked against them, and the White House refusal to accept their resolutions inspired Gilson Gardner to comment: "The President seemed to think the women were going to steal his grass roots."[43]

As the months wore on, the pickets became one of the Washington sights. Tour bus guides pointed them out; tourists often said, "We weren't quite sure where the White House was until we saw you pickets." Police urged the suffragists to "Stick to it. We're with you." Some passersby saluted them; some wanted to shake their hands. A Confederate veteran told them: "Girls, you are right. I have been through wars, and I know. You-all got to have some rights."[44]

Many women asked to hold a banner for a moment. A bride and groom stopped: While he was puffily announcing that he would never allow *his* wife . . . she rushed up, radiant, "Oh, do you mind if I hold one of these banners for a while?" Another bridal couple involved themselves more extensively: She spent her honeymoon in jail for picketing, and he spent his indignantly lobbying his congressman. [45]

Women from all over the country took their turn on line. "I have no son to give my country to fight for democracy abroad," wrote Mrs. S. H. B. Gray of Colorado, "and so I send my daughter to Washington to fight for democracy at home." Nineteen-year-old Edna Mary Purtell took a vacation from her file clerk's job at Travelers Insurance in Hartford, Connecticut, to demonstrate in Washington. She was arrested four times in one day and served five days on hunger strike in jail. Back at her job, warned by the president of Travelers against talking about suffrage, she told him that she would do her job responsibly but concluded, "Once I get in that elevator [or take a] coffee break . . . I'll talk about anything I want."[46]

After the United States entered the war, and as the messages on the banners accused the president in more and more hostile terms, official respect for the civil rights of the marchers ended, and young males rioted. The police who made

"AN INDIGNANT CROWD OF REAL AMERICANS" MOBBING SUFFRAGE PICKETS.
(NATIONAL ARCHIVES)

the first arrests of pickets didn't know the charge, and indeed officialdom never did get the theoretical basis for the arrests quite straight, most often using a charge of obstructing traffic. Time and again they arrested the pickets and the chivalrous males who came to their defense, but not the ruffians who assaulted them, tore the banners out of their hands and destroyed them, tried to rip off their sashes, struck them, knocked them to the ground, and dragged them along the sidewalk.

Judges ruled inconsistently, often convicting some women and dismissing others brought in on the same charge and with the same evidence against them. Suffragists typically refused to recognize the jurisdiction of the court. "We do not wish to make any plea before this court," said Alice Paul. "We do not consider ourselves subject to this court, since as an unenfranchised class we have nothing to do with the making of the laws which have put us in this position."[47] Sometimes judges begged the pickets to pay fines, even nickel and dime fines, but almost always the pickets chose jail or the workhouse instead. Altogether, 168 American women served jail sentences.[48]

Their choice took courage for all the pickets, but especially for the gently bred, the very young, and the very old. For they faced the conditions that have long disgraced our prison system: wormy food, open toilets that could only be flushed from outside their cells, dirty sheets and blankets washed once a year, cockroaches and rats, quarters shared with syphilitics, fetid air, filth, drinking water in an open pail. Some women were put in solitary confinement. A young girl was threatened with being put alone among male prisoners. Sometimes the suffragists were held incommunicado, without counsel. Yet they endured. "Strange ladies," the other woman prisoners called the suffragists.

Some women hunger-struck, usually to protest not being treated as political prisoners. Officials resorted to force-feeding. Mrs. Lawrence Lewis, a grand-mother, described her experience: She was seized, laid on her back, held down by five people. A doctor forced a tube through her lips and down her throat. As the fluid poured through the tube, everything turned black. She came to herself to realize that she was making terrible sounds against her will. Often the women vomited continuously during the feedings. So brutal was the process that when, despite a writ of habeas corpus, authorities refused to produce Lewis and Lucy Burns in court, on the grounds that they were too weak, their counsel destroyed this excuse by inquiring how many men it took to hold them for forcefeeding?

Yet Alice Paul hunger-struck for 22 days, during the last two weeks of which she was force-fed. Finally she was removed to a hospital and interviewed by an alienist in an effort to prove her mad. The alienist asked whether Paul would talk, whereupon she laughed, said that talking was her business, and gave him an hour-long history of the suffrage movement. When he speculated that she suffered from a persecution mania, she answered no, she did not think the president was responsible in her case, that he was perhaps uninformed about what was going on. Despite the alienist's certification of her sanity and warning that she would never break, for she had the spirit of Joan of Arc, she was kept in the psychopathic ward for a week incommunicado, while insane patients peered in at her door and nurses kept her awake with hourly examinations by flashlight.

From August to November 1917 the severity of treatment inflicted on the women prisoners escalated, on the streets, in the courts, and in the jail. It culminated in the November "Night of Terror." That night squads of guards beat the suffragists unmercifully. Two seized the 70-year-old Mrs. Nolan, dragged her away, as she pleaded with them to be careful of her lame foot, and threw her onto a bed. Two others twisted Dorothy Day's arms above her head, lifted her, and brought her body down twice over the back of an iron bench. Others threw Mrs. Cosu against the wall of a cell; she suffered a heart attack but was refused a doctor. When Lewis, doubled over like a sack of flour, was thrown in, her head struck an iron bed; she was unconscious; the other women thought her dead. Once five men had deposited her in a cell, Lucy Burns began calling the roll, despite their threats; they then handcuffed her wrists and fastened the cuffs above her head to the cell door and threatened her with a buckle gag. Mrs. Henry Butterworth was taken away from the rest and told she was alone with men prisoners and that they could do what they pleased with her.[49]

Of course the WP saw to it that the pickets' suffering did not go unnoticed. They asked congressmen to visit the cells of constituents. They dispatched speakers all over the United States to report, speakers who read aloud to their audiences telegrams recounting new abuses. In the hysteria of World War I America, which accused anyone who disagreed with officialdom of treason and pro-Germanism, these speakers were opposed by bar associations, civic officials, and home defense leagues, but they got the message out—often with the assistance of labor unions. And of course such treatment of middle- and upper-class women inflamed public opinion.

President Wilson, by his own account, remained in ignorance longer than most—a remarkable ignorance, really, in view of the several influential people who attempted to inform him. Among them was Dudley Malone, Wilson's own appointee, who in a detailed letter of resignation to Wilson explained that as a matter of conscience he could no longer be associated with a government that employed such tactics. Malone then became the counsel for the imprisoned women. Finally in the late fall of 1917 Wilson pardoned all the suffragists and the arrests ended—only to be resumed in the summer of 1918. In this round, although women still suffered imprisonment and hunger-struck, officials warily avoided the excesses of the earlier imprisonments—particularly after the WP sent out a *Prison Special* train carrying speakers, clad in duplicates of their prison clothes, to inform the country of what was going on.

The suffragists never used violence. But amid the hysteria of wartime the Democratic administration ignored the violence inflicted upon the suffragists by ruffians and disgracefully breached their civil rights and wreaked its own violence upon them. Yet by the time picketing began, almost everyone, including the president, agreed that woman suffrage was inevitable.

Apparently Alice Paul's tactics struck home all too effectively. Her election campaigns against candidates frightened them for their political lives. Those among them with consciences flinched at the knowledge that no logical argument existed for continuing to deny women the vote.

The supremely self-righteous Wilson, leading the fight for democracy abroad, detested being reminded of its absence at home. Over and over again the suffragists drove home that point. Even before the war when Wilson ringingly declared himself for the interests of all classes, a woman in the audience would call out, "Mr. President, if you sincerely desire to forward the interests of all the people, why do you oppose the national enfranchisement of women?"[50] They embarrassed Wilson in the presence of foreign delegates with banners proclaiming that the United States was no true democracy.

Finally the WP took to burning Wilson's words. Sometimes they made these occasions impressively ceremonious: On December 16, 1918, for instance, they were led by a woman carrying the American flag, followed successively by women bearing the purple, white, and gold banners of the suffrage cause, by 50 more women carrying lighted torches, and then by a procession of 300 more, to a cauldron before Lafayette's statue, where the 84-year-old Reverend Olympia Brown burned Wilson's latest speech. The press took notice.

TO THE RUSSIAN ENVOYS
President Wilson and Envoy Root are deceiving Russia.
They say We are a democracy. Help us win a world war.
so that democracies may survive.
We, the women of America, tell you that America is not a democracy.
Twenty million American Women are denied the right to vote. President
Wilson is the chief opponent of their national enfranchisement.
Help us make this nation really free. Tell our government that it
must liberate its people before it can claim free Russia as an ally

PICKETS BECAME EXPERTS IN EXPOSING THE PRESIDENT'S LACK OF LOGIC.
(NATIONAL ARCHIVES)

Catt and NAWSA privately lamented and publicly condemned Paul's methods, believing that they undermined NAWSA's tactful persuasions. Probably, though, the bad cop/good cop combination that emerged from the different approaches of the WP and NAWSA served the cause well. Even the meanest masculine intelligence could grasp that nothing was going to stop the WP, beside whom NAWSA seemed a refuge of sweet reason. Between them they brought a reluctant Wilson in January 1918 to a pro-suffrage statement and then over another year to actual work for the suffrage cause. The House of Representatives having long since passed the suffrage amendment, the Senate, at Wilson's urging, finally agreed on June 4, 1919.

"Help Mrs. Catt Put Rat in Ratification"

The suffragists realized the critical importance of moving quickly toward ratification, before postwar America spun out of its reforming mood. All the same, the ratification process was a cliff-hanger.

Early on, states competed to be the first to ratify. Wisconsin won, with an extravaganza of personal messengers racing to Washington to announce their state's acceptance. The burst of enthusiasm soon wore itself out. Both NAWSA and the WP worked frantically to get the state legislatures then meeting to ratify, and to persuade the governors in other states to call their legislatures into session. In Utah Alice Paul maneuvered a Republican senator into expressing his disappointment that the Democratic governor had not called a special session. Paul gave his letter to the press, waited a while, then informed Utah's Democratic congressmen that the responsibility for the delay was on their party—a message that coming from the WP carried an implicit threat. The suffragists got their session, and Utah ratified.[51]

In just such struggles in state after state, women whose names few have ever heard, ordinary women on an extraordinary mission, saved the day, saved the vote for the women of America. Tennessee finally became the storm center, the last state necessary to ratification, and in the judgment of the WP, the last possible state in which ratification could be won. The suffragists used a three-pronged approach. Sue White, the WP state chair, assisted by other state members and national organizers, conducted the Tennessee campaign. In Ohio Abby Scott Baker pressured presidential nominees Cox and Harding—frequently reminding Cox that if Tennessee's Governor Roberts permitted ratification to fail, women would hold the Democrats responsible. From Washington Paul masterminded the campaign and lobbied political leaders who could influence Cox and Harding.

When pro-suffrage votes began to drop, on the excuse that the state constitution forbade consideration of ratification at this legislative special session, the suffragists staved off the crisis by appeals to eminent constitutional lawyers. When they could not reach a crucial state legislator by phone, a suffragist called the operator in Athens, Tennessee, and said, "This is a matter of life and death. . . . I have been in Athens myself and I know it is such a tiny place that you have only to look out of the door to know where Senator Candler is. You must find him."

Members of the legislature thought to hide behind a referral of the amendment to mass meetings of Tennessee citizens, only to be sternly reminded that the WP would hold them responsible for a hostile vote. Rumor whispered everywhere that members of the legislature were being bribed, one way or another. On the morning of the vote, suffragists rounded up all their legislators, saw to it that they arrived safely at the capitol, and reminded them of their commitment.

To the end the vote of the popular Harry Burns, youngest member of the legislature, was in doubt. On the day he wore the red rose of the antisuffragists. The suffragists knew that his mother had written him: "Hurrah—and vote for suffrage and don't keep them in doubt. . . . I have been watching to see how you stood, but have noticed nothing yet. Don't forget to be a good boy and help Mrs. Catt put 'Rat' in Ratification."[52] But, as they eyed his red rose, the suffragists could extract from him no more than this promise: "My vote will never hurt you." It didn't. Young Harry Burns obeyed his mother, voted to ratify, and the 19th Amendment became the law of the land.

The Taste of Triumph

In its progress from a gleam in the eye of Elizabeth Cady Stanton to a political reality, woman suffrage caused even those women who did not commit themselves to or against it to reexamine their identities and their roles. It drew on the time, money, and energy of millions. And it transformed the lives of thousands, who labored for it day and night, year after year, through hope and despair.

The suffragists, of course, were neither saints nor seers. Some, though by no means all, wildly exaggerated the benefits that the vote would bestow on women and society. Some were afflicted by racism, and some by an equally ugly nativism. Some without such prejudices deliberately appealed to them in others. Sometimes suffragists compromised their principles, particularly their belief in pacifism, to achieve their ends. Suffragists, that is, won the vote not purely through enthusiasm, dedication, and unending hard work but also by political means.

Part of what kept them toiling away through such discouragements and for so long was the sheer fun of it. Women in every state in the Union found themselves undertaking tasks they had never dreamed of and meeting interesting people, with new things to think and talk about—and laugh about: "There's more real humor in a little anteroom before a suffrage meeting than anywhere else I've ever been where a lot of women get together," wrote Max Eastman. "They're different from many reformers—they're the people that want to live."[53] Alice Duer Miller in 1915 wrote a tongue-in-cheek piece on "Why We Don't Want Men to Vote":

1. *Because man's place is in the army.*
2. *Because no really manly man wants to settle any question otherwise than by fighting about it.*
3. *Because if men should adopt peaceable methods women will no longer look up to them.*
4. *Because men will lose their charm if they step out of their natural sphere and interest themselves in other matters than feats of arms, uniforms and drums.*
5. *Because men are too emotional to vote. Their conduct at baseball games and political conventions shows this, while their innate tendency to appeal to force renders them unfit for government.*[54]

Suffragist humor gleamed in valentines that they sent to congressmen, complete with homemade jingles. The one for Congressman Pou, their sometime nemesis in the House Rules Committee, showed a little maiden curtsying to a stocked and beruffled gentleman presenting her with a bouquet, with the jingle: "The rose is red, / The violet's blue, / But VOTES are better / Mr. Pou." President Wilson received a May basket brimming with purple, white, and gold flowers—and a plea for the federal amendment. The witty Maud Younger, the WP's chief lobbyist, commented: "The hardest Congressmen to deal with were those who said, 'I will not vote for it if every voter in my State asks me.' To such a one, we would send a woman from his own district. In one case, the Congressman was so rude to her that she came back to Headquarters, subscribed a hundred dollars to our funds, departed, and became a staunch Suffragist. We kept a list of men of this type and we sent to them any woman who was wavering on Suffrage."[55]

With the ratification of the 19th Amendment, American women set a capstone on their achievements of the Progressive Era. For themselves and for American women to follow them they won the right that symbolizes democratic control and full citizenship. No wonder Harriot Stanton Blatch said with pride: "All honor to women, the first disfranchised class in history who unaided by any political party won enfranchisement by its own effort alone, and achieved the victory without the shedding of a drop of human blood."[56]

Source Notes

1. Inez Haynes Irwin, *Angels and Amazons: A Hundred Years of American Women* (1933; reprint, New York: Arno Press, 1974), p. 336.
2. Quoted in William L. O'Neill, *Everyone Was Brave: The Decline and Fall of Feminism in America* (Chicago: Quadrangle Books, 1969), p. 56.
3. A 1906 "secret" circular of the Brewers' and Wholesale Liquor Dealers' Association in Oregon reasoned: "It will take 50,000 votes to defeat woman suffrage. There are 2,000 retailers in Oregon. That means that every retailer must himself bring in twenty-five votes on election day." Irwin, *Angels and Amazons*, p. 337.
4. Molly Elliot Seawell, "The Ladies' Battle," *Atlantic Monthly* 106 (September, 1910):303.
5. Harriet Connor Brown, *Grandmother Brown's Hundred Years, 1827–1927* (New York: Little, Brown, 1929), p. 333.
6. For a sophisticated discussion of the numbers and the antisuffragist movement as a whole, see Jane Jerome Camhi, "Women Against Women:

American Antisuffragism, 1880–1920," Ph.D. dissertation, Tufts Univ., 1973.

7. Harriot Stanton Blatch and Alma Lutz, *Challenging Years: The Memoirs of Harriot Stanton Blatch* (1940; reprint, New York: Hyperion, 1976), p. 96.

8. Quoted in Irwin, *Angels and Amazons*, p. 256.

9. The antisuffragists incorporated a lot of satire in their campaign materials. Nelson Harding of the *Brooklyn Daily Eagle* entitled his collection of cartoons and verse "Ruthless Rhymes of Martial Militants": "Rock-a-bye baby, thy cradle is frail / Mother's a militant, locked up in jail. / Grandma's another, and so is Aunt Sue, / Off fighting 'bobbies,' and nurse is there too!" Quoted by Camhi, p. 159.

10. Quoted in Sara Evans, *Born For Liberty: A History of Women in America* (New York: Free Press, 1989), p. 154.

11. Irwin, *Angels and Amazons*, p. 319.

12. Quoted in Andrew Sinclair, *The Emancipation of American Women* (New York: Harper and Row, 1965), p. 228.

13. Agnes Nestor, *Woman's Labor Leader, The Autobiography of Agnes Nestor* (Rockford, Ill.: Bellevue Books, 1954), p. 170.

14. Belle Kearney, *A Slaveholder's Daughter* (St. Louis: St. Louis Christian Advocate Press, 1900), pp. 111–12.

15. Jane Addams, *Twenty Years at Hull House, with Autobiographical Notes* (1910; reprint, New York: Macmillan, 1924), p. 339.

16. Quoted in Frances Weitzenhoffer, *The Havemeyers: Impressionism Comes to America* (New York: Harry N. Abrams, 1986), p. 220.

17. Irwin, *Angels and Amazons*, p. 349.

18. Max Eastman, *Enjoyment of Living* (New York: Harper, 1940), p. 351. One male argued for woman suffrage on the grounds that "women ought, if only for the sake of their husbands, to try to be more intelligent than they are." Eastman, p. 307. Mary Kingsbury Simkhovitch noted that only 89 men marched in the first New York parade, but when these veterans were asked to march separately in later parades, after public sentiment had shifted, "five hundred and twenty of the original eighty-nine appeared!" *Neighborhood: My Story of Greenwich House* (New York: Norton, 1938), p. 174.

19. Quoted in Inez Haynes Irwin, *The Story of the Woman's Party* (1921; reprint, New York: Harcourt, Brace, 1971), pp. 85–86.

20. Eleanor Flexner, *Century of Struggle: The Woman's Rights Movement in the United States* (Cambridge, Mass.: Belknap Press of Harvard Univ. Press, 1968), p. 292.

21. Irwin, *Woman's Party*, p. 468.

22. Anna Howard Shaw with Elizabeth Jordan, *The Story of a Pioneer* (1915; reprint, New York: Kraus Reprint, 1990), p. 151.

23. Quoted in Blatch and Lutz, p. 222.
24. For a rousing account of this spectacular trip, see Irwin, *Woman's Party*, pp. 105–116.
25. Sherna Gluck, ed., *From Parlor to Prison: Five American Suffragists Talk About Their Lives* (New York: Vintage, 1976), p. 44.
26. Gluck, pp. 147–48.
27. Ibid., p. 203.
28. Ibid., p. 149.
29. Mari Jo Buhle and Paul Buhle, eds., *The Concise History of Woman Suffrage: Selections from the Classic Work of Stanton, Anthony, Gage, and Harper* (Urbana: Univ. of Illinois Press, 1978), Document 69.
30. Martha Farnsworth, *Plains Woman: The Diary of Martha Farnsworth, 1882–1922*, ed. Marlene Springer and Haskell Springer (Bloomington: Indiana Univ. Press, 1988), p. 217.
31. Blatch and Lutz, p. 92.
32. Ibid., p. 160.
33. Ibid., p. 192.
34. Ibid., p. 193.
35. Buhle and Buhle, Document 71.
36. Quoted in Gluck, pp. 197–98.
37. Blatch and Lutz, p. 220.
38. Quoted in Barbara Meyer Wertheimer, *We Were There: The Story of Working Women in America* (New York: Pantheon Books, 1977), pp. 281–82.
39. Irwin, *Angels and Amazons*, p. 356.
40. Anecdotes and quotations in this and next three paragraphs in Irwin, *Woman's Party*, pp. 20–23.
41. Ibid., pp. 78–82, passim.
42. Irwin, *Angels and Amazons*, p. 363.
43. Irwin, *Woman's Party*, p. 214.
44. Quoted in Irwin, *Woman's Party*, p. 216.
45. Ibid., pp. 216, 220.
46. Quoted in Carole Nichols, *Votes and More for Women: Suffrage and After in Connecticut* (New York: Haworth Press, 1983), p. 25.
47. Quoted in Doris Stevens, *Jailed for Freedom* (New York: Schocken Books, 1976), p. 212.
48. Nichols, p. 19.
49. For a description of the "Night of Terror," see Irwin, *Angels and Amazons*, pp. 381ff.
50. Irwin, *Woman's Party*, pp. 166–67.
51. Irwin, *Angels and Amazons*, pp. 428–29. Irwin details the Woman's Party's work in the ratification precess, pp. 393ff.
52. Flexner, p. 323.

53. Eastman, p. 316.
54. Reprinted in the *New York Times*, Sept. 30, 1990.
55. Quoted in Irwin, *Woman's Party*, pp. 324–25.
56. Blatch and Lutz, p. 293.

CHAPTER 8

Women's War Against War

The outbreak of World War I in August 1914 stunned most Americans. Women and men within the pacifist movement had convinced themselves that war was outmoded, passé. Even in the face of the Spanish-American War and the bloody crushing of the Philippine insurrection and the Boxer Rebellion, they argued that Western civilization had so far evolved that nations would no longer descend to force to settle their differences. Jane Addams thought of "war as a throwback in the scientific sense."[1] Emily Balch considered it "as obsolete as chain armor."[2] And young Nettie Elizabeth Mills assured her father, "We would never have any more wars. I said, 'You know, Daddie, people are more educated and realize fighting is for beasts—not men.' I felt my life would be different and I would not have to think about wars."[3]

Men and Women, War and Peace

Of course die-hard apostles of virility like Teddy Roosevelt compared the nation to the human body and war to an exercise necessary to its development. To escape emasculation and effeminacy, they said, an affluent society must periodically engage in battle. This kind of talk about war as masculine and peace as feminine influenced the ways people thought about war. Those who wanted the United States to go to war said that manly men could not let insults and injustices go unavenged. And women pacifists said that womanly women, representing humankind's higher nature, must teach men peaceful ways to resolve their conflicts.

Jane Addams pondered ways that industrial societies could maintain both virility and peace, visiting Tolstoy in her quest. The idea still dominated even sensitivities like hers that through the ages war had provided opportunities for men to rise to the heights of chivalry and self-sacrifice. Could humanity discover another activity that would inspire equal nobility? Perhaps, Addams thought, reform efforts could provide a "moral substitute for war."

Reinforcing the association between femininity and pacifism, women asserted that they, the creators of life, had special interests in peace. Many woman suffragists insisted on the interdependence of pacifism and the rights of women. Women and children, said Harriot Stanton Blatch, suffer most in war, war "caused because the masculine ideas of physical force are not balanced in government by the ideals and practical common sense of women."[4] Accordingly Charlotte Perkins Gilman urged women to use their influence to establish an international government as a center for growth in art, science, industry, and education. The Women's Political Union wanted to force "the mother viewpoint into the diplomacies of nations" by having women participate in fashioning the peace treaty.[5]

In the long run the identification of war as masculine and peace as feminine helped to push the United States into World War I. Whatever lip service the country paid to the feminine virtues, Americans were not about to let go of their claims to physical courage, hardihood, and ability to repay insult with injury.

Peace societies had flourished from the late 1880s up to 1914, though they wielded no great influence. "When the W.C.T.U. adopted a peace program [in 1887], even when in 1907 May Wright Sewall temporarily ranged the National Council of Women behind the embryo American [pacifist] movement," wrote Inez Irwin, "it did not achieve even the dignity of unpopularity. The average citizen still considered it a joke."[6] Undeterred, women in this prewar era worked hard for peace in groups of men and women, as well as in their own organizations. But by 1914 women had learned the lesson taught them before and since in so many organizations with members of both genders. As Anna Garlin Spencer told Carrie Chapman Catt, the national peace societies seemed to have "as little use for women and their points of view, as have the militarists."[7] Women's outrage at this exclusion was excited particularly because "women are mothers, or potential mothers, [and] therefore have a more intimate sense of the value of human life. There can be more meaning and passion in the determination of a woman's organization to end war than in an organization of men and women with the same aim."[8]

Women Pacifists to the Front

So when war flared in Europe, women pacifists rushed into action on their own. And throughout the war, women spearheaded the efforts for mediation. They created a range of pacifist organizations propelled by womanpower or with a membership of women only.

On August 19, 1914, almost immediately after war's outbreak, Lillian Wald led a New York City protest parade of 1,200 social workers.[9] And that year the social workers organized the American Union Against Militarism (AUAM) with Wald as president. In this organization with members of both genders, women were the prime movers. With attorney Crystal Eastman as executive secretary, the AUAM became the most daringly effective wartime advocate of peace. In a time after the United States' entry into the war when young men out of uniform were targets for persecution, when conscientious objectors were treated like traitors, when the freedoms of speech and the press were abridged by law, the AUAM defended civil liberties. They supported a lobbyist in Washington, established local committees in 22 American cities, and maintained the only nationwide press service for peace.

The Woman's Peace Party (WPP) attracted more middle-of-the-road women. The British Emmeline Pethwick-Lawrence, the Hungarian Rosika Schwimmer, Crystal Eastman, and Carrie Chapman Catt among them persuaded Jane Addams to call a meeting in January 1915 to discuss forming a women's peace group. Eighty-six delegates from most of the major women's organizations rallied to hear Catt explain the need for separate action by women. When the "Great War" broke out, she said, American women, lulled into inattention by the assurance that there could never be another war, heard nothing from the pacifist organizations. All too late, women now came together at the 11th hour. In two days the delegates constructed a bold platform, declaring for a conference of neutral nations to enable an early peace; limitation of armaments and nationalization of their manufacture, so that war would no longer bestow windfall profits; democratic control of foreign policies; and universal suffrage. Most significant, they proposed an international organization and an international police force to replace national armies and navies and "to substitute Law for War"—a foreshadowing of the League of Nations and the United Nations. ". . . as human beings and the mother half of humanity," wrote Anna Garlin Spencer in the preamble to the platform, they proclaimed their "right to be consulted in the settlement of questions concerning not alone the life of individuals but of nations."[10]

The names of well-known women studded the rolls of the officers and sponsors of the new party: Jane Addams as president, Sophonisba Breckinridge as treasurer, Carrie Chapman Catt, Anna Howard Shaw, Ellen Henrotin, Margaret Dreier Robins, and Mrs. Booker T. Washington as sponsors. The WPP gained 25,000 members in their first year. They concentrated their most vigorous efforts on a campaign for American mediation and arbitration among the warring nations.

Catt had her doubts: In her view the world had literally gone mad, and trying to get the embattled countries to an international meeting would "be too much like trying to organize a peace society in an insane asylum."[11] But aside from wringing their hands, what else were the WPP members to do? By mid-November 1914, three months into the war, the Allies and Central Powers had already settled into a near deadlock. The trench warfare, which was to last for four years more, sacrificed millions of lives without a significant gain or loss of territory. For the neutral nations not to try to intervene was to connive at chaos. Of all the neutral nations, the United States was the most powerful, the best positioned to mediate—if necessary with clout. Yet Wilson, though repeatedly proclaiming his commitment to neutrality and to peace, did not offer to mediate.

The International Congress of Women

So the women of the WPP and their sympathizers welcomed the invitation of Dr. Aletta Jacobs of the Netherlands and the International Woman Suffrage Association to an International Congress of Women to be held at The Hague in late April 1915. Jane Addams was asked to preside, partly, no doubt, in recognition of the unique position of the United States as a potential mediator.

Improbable as it seems, in the midst of one of the most widespread wars in human history, the women pulled it off. Against high odds, the opposition of several governments, and the jeers of the press, some 2,000 women participated, women from 12 countries, several of them at war. British, German, Austrian, Hungarian, Italian, Polish, Belgian, Dutch, American, Danish, Norwegian and Swedish women attended, representing 150 different organizations. Putting aside their very real grievances against the enemy countries of their co-delegates, they achieved consensus. Had their governments emulated their efforts, they could have changed the course of history, perhaps averting World War II.

Women in the United States sent 47 delegates, a mixed lot representing diverse backgrounds and convictions but united in their determination to do whatever they could to end the "Great War." Forty-seven independent-minded women, accomplished, used to leading, and unafraid to rebel.

Rosika Schwimmer, Hungarian social reformer and feminist, sailed with them. In Hungary she had organized women agricultural laborers and office workers. In England she had acted as a correspondent for European newspapers and press secretary for the International Woman Suffrage Alliance and published a plan for mediation. In America she already had impelled the founding of the Woman's Peace Party and was to go on to more spectacular peace activities. A marvelous rhetorician, she could persuade almost anybody (with the notable exception of Woodrow Wilson, who seemed to owe his guidance only to God and Colonel House) to do almost anything. But heaven help the project of which she took charge: She and power simply couldn't live together. As an administrator, she evoked chaos.

The formidable array of delegates to the International Congress on the *Noordam*, however, under the firm guidance of Jane Addams, had nothing to fear from Schwimmer. Too intelligent and politically practiced to overrate the likelihood of stopping the war, or to underestimate the odds of ridicule, they nonetheless had to do what they could for peace. "We know we are ridiculous," said Professor Emily Balch, "but even being ridiculous is useful sometimes and so too are *enfant terribles* that say out what needs to be said but what it is not discreet or 'the thing' to say and which important people will not say in consequence."[12] Labor organizer Leonora O'Reilly spoke for the other delegates when she proclaimed her determination to attend the congress if they blew her to atoms, as long as there was "a ghost of a chance of bringing peace on earth or anything lastingly useful by going." For, she said, ". . . the reason women succeed in doing new things while men stay put in ways that are old, is that the women are such darn fools they don't know the thing can't be done. . . . maybe . . . the future will show how the God of War was vanquished forever by the Goddess of Peace."[13]

On shipboard the delegates set about preparing themselves for the congress by lectures, discussion, and study. Alice Hamilton comparing the voyage to "a perpetual meeting of the Woman's City Club," remarked, "It is interesting to see the party evolve from a chaotic lot of half-informed people, and muddled enthusiasts, and sentimentalists, with a few really informed ones, into a docile, teachable, coherent body. . . . We have long passed the stage of poems and impassioned appeals and 'messages from womankind' and willingness to die in the cause, and now we are discussing whether it is more dangerous to insist on democratic control of diplomacy than it is to insist on the neutralization of the seas."[14]

One of their number, Julia Grace Wales, who taught at the University of Wisconsin, won support for her plan to provide continuous, ongoing mediation among the warring powers. Experts from neutral countries appointed by their governments would form a commission to offer all the belligerents one proposal after another to end the war. Their activities would be publicized, to afford the peoples hope, to encourage public opinion for the adoption of a peace settlement, and to avoid the secret diplomacy that many held responsible for the war. After the war an international organization would be created to keep the peace. In Wisconsin, a bastion of Progressivism, the state legislature had already endorsed this plan and recommended it to the United States Congress. The delegates on the *Noordam* in their turn decided to advocate it at the International Congress of Women.

First, though, they had to get there, and the British didn't make it easy. Their government stuffily prevented all but three of the British delegates from getting to The Hague. Their press virulently labeled all delegates to the congress "Pro-Hun Peacettes." To top it all off, the British navy intercepted the *Noordam* and detained it incommunicado for an unstated period. The delegates could hardly avoid suspecting a British plot to keep them from the congress.

Their spirits lifted when after four days the British allowed them to proceed. They soared as the Americans met the delegates from other countries and sensed the remarkable openness that infused and united the congress. Here were women whose countries had been clashing for eight months in perhaps the bloodiest war in history, trying to communicate with one another, to put aside their keen grievances for the atrocities committed on both sides, in order to work together for peace. Here were women who had braved the ridicule, disapproval, and prohibitions of their own governments and people in an effort to save Western civilization.

They made up their minds to avoid clashes along national lines. They refrained from discussing who had caused the war or allotting blame for its conduct. Self-discipline and patience governed their behavior. "All the speakers," Leonora O'Reilly reported, "were filled with altruistic cosmopolitanism, rather than narrow, egotistical patriotism."[15] And the Quaker Lucy Biddle Lewis remarked, ". . . all seem willing to give up the ideas that hurt someone else in this time of terrible stress."[16]

Of course the delegates sometimes didn't agree. Some were willing to sacrifice anything for immediate peace; others held out for a "just peace." They disagreed in principle about the possibility of a "good war." They differed too on procedural matters—matters that, as every experienced committee member knows, cause most agreements to founder. In the chair Addams was exasperated by the European rigidity about parliamentary procedure, which stifled debate and discussion.

But the delegates' will to peace overrode their differences. That will was symbolized on the second day of the assembly by the reception given five Belgian women who had wangled permission to attend from the German forces occupying their country. A German delegate to the congress rose to welcome them and asked that they be seated on the platform.

Only such a spirit could have enabled these diverse women with clashing national interests to discover and agree on a set of principles as conditions of a permanent peace.[17] Concerned that women should contribute to the treaty making at war's end, whenever it came, the congress also created the International Committee of Women for Permanent Peace, soon afterward and today known as the Women's International League for Peace and Freedom. They scheduled it to meet after the war, when and where peace terms were negotiated.

Most spectacularly, perhaps most usefully, certainly most controversially, the congress voted to send two delegations to sound out the heads of government of neutral and belligerent countries. Would they listen to mediation? Addams at first called this proposal "hopelessly melodramatic and absurd," and Hamilton initially thought it "a singularly fool peformance."[18] But they went along when its proponent, none other than Rosika Schwimmer, persuaded the congress to embrace it and when they realized how much it meant to some of the European delegates, for whom it was the last, best hope of peace.

Events indeed proved those European delegates right. No one else was willing to intervene—either women acted, or no one would. Just possibly they might provide channels of communication among warring nations. Just possibly they might help a politician who wanted peace to build popular support. Just possibly they could furnish the public with information otherwise denied them, correcting the propaganda gushing from both sides. Looking back 25 years later, Hamilton asked, "Can anyone believe that soldiers could have been held in the trenches through 1916 and 1917, if they had known that their governments were refusing peace terms which were fair and reasonable?"[19] Probably not, given the mutiny of the French army in 1917.

In any case, two delegations from the International Congress of Women set off, at the members' own expense. Jane Addams, Rosa Genoni, Aletta Jacobs, and Alice Hamilton called on the officials of Austro-Hungary, Belgium, France, Germany, Italy, Switzerland, and Great Britain. Rosika Schwimmer, Cora Ramondt-Hirschmann, Christal Macmillan, Emily Balch, and Julia Wales visited the Scandinavian countries and Russia. In five weeks the delegates among them interviewed 22 prime ministers and foreign ministers, two presidents, a king, and the pope.

It must have been an astounding experience, touched by a sense of unreality, as they endured spy scares, body searches and confiscations of their personal possessions in their travels through war-torn Europe, as they gazed at the ruins of the great library of Louvain burned by the Germans, as they tried to sort out truth from diplomatic politesse.

The book about the experience that Addams, Balch, and Hamilton wrote together reveals the great effort they made toward sympathy, patience, and objectivity. Clearly they desperately wanted to find out whether a will to peace existed among the warring countries and a willingness to mediate among the neutrals. They tried hard not to let their own urgent hopes mislead them, even at such heart-stopping moments as when Addams remarked to one highly placed official, "It perhaps seems to you very foolish that women should go about in this way," and, banging his fist on the table, he replied: "Foolish? Not at all. These are the first sensible words that have been uttered in this room for ten months."[20]

How much did their own natures and convictions conspire against an accurate perception? Everywhere they went the siren song of the need for women's action sounded in their ears. They had heard about how German trainmen begged American women traveling through Schleswig-Holstein "to do their utmost to stop this war, saying they & everyone else they came in touch with [were] heartily tired of it & pray[ed] to God it be ended."[21] On their way through Europe the delegates heard "of soldiers who [said] to their hospital nurses: 'We can do nothing for ourselves but go back to the trenches so long as we are able. Cannot the women do something about this war? Are you kind to us only when we are wounded?'" A statesman they interviewed "said that he had wondered many times since the war began why women had remained silent so long, adding that as women are not expected to fight they might easily have made a protest against war which is denied to men."[22]

The delegates also had to try to counterbalance the weight of the reports of their European friends from the international pacifist and woman suffrage movements. These Europeans repeatedly told the American women stories about the unwillingness of soldiers to fight and their demands for peace. Soldiers killed themselves, it was said, to avoid killing others. A mother professed her gratitude that her soldier son had died early, "before he harmed the son of any other woman called an enemy."[23] Even in the kaiser's Germany workers were conducting mass demonstrations for peace.

Most difficult of all—and probably with the least success— the Americans had to struggle against their own idealism. Idealistic people, judging others by themselves, generally hold to the view that most humans are basically good. Thus Jane Addams was shocked when she received from Hans Delbrueck of the German foreign office the solid practical advice that only American power could end the war. Wilson, Delbrueck said, should threaten to embargo England unless England accepted reasonable terms of peace and offer to lift the embargo against Germany if, and only if, Germany would accept them. Addams, apparently unable to apply on the international scene the political lessons she had learned at Hull House, repudiated the advice. Such a response, she said, would be blackmail and totally un-American; President Wilson would lose his power of moral suasion if he resorted to coercion. Delbrueck didn't give a snap of his fingers for moral suasion and said so—a reaction that only convinced Addams of his "Prussian depravity."[24]

The delegates conscientiously tried to listen to people who disagreed with them. Hamilton stressed, for instance, the conviction of almost all Germans that they were fighting simply in self-defense. They labeled as criminals Belgian guerrilla sharpshooters defending their own country after the German invasion. And Hamilton noted, "Even the very best of [the Germans] accepted the *Lusitania* incident [in which neutral Americans lost their lives after a German submarine attack] without questioning. . . . One really lovely young married woman told us that the day the news came she declared a holiday and took her children on a picnic to the country to celebrate."[25]

The delegates also wisely reminded themselves that among both the Allies and the Central Powers enthusiastic supporters of the war who demanded a crushing military victory far outnumbered those who wanted peace through mediation. But to this smaller group the women from the International Congress gave a voice, when no one else would, when governments and media united to suppress the ideas they advocated.

In the end what they heard convinced the delegates, they wrote in a joint statement, "that the belligerent Governments would not be opposed to a conference of neutral nations; that while the belligerents have rejected offers of mediation by single neutral nations, and while no belligerent could ask for mediation, the creation of a continuous conference of neutral nations might provide the machinery which would lead to peace."[26] This was their message to the world, a message that they wanted particularly to convey to the man who could do most about it—Woodrow Wilson.

But Wilson, busily touting himself as the ultimate pacifist, had apparently convinced himself that he knew more than any other man in the world about how to end the war—let alone any woman. Politically he wanted the support of Jane Addams and her kind, and he granted them audiences. But he was to say, "My heart is with them, but my mind has a contempt for them. I want peace, but I know how to get it, and they do not."[27] The record and the expenditure of 116,708 American servicemen's lives in World War I comment on his wisdom.

The Peace Ship

As Wilson's intransigence corroded their hopes, pacifists had to consider alternative means to continuous mediation. Here actuality defies fantasy. Rebecca Shelley, a young schoolteacher who had finagled her way to the International Congress of Women, now alleged that she had received a message direct from the Deity instructing her to "Go to Ford."[28] She went as near as she could get, to Detroit, where (providentially?) she met a young reporter, through whom she arranged a meeting between Henry Ford, the quintessential self-made, politically naive, anti-Semitic American tycoon, and Rosika Schwimmer, the sophisticated, radical European Jewish woman. Between them, this bizarre pair, both brilliantly entrepreneurial, concocted the idea of a Peace Ship. It was, they decided, to carry from the New World a delegation to resolve the difficulties in which the Old World had embroiled itself.

Ford, a magnate used to telling other people what to do and having them do it, saw no reason that this goal could not be reached with dispatch. Announcing to the press that he could have the soldiers out of the trenches in a month, he gave Wilson one more chance at participation by offering unlimited financial backing for a neutral commission to mediate among the warring powers. When Wilson refused, Ford let Schwimmer, who was as much in a hurry as he, forge ahead. He contented himself with calling for a general military strike on Christmas Day, furnishing lots of money and leaving the rest in Schwimmer's hands. The Peace Ship, the chartered *Oscar II*, was to carry an American delegation to Europe, there to meet with others who desired peace and to convene an assembly of neutrals.

The press roared with laughter, satirizing the undertaking unmercifully and destroying any credibility that it might have had.[29] Addams and the other women who had worked so responsibly and patiently for peace were appalled, both at

Ford and Schwimmer's headlong attack and at the damage to the reputation of pacifism. But, with Wilson still refusing to move and no other prospect for peace on the horizon, they had few options. Settling for what she could get, Addams agreed to go along; she later said, "I was fifty-five years old in 1915; I had already 'learned from life' that moral results are often obtained through the most unexpected agencies."[30] Julia Grace Wales, seeing no other way to implement her plan of continuous mediation, also consented.

With slapdash haste, invitations went out just a week before the Peace Ship was to sail, in early December 1915. All of the socialists invited refused; so did the entire executive board of the Woman's Peace Party. But many others, including 25 student observers, 44 members of the press, and a few adventurers, were delighted to travel to Europe at Mr. Ford's expense. The 55 delegates, about half men and half women, numbered among them one governor, one lieutenant governor, six gubernatorial representatives; Helen Ring Robinson, the first woman elected to a state senate; the septuagenarian suffragist organizer May Wright Sewall; and the competent and exquisite Inez Milholland, lawyer, flamboyant feminist, pacifist, and war correspondent, adored and censured for leading a suffragist parade down Fifth Avenue in a Grecian gown on a white charger, with her hair down her back. What a contrast this was to the American delegation to the International Congress of Women, who described themselves as "forty elderly females!"[31]

Young Lella Secor (Florence), "pretty, piquant, blessed with a mop of golden red curls and total self-confidence," reported the voyage for the *Seattle Post-Intelligencer*, an experience that converted her to pacifism.[32] With a faked passport acquired with some flutterings of eyelashes and tosses of that red hair, she boarded the ship on "the heels of William Jennings Bryan who had [gone] along to wish the venture God-speed. . . . [She] hadn't the slightest idea what the Ford Peace Ship was designed to do—they seemed to want the war to stop and that was sensible enough. . . . The whole scheme had been organised in such haste that many of its details had to be worked out after the *Oscatwo*, as the ship came to be known, had got under way."[33]

Jane Addams was not aboard; at the last minute illness prevented her sailing, but she sent Emily Balch as her surrogate. Ford himself was of no use. Accustomed to factory autocracy rather than participatory democracy or international anarchy, he could not see the problem: "I doubt," wrote Lella Secor, "if he ever gave much thought to the plans and purposes of the Neutral Conference once he had decided to support the venture. It seemed a silly thing for the war to go on, and he felt that people would be reasonable and stop it if you got hold of them and talked it over."[34] Schwimmer's devious, dictatorial, secretive methods of administration fed dissension and disrupted the earnest conversations and well-attended meetings of the early part of the voyage, pitting the delegates against one another. Fatally, she also spatted with the press, a group already disposed to sneer and ridicule.

Once on the Continent, still with no clear idea of what they were to do, let alone how to do it, the delegates faced Europeans unprepared for their arrival, skeptical of their intentions, and wary of American interference. The International Committee of Women for Permanent Peace rejected Ford's offer of support for their peace plan. Elsewhere pacifists enjoyed what his money could buy in the shape of meetings, dinners, and several $10,000 contributions to local causes but remained uncommitted—partly because Schwimmer's maneuvers alienated them.

Ford, excusing himself on the grounds of minor illnesses, went home on December 21. By mid-January 1916, so had most of the delegates.

But not all—amazingly, in view of the odds, others did manage to set up a Neutral Conference for Continuous Mediation. After a fashion, it functioned, but never without internal disagreements and convulsions so severe as to stymie efficiency. The able women who had participated in the International Congress of Women never gained real power, and the spirit of the International Congress went down to defeat in the political infighting of the Neutral Conference. Ford's stateside representatives, to whom he had given financial control, cut back funds. Yet in its brief life delegates did manage to formulate tentative peace proposals, submit them to the belligerent powers, and publicize them.

Perhaps the jury is still out on the whole effort. Contemporary reports, not without bases, damned the Peace Ship and the Neutral Conference as silly liberal pacifist efforts. By the summer of 1916, the conference had effectively ceased to function. Ford cut his losses and abandoned its support on February 1, 1917.[35] And yet, for good or ill, these pacifist efforts prepared the way for both the League of Nations and the United Nations.

Against the Odds

Even while the United States edged toward active involvement in Europe, American pacifists at home did manage to avert war with Mexico, chiefly through the agency of the American Union Against Militarism (AUAM). When in 1916 American forces chasing Pancho Villa had exchanged fire with the Mexican army, Wilson asked Congress to empower him to occupy northern Mexico. The AUAM, assisted by the Woman's Peace Party and other pacifist groups, swung into action, publicizing an American army officer's eyewitness allegation that American troops had been the aggressors, holding meetings, and organizing a letter and telegram campaign. They turned around public opinion, and Wilson changed course. If not a unique victory, certainly it was a rare one.

More and more, though, unrestricted German submarine warfare, British and French propaganda, a gung ho American press, the self-interest of the manufacturers of war supplies and their employees, and Wilson's shifts of stance toward "preparedness" moved the United States toward participation in the European war.

American entry into the war in April 1917 further splintered the peace movement. The WPP, faced with the desire of many members to work in war relief projects, finally decided that each branch could do as it liked—a decision that caused Zona Gale, with reason, to complain that the WPP would be reduced to a food dehydration center in Massachusetts, and somewhere else to a "bureau for getting messages through to relatives beyond the lines."[36] In fact, the WPP split three ways. Many members hailed the war as a crusade for liberty and justice, which they enthusiastically supported. Others, like Jane Addams, compromised by choosing to work for internationalism and meanwhile to support humanitarian projects connected with the war.

And a small intransigent radical minority, led by Crystal Eastman, furiously opposed the war. For a while, until the Post Office refused it, this group published a monthly journal, in which they called female relief work a "peculiarly infantile form of patriotism" and claimed that hand knitting was not only unnecessary but also deprived women workers in knitting mills of their livelihood and urged that knitters be "legally restrained."[37] They lobbied against the Espionage Bill and universal military training. They tried to unseat Fiorello LaGuardia, who accepted an army commission without resigning from Congress. Under the aegis of this segment of the WPP people like Emily Balch taught classes on world politics. In every way they could these determinedly pacifist women refused war work and agitated for peace. That took courage in the United States of World War I, when other women were handing out white feathers to men not in uniform and vigilantes were painting a bright shade of yellow the doors and gates of men who did not volunteer for the military.

The AUAM split not over relief activities but over the protection of civil rights. Against pacifist opposition, the U.S. Congress passed a Selective Service Act that made no provision for conscientious objectors, and an Espionage Act that made short shrift of the civil liberties of those who objected to the war. The AUAM's efforts to protect the victims of these acts came close to destroying the organization.

In this atmosphere people paid a high price for not participating in the general hysteria. Addams's compromise did not exempt her. When she, whom many had reverenced as almost a saint, accurately reported that the European Allied armies commonly bolstered their soldiers' courage with alcohol or drugs before a bayonet charge, her reputation suffered an attack from which it never recovered. Women with German names like Unitarian minister Adele Fuchs were made to feel like aliens. And more than one woman, like Dr. Marie Equi, went to prison for "sedition" because of her pacifist beliefs.[38]

Aftermath

The post–World War I era let people down, women as well as men. Those idealists who had bought the Wilsonian rhetoric about making the world safe for democracy and fighting a war to end war suffered their Gethsemane in the disastrous Treaty of Versailles. Those feminists who had assured themselves that wars would never be fought if women were in positions of authority had to face the actuality that many women had at least verbally revealed a frightening degree of belligerence. Those women who, judging others by themselves, had assumed an international community among women found themselves without a base on which to rely.[39]

Nevertheless, and to their credit, a substantial number of American women emerged with enough energy to carry on. Some of them urged the participation of women in the peace conference—which welcomed neither the presence nor the advice of the International Committee of Women for Permanent Peace. Some of them continued to try to defend constitutional rights. They protested against the deportation of radical aliens like Emma Goldman. They advocated the release of conscientious objectors imprisoned during the war. They opposed compulsory military training. They hoped to infuse the Americanization process with an appreciation of the many cultures represented by recent immigrants. Postwar hysteria defeated them.

Some of them went in May 1919 to the second International Congress of Women. Despite the unwillingness of the German women to acknowledge their country's share of the guilt or to express regret for the sufferings inflicted on

AMERICAN WOMEN SEEKING REPRESENTATION IN THE PEACE CONFERENCE: MRS. J. BORDEN HARRIMAN OF THE RED CROSS, MRS. JULIETTE BARRETT RUBLEE, DR. KATHARINE BEMENT DAVIS OF THE YWCA.
(NATIONAL ARCHIVES)

others, this congress did achieve consensus in calling for an end to the blockade of Germany, a sharing of the world's resources, and an international organization for peace. But the Senate of the United States soon destroyed their hopes by refusing to commit the country to the League of Nations.

Despite these many failures, two important organizations emerged from the wartime women's peace movement. Out of the Civil Liberties Board of the AUAM grew the modern American Civil Liberties Union.

The Women's International League for Peace and Freedom (WILPF), spawned by the Women's International Committee for Permanent Peace, met for the first time in Switzerland in 1919. Its work at that time had many supporters. Carrie Chapman Catt and her followers, for instance, were devoting themselves almost completely to the pacifist cause. For their first two years the meetings of the League of Women Voters were mostly antiwar rallies, and the General Federation of Women's Clubs also interested itself in peace. WILPF survives today—now, as then, a voice crying in the wilderness.

Source Notes

1. Jane Addams, *The Second Twenty Years at Hull House, September 1909 to September 1929* (New York: Macmillan, 1930), pp. 117–18.
2. Mercedes M. Randall, *Improper Bostonian: Emily Greene Balch* (New York: Twayne, 1964), p. 134.
3. *The Lady Driller: Autobiography of Nettie Elizabeth Mills* (New York: Exposition Press, 1955), p. 44.
4. Harriot Stanton Blatch and Alma Lutz, *Challenging Years: The Memoirs of Harriot Stanton Blatch* (1940; reprint, New York: Hyperion, 1976), p. 251.
5. Ibid., p. 252.
6. Inez Haynes Irwin, *Angels and Amazons: A Hundred Years of American Women* (1933; reprint, New York: Arno Press, 1974), p. 415.
7. Quote in William L. O'Neill, *Everyone Was Brave: The Decline and Fall of Feminism in America* (Chicago: Quadrangle Books, 1969), p. 173.
8. Crystal Eastman to Jane Addams, Jan. 16, 1915, Papers of the Woman's Peace Party, quoted in O'Neill, p. 176.
9. Allen F. Davis, *Spearheads for Reform: The Social Settlements and the Progressive Movement, 1830–1914* (New York: Oxford Univ. Press, 1967), p. 219.
10. Quoted in O'Neill, p. 176.

11. Catt to Addams, Jan. 16, 1915, Papers of the Woman's Peace Party, quoted in O'Neill, p. 177.

12. Quoted in Randall, p. 151.

13. Leonora O'Reilly, "Report on the International Congress of Women," in *Proceeding of the Fifth Biennial Convention of the National Women's Trade Union League of America, New York City, June 7–12, 1915*, pp. 1, 3.

14. Letter of April 22, 1915, in Barbara Sicherman, ed., *Alice Hamilton: A Life in Letters* (Cambridge: Harvard Univ. Press, 1984), pp. 185-86.

15. O'Reilly, p. 5.

16. Letter of April 26, 1915, Biddle MSS, Friends' Historical Library, Swarthmore, Pa.

17. These principles include these points, among others:

    1. No territory should be transferred without the consent of the men and women in it. The right of conquest should not be recognized.
    2. Autonomy and a democratic parliament should not be refused to any people.
    3. The governments of all nations should agree to refer future international disputes to arbitration or conciliation and to bring social, moral, and economic pressure to bear upon any country which resorts to arms.
    4. Foreign policies should be subject to democratic control.
    5. Women should be granted equal political rights with men.

    Randall, p. 159.
    Wilson described these proposals as "by far the best formulation which up to the moment has been put out by any body" and borrowed from them for his Fourteen Points. Randall, Introduction.

18. Letter of May 5, 1915, in Sicherman, p. 190.

19. Alice Hamilton, *Exploring the Dangerous Trades: The Autobiography of Alice Hamilton, M.D.* (1943; reprint, Boston: Northeastern Univ. Press, 1985), pp. 165–66.

20. Addams, in Jane Addams, Emily G. Balch, and Alice Hamilton, *Women at the Hague: The International Congress of Women and Its Results* (1915; reprint, New York: Garland, 1972), p. 96.

21. Lucy Biddle Lewis, letter of April 26, 1915, Biddle MSS, Friends' Historical Library, Swarthmore, Pa.

22. Addams, Balch, and Hamilton, pp. 127, 96.

23. Addams in Addams, Balch, and Hamilton, pp. 128–29.

24. O'Neill, p. 181.

25. Hamilton, *Exploring the Dangerous Trades*, p. 172.

26. Joint statement of Aletta Jacobs, Chrystal Macmillan, Rosika Schwimmer, Jane Addams, and Emily Balch, October 1915, quoted in Randall, pp. 208–09.

27. Quoted in Randall, p. 212. Steinson concludes that women advocates of mediation never influenced Wilson the politician but did touch Wilson the idealist. Barbara J. Steinson, *American Women's Activism in World War I* (New York: Garland, 1982), pp. 111–12.

28. In the Progressive Era mysticism and spiritualism attracted considerable interest even among such sophisticates as the philosopher-psychologist William James.

29. The definitive work on the Peace Ship is Barbara S. Kraft's *The Peace Ship: Henry Ford's Pacifist Adventure in the First World War* (New York: Macmillan, 1978). For an account of the press attitude, see Burnet Hershey's *The Odyssey of Henry Ford and the Great Peace Ship* (New York: Taplinger, 1967). Lella Secor Florence's "The Ford Peace Ship and After" in *We Did Not Fight* (1935; reprint, New York: Burt Franklin Reprints, 1974) helpfully presents the point of view of a journalist converted to pacifism by the experience.

30. Quoted in Hershey, 68. And Addams was willing to risk error and ridicule for herself when she would not for others; she advised the Woman's Peace Party and the International Committee of Women in Europe of her doubts about the whole operation.

31. Letter of Alice Hamilton, April 22, 1915, in Sicherman, p. 186.

32. Eleanor Flexner's foreword to Florence, p. xi.

33. Florence, pp. 275–76, 281–84 passim.

34. Ibid., p. 282.

35. "Ford also stated some years later that the peace ship, by making the Ford name known through Europe, had enabled the company to break into the post-WWI European market at about 1/20th of what Ford thought it would have cost without the peace ship." David L. Lewis, "Henry Ford: A Study in Public Relations, 1896–1932," PhD. dissertation, Univ. of Michigan, 1959, p. 167; quoted in Steinson, p. 79, note 42.

36. Quoted in Steinson, pp. 258–59.

37. They called knitting "sex antagonism released." Steinson, p. 262.

38. Ruth Barnes Moynihan, *Rebel for Rights: Abigail Scott Duniway* (New Haven: Yale Univ. Press, 1983), p. 218.

39. Jane Addams "had tried to create an international community of women where one did not exist. . . . The War had not demonstrated the existence of any special feminine consciousness which could be tapped and directed toward international harmony. Indeed, the *vox feminarum* spoke in international conflicts in an alarming babble of tongues. . . . women had actually seemed as aggressive as men in a situation where it was deemed proper for women to display violent feelings." Jill K. Conway, *The First Generation of American Graduates* (New York: Garland, 1987), pp. 390–91.

CHAPTER 9

War Work:
Not Just Tending to Their Knitting

When in 1914 Kaiser Wilhelm sent his armies trampling through Belgium to invade France, he assumed that many Americans would sympathize with Germany. Many German-American citizens preserved close ties with the Old Country, spoke German among themselves, read German-language newspapers, and attended church services conducted in German. Not only they but other Americans as well thought of Germany as *a*, if not *the*, natural home of music and philosophy, and American students flocked there to study. The young Willa Cather moving from her prairie home in Nebraska found in a German household in Lincoln a concern for ideas and a love of the arts that educated and delighted her.

War Fever

But the kaiser had underestimated the number of American Francophiles and Anglophiles, particularly on America's East Coast. Besides, with a talent dating from the time of the Visigoths, and with clever assists from British and French propaganda, the Germans by such barbarities as the burning of the library at Louvain and the sinking of the *Lusitania* soon managed to alienate most Americans. Even Americans visiting their German relatives turned away, like Helen Hooven Santmyer's young Jennifer: "I'm sorry, Mother, but I *can't like them*. They think the earth belongs to them, or should."[1] The Americans' democratic gorge rose at such sights as German women stepping off sidewalks to give place to German officers or carrying packages for them so that the officers' military bearing might remain unsullied.

At the same time, American sentiment for neutrality waned as a demand for preparedness waxed, but only gradually. In 1916, two years after the outbreak of hostilities, Wilson ran for a second term on the slogan "He kept us out of war." But less than six months after that election he took the country into that catastrophic war, which engendered a hysteria since unparalleled in the United States (except possibly in the treatment of Japanese-Americans in World War II).

That hysteria was encouraged by the government's suspension of the constitutional rights of dissidents, whom it jailed; conscientious objectors, whom it persecuted; and writers and publishers, whose books it censored and/or confiscated. The general populace spread rumors about German agents. Aurie Carreau, for instance, wrote in 1918: "Dr Barth is in awfully bad, he they say was injecting and spreading the Spanish influenza in the local camps here and his uniform was taken from him he had no authority to have a uniform they say at all, he is a German Jew."[2] Newspapers promoted spy scares. Academics banned the teaching of German in schools and universities. Charities rejected volunteers with German names. Christian ecclesiastics denied denominational aid to the churches of ministers who were not "earnest and outspoken" supporters of the war.[3] Ministers like the 65-year-old cleric-suffragist Mary Safford declaimed that "The ballot, the biscuit, and the bullet are now leagued together for national defense."[4]

Few could stand up to such hysteria. Most American women, like most American men, sympathized with the Allies and supported the war. Even many pacifists soft-pedalled their opposition. Particularly after the United States' declaration of war in April 1917, they searched their souls for a response that would proclaim their love of country but not violate their consciences. Jane Addams found her compromise in working to conserve food, Florence Kelley hers in trying to ensure good labor conditions in the factories that manufactured military uniforms.

Single-minded, one-issue reformers were in a sense luckier. A little cynically, perhaps, they yielded to the war effort only as much as was politic but kept their eyes fixed on what mattered to them most, be it prohibition or woman suffrage.

Many women simply joined in the hue and cry, plunging unashamedly into the prevailing spirit. They put their vaunted moral superiority into the service of the war, self-righteously denouncing other Americans for "lack of patriotism" and at the behest of the government nagging their menfolk to enlist. They indulged in what Alice Hamilton described as the "strange spirit of exaltation among the men and women who thronged Washington, engaged in all sorts of 'war work' and loving it." Hamilton sensed "an impression of joyful release in many of them, as if after all their lives repressing hatred as unchristian, they suddenly discovered it to be a patriotic duty and let themselves go in for an orgy of anti-German abuse."[5]

In the outburst of chauvinism all sorts of people signed all sorts of pledges. The members of the Women's National War Economy League pledged "to buy 'no jewelry or useless ornaments,' to buy fewer clothes and cut their entertaining, and 'to abstain from cocktails, highballs and all expensive wines, also from cigarettes, to influence husbands, fathers, brothers, sons and men friends to do the same, and to contribute the amount thus saved to the Women's National War Fund.'"[6] And more than 1,000 "fallen women," the Florence Crittenden Mission reported, pledged not to go near military camps.[7]

Volunteers for Uncle Sam—and for Humanity

In Washington, and all across the country, women who would not be denied participation in the "central crucible of experience of their time" threw themselves into war work.[8] As in earlier wars, their efforts were impeded by the government. Most men in government, insofar as they had thought about women at all, seem to have assigned to them the duty of "giving their sons" and putting flags for them in their windows, or perhaps shaming reluctant men into joining up.

The outpouring of volunteerism from women and their obvious expectation of serving in the war effort staggered men who had been happily going about men's business of conducting war. They dared not reject women completely, for they uncomfortably sensed that they might eventually need women's labor. And the women did seem to be astonishingly well organized and experienced

LADIES RELIEF CORPS, MEMORIAL DAY, 1913.   (CLINTON [CT] HISTORICAL SOCIETY)

in working together for the public weal. Long before the United States entered the war, they had formed a multiplicity of relief committees to send aid abroad.

The government's response was minimalism, a sort of kindergarten approach. Women could be womanly, cheering the men up and on. They could knit. They could grow food, preserve it, conserve it, restrict their families' diets with meatless days and wheatless days. The absurdity of the demands upon women was epitomized by the still-naive Eleanor Roosevelt, who, in a disastrous newspaper interview, remarked: "Making ten servants help me do my saving has not only been possible but highly profitable."[9]

The redoubtable Dr. Anna Howard Shaw ironically remarked,

> There is no end to the things that women are asked to do. I know this is true because I have read the newspapers for the last six months to get my duty before me. The first thing we are asked to do is to provide the enthusiasm, inspiration and patriotism to make men want to fight, and we are to send them away with a smile! That is not much to ask of a mother! We are to maintain a perfect calm after we have furnished all this inspiration and enthusiasm. "Keep the home fires burning," keep the home sweet and peaceful and happy, keep society on a level, look after business, buy enough but not too much and wear some of our old clothes but not all of them or what would happen to the merchants?[10]

As a visiting British major told a group of American clubwomen, "Do not think that this war is being fought entirely by men. We [men] bear the brunt of it, of course, the actual fighting. But ladies, I want to tell you that you have a definite part to play. Your part, ladies, is to *smile*."[11]

When American women made it unavoidably plain that they expected to participate responsibly in the war effort, that, as Helen Ring Robinson expressed it, "we can not win this war by shutting up women's energies in a garbage can," the government threw them a bone by establishing a Woman's Committee of the Council of National Defense—itself only an advisory body.[12] And the Woman's Committee, wrote member Harriot Stanton Blatch, "are not allowed to do anything without the consent of the Council of National Defense. There is no appropriation. . . . now, as always, men want women to do the work while they do the overseeing."[13]

To chair the Woman's Committee the government appointed the septuagenarian Dr. Shaw. If the government entertained the hope that age had tempered her spirit or softened her brain or her voice, they erred. In the disadvantageous situation of one with heavy responsibility and no power, Shaw fought every inch of the way, struggling to protect laboring women against exploitation, outspokenly resisting tokenism, nagging and chivying to get a little control, rebutting government rhetoric and cover-ups with frankness.

She willingly used her famed oratorical powers to inspire women to work in the war effort, but she also warned them against governmental manipulation. "I want to say to you women," she declaimed at a NAWSA convention,

do not meekly sit down and make all the sacrifices and demand nothing in return. It is not that you want pay but we all want an equally balanced sacrifice. The Government is asking us to conserve food while it is allowing carload after carload to rot on the side tracks of railroad stations and great elevators of grain to be consumed by fire for lack of proper protection. . . . we women have Mr. Hoover looking into our refrigerators, examining our bread to see what kind of materials we are using, telling us what extravagant creatures we are, that we waste millions of money every year, waste food and all that sort of thing, and yet while we are asked to have meatless days and wheatless days, I have never yet seen a demand for a smokeless day! . . . [I]f men want the soldiers to have tobacco, let them have smokeless days and furnish it![14]

With power and a mandate to help the nation's women perform significant war work efficiently, the Woman's Committee could have accomplished miracles. Its structure properly took advantage of the sophisticated networking that women had been doing ever since the late 19th century. Its members included the heads of the National Council of Women, the General Federation of Women's Clubs, the National League for Woman's Services, the National American Woman Suffrage Association, the International Glove Workers' Union, and the National Society of Colonial Dames, as well as the muckraker Ida Tarbell and the antisuffragist Mrs. Joseph R. Lamar.[15] The committee's purpose, Secretary of War Newton Baker said, was to coordinate the women's preparedness movement.

Unfortunately no one knew what the "women's preparedness movement" should be. "[E]very blessed woman in the country was writing Washington, or her organization was writing for her, asking the Government what she could do for the war and of course the Government did not know."[16]

Efforts duplicated one another chaotically. The National League for Woman's Service was already *registering* women for the war effort when the Woman's Committee of the Council of National Defense undertook to *enroll* them. Women importuned by four or five different organizations to enlist in the war effort began to listen to rumors that they were to be drafted and taken involuntarily from their homes for government service, or to fear that registering might jeopardize their jobs or incur punishment if they later found they could not serve. The arduous food conservation pledge campaign made some poor souls believe that government agents would confiscate their canned fruits and vegetables.[17]

Committee members envisaged the kind of work that British women were performing. Anna Howard Shaw had directly warned officialdom: Women would respond magnificently, she said, "if you put before them an incentive big enough, if you appeal to them as a part of the Government's life, not as a by-product of creation or a kindergarten but as a great human, living energy."[18] Instead the government assigned the committee such time-consuming, draining, and pointless tasks as registering hundreds of thousands of women as volunteers for tasks they were never called on to perform and collecting from all households unenforceable pledges to conserve food.

What a travesty—energetic women experienced in working for the public good, aglow with patriotic enthusiasm, already organized, with expert leadership, were now told in effect to tend to their knitting, their kitchens, their menfolk, their babies, and women's business generally. What happened, of course, was that they promptly discovered work for themselves.

They did attempt all that the government asked. They did indeed sell war bonds. The volunteers did indeed knit, everywhere they went, in college classes, in opera boxes, on picket duty in front of the White House, thereby no doubt sparing themselves many an hour of boredom but accomplishing nothing for the war effort that could not have been done at least as well and much faster in a knitting mill.[19]

They did indeed valiantly try to conserve food. Posters throughout the country exhorted women to make "Every Garden a Munition Plant" and to remember that "We Can Can Vegetables and the Kaiser Too."[20] Women workers held food conservation meetings. They offered prizes for the best wheatless, meatless menus. They propagandized everyone who could conceivably influence a menu, from housewives to cooks' unions to butlers serving wealthy families. The mostly middle-class women volunteers conscientiously traded recipes for wheatless and meatless meals while the consumption of beef actually rose: With full employment and lots of overtime working people were making more money, and they knew just where they wanted to spend it—on the meat of which poverty had long deprived them.

But more important, on their own, the hardworking women volunteers continued and expanded the efforts they had begun before the United States entered the war to send enormous quantities of food and relief supplies to the pitiable refugees in Europe, to the ill-supplied and ill-run institutions the French, Italians, Russians, and Serbians called military hospitals, to the war-struck European women deprived of their livelihoods, to war widows and war orphans, to maimed and disfigured and blinded soldiers. Many gave their full-time services as well as their money, from the sculptor Gertrude Vanderbilt Whitney, who donated, equipped, and ran a whole hospital in France, to nameless women who used their entire savings to cross the Atlantic to nurse or to scrub floors.[21]

Within the United States, women undertook volunteer work ranging from the essential to the absurd. The efforts of the Association of Collegiate Alumnae (ACA) displayed both the variety of women's activities and the adaptability of their already established organizations in finding work that met their members'

DISTRIBUTING FOOD CONSERVATION POSTERS IN ALABAMA. (POSTER READS: "THEY ARE GIVING ALL. WILL YOU SEND THEM WHEAT?") (NATIONAL ARCHIVES)

interests and competence—and their eagerness to support the war effort.[22] As their main project, they formed a speakers' bureau to deliver before women's clubs and in movies, community centers, and churches four-minute speeches to instruct their audiences about the causes of the war and to whip up enthusiasm for it. In this way they helped in drives for the war work of the Red Cross, the YMCA, and the YWCA; sold war savings stamps and liberty bonds; and propagandized for food conservation. Speech giving led naturally to immigrant "education" to Americanize immigrants and ensure their support for the war. The Minneapolis branch alone made more than 6,100 addresses on American history and government to immigrants, and in Hawaii members of the ACA spoke through interpreters to people of Japanese, Korean, and Chinese heritage.

But ACA members did much more than speechify. They distributed government publications. They brought more than 100 French women to be educated in American colleges. They identified qualified women to go overseas for the Red Cross and the YMCA and to work stateside in the War Camp Community Service. They adopted French and Belgian orphans, supervised hostess houses near army camps for families visiting servicemen, provided ambulance units, demonstrated food conservation, ran a liberty bread shop (with politically correct wheatless bread), maintained recreation centers for men in uniform, and recruited women to make surgical dressings for the Red Cross.

All women's organizations faced the problem of whether to suspend their normal activities in order to support the war effort. Although a very few, like Alice Paul's suffragists, refused to divert one iota of effort from their own causes, most, like the Women's Trade Union League (then waging a campaign for the eight-hour day), decided simply to work harder, to do both. So with the ACA—along with all their war-related activities, the Toledo branch conducted training classes for speakers on child welfare. In cooperation with the Children's Bureau, ACA members helped weigh and measure thousands of school children. They went into the schools as substitute teachers. In Superior, Wisconsin, they helped maintain an emergency workshop for unemployed women. They established cooperative houses where women students might live economically during their college courses. The Washington, D.C., branch ran a rooming house for college women in government work. Missoula, Montana, and other branches seized their opportunity while men were away to get women onto school boards.

Besides their work in their existing organizations, women organized literally hundreds of new war-oriented committees and councils. Cities, states, and the Woman's Committee of the Council of National Defense struggled vainly all

WORLD WAR I TROOPS AT A RECREATIONAL CLUB ORGANIZED BY BLACK WOMEN FOR THEIR SERVICEMEN. (NATIONAL ARCHIVES)

through the war to coordinate them. Women's efforts were never satisfactorily coordinated, and their undertakings overlapped and duplicated one another.

But among them all they identified and met needs that would never have been recognized otherwise. In Atlanta, for instance, the Colored Women's War Council led public protests against mistreatment of black soldiers on streetcars and police harassment of black civilians and soldiers.[23] In St. Louis, with the support of the Woman's Committee of the Council of National Defense, Miriam C. Senseney launched a public kitchen for immigrant women workers in defense industries, with a workers' dining room for 60 and takeout service to nearby factories. The women customers themselves helped with furnishing the place, scrubbing, and food buying. A model apartment, an old-clothes clinic, and a laundry were set up in the same building, with a backyard model poultry unit. Four day nurseries operated in the area. A wartime food conservation committee established a cannery and cooking school nearby.[24]

When women took literally the government's language about the "women's preparedness movement," they stooped to silliness. Particularly early on in the war, some of them helped organize local defense councils. Women who had blushed for their sisters parading for woman suffrage now unashamedly paraded for preparedness and flocked to luncheons featuring speakers discussing military needs. At one of these "above the center of the table hung an armored Curtis biplane with a model machine gun and bombing apparatus, and suspended from this was an armored dirigible, also equipped for war. At one end of the floral

WAR HYSTERIA. "MAY BE CALLED FOR DUTY ANY TIME," NOTED THE NEWSPAPER CAPTION FOR THIS PICTURE OF THE WOMEN'S SANITARY DETACHMENT IN TRAINING IN CHICAGO. (NATIONAL ARCHIVES)

WAR HYSTERIA. MEMBERS OF THE NATIONAL LEAGUE FOR WOMEN'S SERVICE PRACTICING WITH A MACHINE GUN.   (NATIONAL ARCHIVES)

WAR HYSTERIA. A CAVALRY TROOP ORGANIZED BY THE AMERICAN WOMEN'S LEAGUE FOR SELF DEFENSE. FOR A WHILE THEY HELD THEMSELVES READY TO JOIN THE RUSSIAN WOMEN'S BATTALION OF DEATH.   (NATIONAL ARCHIVES)

shield on the table was a model of a super dreadnought and at the other a submarine, with guns representing the latest models of coast defense."[25] The American Woman's Hat Fund asked women to contribute the price of a spring hat toward the purchase of planes for the New York National Guard. Boston women stored blankets for "our boys" to use in case of invasion and perfected plans to transport virgins (presumably female) inland. Well-off young women attended national service training camps set up by preparedness advocates. There they drilled and studied dietetics, camp cookery, map reading, motor car driving and repairing, bicycling, advanced signaling, and agriculture. At least it was a healthy life, kept them off the streets, and encouraged female bonding.

Enforcing Purity

Almost equally silly, and much more damaging, were women's stabs at backing up military efforts to discourage the troops' sexual activity. The military had two concerns. First, they wanted to reassure anxious mothers that American boys didn't indulge: Secretary of War Newton Baker announced that at the front no American soldier was "living a life which he would not be willing to have mother see him live."[26] On the other hand, frightened by the soaring rate of venereal disease within the military, the authorities wanted to ensure that no lascivious ladies corrupted these pure lads. Prostitutes, they alleged, could more greatly harm American soldiers "than any German fleet of airplanes."[27]

Accordingly, in hardened disregard of the constitutional rights of American citizens, the government empowered the arrest and detention, without trial, of any unaccompanied woman in the environs of a stateside training camp.[28] Municipal and state authorities hired vice agents to arrest *potential* carriers of venereal disease, sending thousands of women to jails and reformatories. Women arrested under this mandate could be forced to submit to a test for venereal disease.[29] (This submission doubly offended advocates of women's rights in that internal examinations of women often caused medical complications: Some women referred to the procedure as "speculum rape.") Suspects could be held without charge and without bail until the results of the test were reported. If they were found to be diseased, they could be held until cured. Most never received medical treatment. Some were remanded into permanent custodial care in homes for the feebleminded. Local communities supplemented the federal law by imposing curfews on women or requiring any woman accompanied by an unrelated soldier or sailor to carry a letter of permission from her parents.[30]

Significant numbers of women suffered deprivation of their rights. The War Department admitted that 18,000 women, of whom 15,000 were diseased, were quarantined in federally supported institutions, and these figures presumably include neither women incarcerated in local jails and workhouses nor many of the women who proved not to be infected. If philanthropist Ethel Dummer was right in asserting that only half the women detained were found to be infected, one must suppose that at least 30,000 women were so persecuted. Many caught in the net were not even suspected of prostitution. They included such pathetic figures as a girl who had gone to New York City to marry a soldier; he had backed out, leaving her infected with gonorrhea, pregnant, and stranded in the city when he shipped out for France.[31]

More women than men protested this egregious "American Plan." Yet all too few dared raise their voices—with notable exceptions like Katherine Bushness, an American doctor and missionary for the Women's Christian Temperance Union, who denounced the plan as a violation of a woman's right to protection "from the vile masturbating hand of a doctor."[32]

Other women undertook to cooperate in the effort to enforce purity. Sometimes their attempts were merely harmlessly optimistic. A Woman's Anti-Vice Committee run by suffragists endeavored to protect soldiers stationed in Texas from alcohol and prostitution.[33] The penal reformer Katharine Bement Davis coordinated a campaign in which women physicians and orators spoke, urging servicemen to be pure and showing them films like "Fit to Fight" and "The End of the Road."[34] Overseas the popular poet Ella Wheeler Wilcox reportedly touched the hearts of thousands of "our boys" with her poem "Come Back Clean." But other women were suborned as "law enforcers attached to the government bureaucracy," violating the civil rights of their suspect sisters.[35]

Women who for years had fought to prevent prostitution by working for higher wages for blue- and pink-collar workers, women who had extended helping hands to prostitutes as victims of men's lust and white slavery, women who had improved prison conditions now allowed themselves to be coopted into the enforcement of laws that put the blame for venereal disease squarely on women and allowed their sexual partners to go scot-free. Many of them simply failed to recognize that the emphasis in combating prostitution had shifted away from protecting women to protecting men—or to a fear of venereal disease.

A War Department Committee for the Protection of Women and Girls, with a national board and local agents near training camps, enrolled women reformers, prison experts, and settlement workers. The committee's actual purpose as an agency of the War Department contravened its ostensible purpose. Yet Martha Falconer, a prominent women's penal reformer, took charge of constructing detention homes proposed by the committee. Field workers from the YWCA and the WCTU patrolled beaches and parks, looking for delinquent women. Social worker Helen Pigeon actually hid in the bushes of the Boston Common late at night, all in the name of protecting women and girls. Some of these guardians, it's good to know, like Maude Miner, former director of the New York Juvenile Probation Department, resigned as they came to recognize the War Department's real goals. Some, like a volunteer from the Boston Society for the Protection of Young Girls, tried to soften the application of the law—she spent two nights in the Lowell town hall with women picked up near Fort Devens rather than allow them to be sent to the city jail. Others, though, like Falconer, deceived themselves with euphemisms, calling the houses of detention "human reclamation centers."[36]

The Woman's Committee of the Council of National Defense formed its own Department of Safeguarding Moral and Spiritual Forces. Guarding chastity was their business but it did occur to these and other concerned women that young girls might be at least as much at risk from the soldiery as the other way around. So they created patrols to save girls from ruin. The Committee on Protective Work for Girls of the Commission on Training Camp Activities, supported by the General Federation of Women's Clubs, went further, trying to rehabilitate camp followers who showed signs of being salvageable. From such efforts it was only a short step to censorship, and some women took it, trying to keep the young away from temptation by banning Theda Bara movies.[37]

The American Way

In those panicky wartime days, Americans looked suspiciously around them, not only at prostitutes, but also at immigrants. Fears that immigrants might not support U.S. participation in the European quarrels they had hoped to leave behind them inspired renewed efforts at Americanization. Ida Clyde Clarke, writing of the need to Americanize women as well as men, pointed to the suffrage states, where the wife automatically assumed citizenship with her husband. What if she were too ignorant to vote? "In these states, therefore, Americanization of the foreign women is a civic and political necessity."[38]

This time around, though, it occurred to some of the Americanizers that condescension might not win the day. The National American Woman Suffrage Association in particular took a new look at the problem after New York City with its throngs of immigrants voted for woman suffrage, and emerged with a new motto: "Don't Preach. Don't Patronize."[39] The politically astute Belle Moskowitz redefined Americanization as transmitting to immigrants "what is best in American culture and civilization, at the same time retaining the finest and best that foreigners have to contribute to this country." Old habits died hard, though, and in fact her program scanted aliens' contributions in favor of providing English-language training, spreading American cultural influences through a community chorus and trying to find out "what the foreign population [was] doing and saying and thinking so that educational propaganda [sic] [might be able to] meet direct needs."[40]

At its best and most pragmatic, Americanization constructed a useful two-way street. Thus at Greenwich House in Greenwich Village, with its well-established relationships with its neighborhood, Margaret Norrie organized the women into a War Service Bureau: "As one drive after another took place this group by its familiarity, each member with her own district, was able to bring to the citizens various messages the government desired brought to their attention."[41] But besides delivering messages for the government and selling war stamps and war bonds, Greenwich House also sold hot dinners to families in which the father was in the service and the mother working, started a day-care center for children, and through its War Service Bureau helped families cope with the military bureaucracy.

New Jobs for Women

As the war diverted the energies of middle-class clubwomen, social workers, and reformers into new channels, it also changed the lives of women wage earners. Opportunities for new jobs and higher pay opened for them. Four times as many women as before the war earned salaries above $1,800 a year. About a million women replaced men in industry.[42] Women substituted for men in all sorts of jobs, on trains and streetcars, in blast furnaces and foundries and refineries, in producing steel plate, high explosives, armaments, and plane parts. " [I]t took four pages of small type in a government publication to list those occupations in which, in varying degrees, women substituted for men in 1917 and 1918."[43]

WAR JOBS: WOMEN REPLACING MEN AT NEW YORK STOCK BOARDS. (NATIONAL ARCHIVES)

These new opportunities changed the lifestyles and the self-image of thousands of women. Domestic servants took factory jobs. Garment makers earned higher pay by shifting to assembling dangerous explosives. Typists rushed to Washington to work for the federal government. Other women abandoned clerical jobs or waitressing to take over "men's jobs" as trolley conductors,

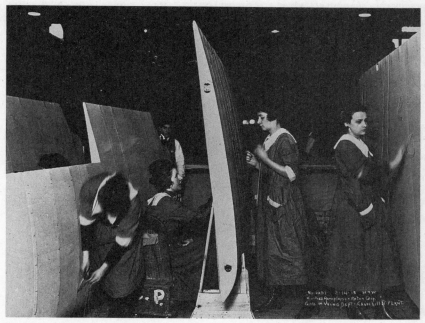

WAR JOBS: STRETCHING CLOTH TO AIRPLANE WINGS, BUFFALO, NEW YORK.
(NATIONAL ARCHIVES)

block house operators, draftsmen, and electrical repairmen.[44]

But during the war organizations like the Women's Trade Union League and the Consumer's League had to struggle against the exploitation of women workers. Employers argued that the war emergency necessitated ignoring or rescinding existing protective legislation. Agnes Nestor and her ilk had to remind the council of National Defense to include a labor representative on its Woman's Committee and Samuel Gompers to include women on the council's Committee on Labor. When Gompers appointed the wealthy Mrs. J. Borden Harriman chair of his Sub-Committee on Women in Industry, he sent a message that trade union women could no more count on his support during the war than earlier on.[45] Nor did the government show much concern for the welfare of women workers.

Many women workers, from laundresses to typists and teachers, took advantage of the labor shortages to look after themselves. Sometimes they cooperated with one another in unions, participating in the more than 6,000 wartime strikes. But more often they acted individually. If conditions didn't suit them, if their pay was too low, they simply quit and found a new job. Constant searching for better work made them upwardly mobile and economically more secure. Com-

WAR JOBS: THE ICEWOMAN COMETH.

(NATIONAL ARCHIVES)

panies paid a high price for the consequent labor turnover. General Electric, for instance, had to hire 125 women in one week to replace 25 operatives. Low-paying telephone companies experienced breakdowns of service.[46]

Black women made some gains. Most government agencies would not hire them as clerical workers, and those that did segregated them. Black women as a group remained marginal workers throughout the war and were the first to be fired after it. But even the meager opportunities the war afforded them, jobs that white women had vacated or would not take, made a difference. Paula Giddings comments,

WAR JOBS: WOMEN TRACKWALKERS, ERIE RAILROAD.   (NATIONAL ARCHIVES)

WAR JOBS: TESTING BLEACH IN AN ELECTROCHEMICAL COMPANY. (POSTER READS: "HALT THE HUN! BUY U.S. GOVERNMENT BONDS. THIRD LIBERTY LOAN.") (NATIONAL ARCHIVES)

For the first time, significant numbers of Black women were earning decent wages in the mainstream of the American labor force. In the metal industries they drilled, polished, punch- pressed, soldered; Black women also upholstered, tinned, and decorated lampshades. In laundries, most did the heavy work, but others used hand and machine irons. In the garment industry, some factories employed only Black women, who were allowed to take any position that needed to be filled. For the first time they were permitted to use machinery, and some even found jobs as clerks, stenographers, and bookkeepers.[47]

These new opportunities enabled them to maximize their earnings "by alternating between jobs as domestics and factory hands. Manufacturers bitterly complained about the high rate of absenteeism among black female wage earners. Whenever they could not make ends meet, they played hooky from their factory jobs and cleaned houses for more money."[48]

This movement of women workers, black or white, into better-paying jobs in industry sent the hopes of feminists sky-high. *Women Wanted: The Story Written in Blood Red Letters on the Horizon of the Great War* screamed the title of a book by Mabel Potter Daggett, prophesying a millennium in which postwar women's talents would be recognized and duly compensated. But the women war workers played out the same scenario later to be reprised by the Rosie the Riveters of World War II: Once the war was over, their services were no longer required. By 1919 most of their jobs had disappeared or reverted to their traditionally male holders. "The federal censuses of 1910 and 1920 show that the First World War primarily occasioned a shift within the female labor force, rather than a movement of non-wage earning women into categories of paid labor. In 1910, 8,075,722 females ten years of age and over were employed, whereas in 1920, there were 8,549,511, an increase of only 6.3 percent."[49]

What did make some permanent difference to women workers was the wartime movement of numbers of social workers and labor reformers into the federal government. By no means did all of them stay on after the war. But during the war women in various governmental agencies networked and fed one another information in the Women's Council that Mary van Kleeck organized. Under their influence the Woman in Industry Service created by the Department of Labor during the war developed into the postwar Women's Bureau, with van Kleeck as its first director.

Not only industry reacted to the pinch of the wartime manpower shortage and the proved competence of working women, but the military did also. In 1916, contemplating the probable lack of sufficient clerical staff if the United States entered the war, Secretary of the Navy Josephus Daniels asked the unthinkable question: Did any law prescribe that a yeoman be a man? That question led to the enlistment of 13,000 women in the navy and 300 in the Marine Corps. Known popularly as Yeomanettes and Marinettes, properly as Yeomen(F) and Women Marines, they literally did yeoman service. Almost all of them did clerical work, though others served as translators, draftsmen, fingerprint experts, camouflage designers, and recruiters. Almost all of them worked in the United States, most often in Washington, D.C. Some labored in munitions factories and some as radio electricians. Assigned to special duty, Yeomen(F) sold liberty bonds in theater aisles.

The whole operation was off the cuff and impromptu. Navy women were known simply as Yeomen until they reported for duty on shipboard when their names turned up on duty rosters, and the navy recognized the necessity of being able to identify its women, whom it certainly did not intend to take to sea. Even with Secretary Daniels's foresight, uniforms were not ready when after the declaration of war women rushed to volunteer for the service. The first pictures show the Yeomen(F) wearing borrowed men's jackets over their civilian skirts. Eventually they had their own uniforms, one white and one blue, fashioned after those of the navy's chief petty officers: Norfolk jackets with pleats front and back, gored skirts all the same height from the ground, black neckerchiefs over the jackets, black or white stockings depending on uniform color, high-buttoned

UNCLE SAM WANTED THEM—300 OF THEM FOR THE MARINE CORPS, AUGUST 1918.
(NATIONAL ARCHIVES)

or laced shoes, and stiff-brimmed "sailor" hats, blue felt for winter and straw for summer, with straps under the chin.

Marie Broglie joined up at 18. "Yes, there was a physical exam," she recalled. "Not too much of a one, I didn't think. They were very careful, because of the doctor, you know, and the girls in those days, everybody was very modest, so they put a sheet and held it while they examined. But they were awfully nice. And the nurse was right in attendance with the doctor."[50] She remembers her navy days as the best in her life; ever since she has been active in the American Legion. "If I were young," she remarked at age 85, "I would go in the navy today." She loved her clerical work and enjoyed the friends she made. Washington born and bred, she lived at home, and her mother let her bring other girls who lived in the barracks home on weekends. The navy raised no questions about enlisted women dating male officers, and she and her friends had a whirl. Saturdays they drilled, and lots of spectators turned out to watch. Joy Bright Hancock recalled learning to drill: "Sometimes there was sharp provocation for changing direction, as, for example, the time when we marched behind beautiful, high-spirited horses that had not been housebroken. After a particularly shabby parade performance, our instructor gave us explicit directions: 'You don't kick it, you don't jump over it, you step in it.'"[51]

Useful as the Yeomen(F) and Women Marines proved, the military did not intend to incorporate them into its peacetime forces. By August, 1919 all of them were off active duty, with no option to reenlist.

Binding Up the Wounds

Nurses were another story. Women have nursed in all American wars. The experience of the Spanish-American War and the persuasive powers of Dr. Anita Newcomb McGee, who had served in it, finally convinced the military of the inefficiency of the hodgepodge, ramshackle system of volunteers, relatives, and contract nurses on whom they had been relying. The Congress finally established the Army Nurse Corps in 1901 and the Navy Nurse Corps in 1908. But the military still was only edging toward recognizing its need of women, for these corps were auxiliaries rather than integral parts of its services. Placed in positions of life-and-death responsibility, the nurses were denied rank and its authority. The confusion about their status, Alma Lutz observed, "sometimes held up their pay, and led to neglect and unfair treatment in matters of transportation and leave. It often interfered with discipline as regards corpsmen. . . . It tended to lessen the respect of Medical Corps officers for the nurses, and in general they were regarded as civilians rather than soldiers."[52] And the Nurse Corps was tiny: At the beginning of the war the Army Nurse Corps had about 400 members on active duty and the navy 150. Another 8,000 registered with the Red Cross were considered reserve nurses for the armed forces.[53]

Yet by war's end 21,480 nurses had served in the Army Nurse Corps (thousands of them overseas) and 1,500 in the Navy Nurse Corps. Several thousand others worked by their side, but as Red Cross rather than military nurses. All in all, military needs preempted more than a third of all American nurses.

Demands for American nurses soared, not only because in wartime they must serve both American civilian and military needs, but also because of the shortage of nurses among the European Allies. France had traditionally depended upon nuns for professional nursing care, but quarrels between church and state had exiled most of them. When the war with its traumas and disease created millions of new patients, countries like France and Serbia and Russia were left almost literally without resources to treat them. To the rescue, long before the United States entered the war, went British and American nurses, the best trained in the world.

In the American military, in foreign medical services both civilian and military, with all sorts of relief agencies and private enterprises, American nurses served heroically. They risked their lives behind the lines as well as near the front. Some were wounded on duty, sheltering their patients, and others in their own beds. They worked beyond their training, beyond fatigue, beyond concern for danger, dirt, and despair. They acted as anesthetists. They assisted in surgery. In emergencies they themselves operated.

Nurse Florence Bullard, rushed to a French army hospital in an evacuated village near the front in March 1918, found herself in "a sort of coal-cellar, completely underground." She reported: "I have not seen daylight for eight days now and the stench in this cave is pretty bad: no air, artificial light, and the cots are so close together you can just get between them. Side by side I have Americans, English, Scotch, Irish, and French, and apart in the corners are *Boche*. They have to watch each other die side by side."[54]

American nurses, some as young as 21, twice daily changed the bandages of soldiers who screamed in agony at their touch. They endured the nauseating stench of gangrene. They watched men gasp for breath and die, their lungs destroyed by poison gas. They tended blind men, men with their faces half shot away, men who because of their disfigurements refused to see their families— victims of the head wounds so common in trench warfare. They worked in improvised Serbian "hospitals," almost without supplies and sanitary facilities, in territory held by the Serbs, then conquered by the Bulgarians. "Twelve hundred patients and we were only two surgeons, eight nurses and some five hospital orderlies!"[55] Overworked nurses had to ignore the doomed to care for the damned. "I used to tumble into bed at two or three o'clock in the morning," wrote Mary E. Gladwin, "and hear those men [in the ward next to her room]. They begged and prayed in all languages for help. They swore, they tore their bandages and the nights when I got up (it took all my strength of mind to stay in bed), I knew exactly what I would find when I went in,—the men in their agony tearing off the dressings, the dark streams of blood on the floor."[56]

In the long nightmarish watches of the night, in an alien land, amid un-imagined horrors, bearing alone the responsibility for the lives of her compatri-ots and of strangers some of whose languages she could not even speak, many an American woman had bitter cause to wonder what she and they were doing there. Olivia E. Hamilton wrote, "I cannot say that I want to see Germany 'crushed' at such a sacrifice. I would rather see the war end now, a tie. What ultimate good is it going to do to crush anyone, for doubtless in a hundred years or less, as it has always been, some new bugbear will arise, that the rest of the world will feel the need of vanquishing. Who knows but it may be one of the crushers of the present war."[57]

To the Rescue

Nurses were by no means the only American women to make the dangerous journey across an Atlantic infested with German submarines. Indeed they constituted fewer than half of the 25,000 women who from 1914–18 went to the aid of the participants in the war and its victims. An extraordinary phenomenon: For the first time in history, significant numbers of women traveled an immense distance to rescue foreign peoples enmeshed in a terrible war. The exodus started years before the United States was to enter the war.

The trickle with which it began swelled to a spate. At first women went singly or with a few companions, sponsored by small ad hoc committees or adventurously setting out on their own to meet whatever needs they discovered. As the war wore on and the numbers of its victims multiplied, the established clubs sent their emissaries to bind up wounds and succor refugees. With the entry of the United States into the war in April 1917, major organizations like the YWCA, the YMCA, and the American Red Cross swung into action. And the U.S. military discovered the need for more and more women overseas—not only technicians and clerks but also bilingual telephone operators.

The YMCA assumed major responsibility for providing American troops with rest and recreation in its huts and leave areas, usually with male YM secretaries in charge, but with women hostesses who actually ran the canteens— some 3,500 women in the course of the war (among whom the YMCA deigned to include only three of the many black women who volunteered).[58] They and the Salvation Army canteeners made gallons of hot chocolate and lemonade, baked thousands of pies, and fried hundreds of thousands of doughnuts. They answered the doughboys' requests to bake a shortcake for a man who had found some wild berries, to fry eggs bought on the local market. They learned, they said, that air cadets could not fly without pancakes for breakfast. Twenty-four of them jerked sodas in the only ice cream soda canteen in France.

In a thousand ways they tried to represent the absent mothers, sisters, sweethearts, and wives of the doughboys. Canteeners sewed on buttons and badges and altered ill-fitting uniforms and mended, some of them even carrying sewing machines with them. They administered first aid, especially in chiropody—everyone's feet hurt in a war. When the terrible Spanish flu epidemic erupted, and in the big military pushes, they nursed. They sang hymns and prayed at graveside services, for American troops, for Frenchmen and Belgians and Annamites, and for the German dead.

They operated banks to transmit servicemen's funds back home. They helped them shop for gifts for the home folks. They testified for men entangled in the military justice system and listened to soldiers' pledges of sobriety and their confidences. They kept money and mementos for men going over the top—to be sent home in case they did not return. They smiled "the eternal canteen smile." They looked at photographs "of most of the women of the United States of America."[59] Time and again they heard, "You look exactly like my wife/sister/mother."

The YMCA also sponsored most of the actors and lecturers who entertained the American Expeditionary Force overseas. On trails pioneered by the boister-

AMERICAN WOMEN PREPARING HOT CHOCOLATE FOR SOLDIERS "SOMEWHERE IN FRANCE." (NATIONAL ARCHIVES)

ous vaudevillian Elsie Janis, these entertainers, more than 500 of them women, trekked through France wherever they could find servicemen, performing on wagon beds, in market squares before cathedrals, on stages constructed of boxes of ammunition, at dusty crossroads platforms. Soldiers stood in deep mud or perched in trees to cheer them.

Elsie Janis swept into railroad stations on the engine's cowcatcher, cartwheeled across the platform, and shouted, "Boys, are we downhearted?" while they roared back, "Hell, no!" Musicians sang everything from grand opera to "If he can fight like he can love, then goodbye Germany." Elocutionist Cornelia Barnes recited her poem "Now That My Boy Has Gone to France," and Rheta Childe Dorr lectured on her recent trip to Russia in the throes of the Bolshevik revolution. Barnstorming actors put on *Macbeth* and Margaret Mayo's Broadway hit *Baby Mine*. Tsianina, daughter of a Cherokee Indian chief and sister of two soldiers, sang and danced in her traditional tribal modes. Neysa McMein, painter, illustrator, and famed party giver, entertained the troops by sketching, by flashlight, candlelight, or searchlight. She and her friends staged an original show, "Orlando Slum, a Man of Mystery," choosing soldiers in the audience to play Harold the Hero and Orlando the Man of Mystery; at the end "the vamping villainous lady spy" played by McMein "eats corn willy [a detested Army dish] and dies."[60] A merry lot, the entertainers enjoyed their tours, turned their adventures into amusing stories, and usually made light of the hardships and dangers they endured. But behind their smiles lurked the knowledge of what awaited the youngsters who cheered them. "It has been hard for me to sing today," wrote Mary Rochester, "realizing that many of these boys will be killed before this time tomorrow. Tears would come and the only way I managed to sing was to look over their heads and not into their faces. . . . If only I knew just the helpful things to say (or sing) to give them courage. I have felt so inadequate."[61]

The American Red Cross served abroad in a thousand different ways. Some overseas workers hated it; some loved it. Its semiofficial status granted it the ability to usurp the power of groups earlier on the scene. Women like the American novelist Edith Wharton detested the Red Cross takeover that came in 1917— Wharton, long a French resident, from 1914 until the entry of the United States had on her own initiative, with money she had raised and with the aid of her friends, succored literally thousands of suffering people. Other workers watched socialites volunteer at their own expense in Red Cross enterprises and condemned it as a rich person's resort. But the huge amounts of money the Red Cross raised, its status as a recruiter of nurses for military hospitals, and its control over shipping space meant that it could shelter under its doorman's umbrella all sorts of undertakings. The Red Cross had a finger in every pie; its people alleviated suffering, and treated and prevented disease among millions of war's victims.

The U.S. military, like every other American organization, depended heavily on women for its clerical work, stateside and overseas, whether military women or civilians. Without really thinking about military or civilian status, it also recruited into the Signal Corps in France a couple of hundred telephone operators, who thought of themselves as "the glamour girls of the AEF" and distinguished themselves by their ability to enable communication among the Allies, even in the face of all the difficulties presented by the French telephone system. Often when they answered the flashing lights on their switchboards with the traditional American "Number, please?" they heard the heartfelt response of American military men, "Thank God! You're here at last!" That gratitude, of course, did not persist after the war long enough for the telephone operators to be recognized as the military veterans they were; only after some of them waged an incredible 60-year battle were they acknowledged by the Congress in 1979 as having been members of the American military forces and awarded veterans' benefits.

Less persistent, or less fortunate, were the occupational and physical therapists, whose military status during World War I was equally ill defined. They were actually forging new professions, as well as pioneering as women in the armed forces. They were apparently included in the army's tables of organization as Reconstruction Aids. Woman after woman among them wrote of taking the oath of office, enlisting, being mobilized, serving overseas. Were they, or were they not, in the Army?[62]

They literally created their jobs as they went. Occupational therapist Mrs. Clyde McDowell Myres wrote of how she and her colleagues turned the wary antagonism of the previously all-male staff of an American military hospital in France into enthusiastic support: "Utilizing two large tin-cans, a little old rusty grate found in a deserted blacksmith shop, and salvaged bricks, we soon had a charcoal furnace for the heating of our soldering irons. From tin-cans, we made drain pipes and lined three huge six-foot tubs for dishwashing built by the patients; fashioned funnels, strainers, biscuit and doughnut cutters, and soap dishes. The eyes of the harassed Commanding Officer grew almost human. The kitchen sink had won him."[63]

In some degree World War I, in which the United States formally engaged for only a year and a half, affected the life of almost every American woman. For a surprising number, from physicians to artists, from librarians to recent college graduates converted into motor corps drivers and mechanics, it meant adventure and a completely new, if temporary, life-style, at home or overseas. For even more, it meant new vocational opportunities at higher pay, in factories or in the federal government—though most of these opportunities too proved ephemeral. For almost every woman, it meant a strengthening of her concept of herself as a citizen with responsibilities to her country, as during the course of the war private charities and government at all levels called on her to sacrifice her time, money, and energies, to invest in liberty bonds, even to regulate her diet for the public weal—or to "give" the life of her husband or son.

Source Notes

1. Helen Hooven Santmyer, " . . . and Ladies of the Club" (New York: Putnam's Sons, 1982), p. 106.
2. Elizabeth Hampsten, Read This Only to Yourself: The Private Writings of Midwestern Women, 1880–1910 (Bloomington: Indiana Univ. Press, 1982), p. 128.
3. Cynthia Grant Tucker, Prophetic Sisterhood: Liberal Women Ministers of the Frontier, 1880–1930 (Boston: Beacon Press, 1990), p. 216.
4. Quoted in Tucker, p. 216.
5. Alice Hamilton, Exploring the Dangerous Trades: The Autobiography of Alice Hamilton, M.D. (1943; reprint, Northeastern Univ. Press, 1985), p. 193.

6. Richard Hofstadter, *The Age of Reform from Bryan to F.D.R.* (New York: Vintage, 1955), p. 292.

7. William L. O'Neill, *Everyone Was Brave: The Decline and Fall of Feminism in America* (New Haven: Yale Univ. Press, 1967), p. 191.

8. Avis Berman, *Rebels on Eighth Street: Juliana Force and the Whitney Museum of American Art* (New York: Atheneum, 1990), p. 111.

9. Quoted in Joseph P. Lash, *Eleanor and Franklin: The Story of Their Relationship* (New York: Norton, 1971), p. 210.

10. Anna Howard Shaw, NAWSA Convention, Washington, D.C., December 12–15, 1917, Document 80 in Mari Jo Buhle and Paul Buhle, eds., *The Concise History of Woman Suffrage: Selections from the Classic Work of Stanton, Anthony, Gage, and Harper* (Urbana: Univ. of Illinois Press, 1978), p. 440.

11. Quoted in Rheta Childe Dorr, *A Woman of Fifty* (1924; reprint, Arno Press., 1980), p. 375.

12. Ida C. G. Clarke, *American Women and The World War* (New York: Appleton and Co., 1918,), p. 6.

13. Harriot Stanton Blatch and Alma Lutz, *Challenging Years: The Memoirs of Harriot Stanton Blatch* (1940; reprint, New York: Hyperion, 1976), p. 290.

14. Quoted in Mari Jo Buhle and Paul Buhle, eds., *The Concise History of Woman Suffrage: Selections from the Classic Work of Stanton, Anthony, Gage, and Harper* (Urbana: Univ. of Illinois Press, 1978), pp. 439–40.

15. O'Neill, p. 186.

16. Anna Howard Shaw, quoted in Buhle and Buhle, pp. 438–39.

17. Ida C. G. Clarke, pp. 187, 56, 268–69; Barbara J. Steinson, *American Women's Activism in World War I* (New York: Garland, 1982), p. 324.

18. Quoted in Buhle and Buhle, p. 439.

19. The absurdity of the fad for hand knitting was exposed by the struggle between the Woman's Section of the Navy League (WSNL) and Navy Secretary Josephus Daniels. The WSNL decided to supply every American warship in the European war zone or on active patrol with hand-knitted hoods, scarves, and wristlets. But Secretary Daniels, out of pique with the men of the Navy League on an unrelated matter, would accept nothing from WSNL, though he welcomed contributions from individuals not associated with it. Thereupon the WSNL sent 23,000 knitted garments a month to the navy in the name of Mildred Dewey, honorary leader of its Comforts Committee. The struggle continued for months, as more and more garments fell from the needles. It reached its ultimate absurdity when the WSNL acquired 10 sock-knitting machines to produce more of the socks that Daniels was refusing. Steinson, p. 334.

20. Charles Pack, *The War Garden Victorious* (Philadelphia, 1919), pp. 1, 15, 128, quoted by Richard Osborn Cummings in *The American and His*

Food: A History of Food Habits in the United States (1941; reprint, New York: Arno Press and *New York Times,* 1970), p. 139.

21. We have told their stories in *Into the Breach: American Women Overseas in World War I* (New York: Viking, 1991). Santmyer in *"... and Ladies of the Club"* relates how the town librarian, who could ill afford it, worked for nothing during the war.

22. These are described in Marion Talbot and Lois Kimball Mathews Rosenberry, *The History of the American Association of University Women, 1881–1931* (Boston: Houghton Mifflin, 1931).

23. Jacquelyn Dowd Hall, *Revolt Against Chivalry: Jessie Daniel Ames and the Women's Campaign Against Lynching* (New York: Columbia Univ. Press, 1979), p. 84.

24. Dolores Hayden, *The Grand Domestic Revolution: A History of Feminist Designs for American Homes, Neighborhoods, and Cities* (Cambridge, MIT Press, 1981), p. 224.

25. Steinson, pp. 212–13.

26. Quoted in O'Neill, pp. 189–90. In actuality the behavior of the AEF overseas vis-à-vis the French was so disgraceful that the American military had to declare Paris off limits.

27. Barbara Meil Hobson, *Uneasy Virtue: The Politics of Prostitution and the American Reform Tradition* (New York: Basic Books, 1987), p. 165.

28. The Chamberlain-Kahn Act of July 1918 authorized local boards of health to detain and examine any person thought to be a carrier of venereal disease. Hobson, p. 176.

29. Estelle B. Freedman, *Their Sisters' Keepers: Women's Prison Reform in America, 1830–1930* (Ann Arbor: Univ. of Michigan Press, 1981), p. 147. See also Hobson, pp. 165–67.

30. Hobson, p. 176.

31. Hobson, pp. 176–77. Rosen says (chap. 2) that by the end of the war 15,520 infected prostitutes had been imprisoned in detention homes for an average of 70 days and in reformatories for an average of 365 days. Ruth Rosen, *The Lost Sisterhood: Prostitution in America, 1900–1918* (Baltimore: Johns Hopkins Univ. Press, 1982).

32. Hobson, p. 170.

33. Hall, p. 35.

34. Rosen, chap 2.

35. Hobson, p. 166.

36. Ibid., pp. 175–79.

37. O'Neill, p. 217.

38. Ida C. G. Clarke, p. 98.

39. O'Neill, p. 205.

40. Elizabeth Israels Perry, *Belle Moskowitz: Feminine Politics and the Exercise of Power in the Age of Alfred E. Smith* (New York: Oxford Univ. Press, 1987), p. 119.
41. Mary K. Simkhovitch, *Neighborhood: My Story of Greenwich House* (New York: Norton, 1938), pp. 186–87.
42. O'Neill, p. 188.
43. Eleanor Flexner, *Century of Struggle: The Woman's Rights Movement in the United States* (Cambridge, Mass.: Belknap Press of Harvard Univ. Press, 1968), p. 288.
44. Maurine Weiner Greenwald, *Women, War, and Work: The Impact of World War I on Women Workers in the United States* (Westport, Conn.: Greenwood Press, 1980), pp. 3, 31.
45. O'Neill, p. 196.
46. Greenwald, pp. 38–41.
47. Paula Giddings, *When and Where I Enter: The Impact of Black Women on Race and Sex in America* (New York: Bantam Books, 1984), p. 143.
48. Greenwald, p. 23.
49. Ibid., p. 13.
50. Personal interview with the authors, March 16, 1985.
51. Joy Bright Hancock, *Lady in the Navy: A Personal Reminiscence* (Annapolis: Naval Institute Press, 1972), p. 25.
52. Alma Lutz, coll. and ed., *With Love, Jane: Letters from American Women on the War Fronts* (New York: John Day, 1945), pp. 194–95.
53. Vern L. Bullough and Bonnie Bullough, *The Care of the Sick: The Emergence of Modern Nursing* (New York: Prodist [a division of Neale Watson Academic Publications], 1978), p. 174.
54. Quoted in Frank Freidel, *Over There: The Story of America's First Great Overseas Crusade* (Boston: Little, Brown, 1964), pp. 266–67.
55. Mabel T. Boardman, *Under the Red Cross Flag at Home and Abroad* (Philadelphia: Lippincott, 1915), p. 208.
56. Quoted in Lavinia L. Dock, Sarah Elizabeth Pickett, Clara D. Noyes, Fannie F. Clement, Elizabeth G. Fox, and Anna R. Van Meter, *History of American Red Cross Nursing* (New York: Macmillan, 1922), p. 179.
57. Olivia E. Hamilton Papers, pp. 21–22, Schlesinger Library, Radcliffe College.
58. In justice it must be said that only the YMCA sent any black women abroad. But 200,000 black male troops served overseas.
59. Eleanor Barnes, "Overseas Women—In the Memory of One," in Helene M. Sillia, ed., *Lest We Forget . . ., A History of Women's Overseas Service League* (n.p., 1978), p. 237.
60. James W. Evans and Gardner L. Harding, *Entertaining the American Army: The American Stage and Lyceum in the World War* (New York: Association Press, 1921), pp. 97–100.

61. Mary Louise Rochester Roderick, *A Nightingale in the Trenches* (New York: Vantage, 1966), p. 184.

62. As Mrs. Clyde McDowell Myres wrote, "We were nondescripts. We were pioneers going out with hardly the military status of scrubwomen." Laura B. Hoppin, ed., *History of the World War Reconstruction Aides: Being an account of the activities and whereabouts of Physio Therapy and Occupational Therapy Aides who served in U.S. Army Hospitals in the United States and in France during the World War* (Milbrook, N.Y.: W. Tydsley, 1933), p. 76.

63. Quoted in Hoppin, pp. 76–77.

CHAPTER 10

Legacy

The zestful, yeasty Progressive Era held out the promise of a fairer, more democratic society. Ambition, application, thrift, and lashings of elbow grease, many Americans believed, could turn today's hard times into tomorrow's prosperity. Good will and intelligent politicking could pass laws and institute reforms that would reduce inequities and injustices. Carrie Chapman Catt was not alone in her belief in social evolution. Progressivists lived with hope and with faith in a better future.

No matter when they arrived in the United States, Americans always have moved around a lot, both literally and figuratively. The Progressive Era accelerated the pace. Black people, with black women in the forefront, moved from southern farms to southern small towns to southern cities to northern cities: Between 1900 and 1920 the black population of the Northeast almost doubled, and in the north central and western states it increased by 60 percent. Their northward move was also economically upward: In northern cities some women earned more in one month than they had ever seen at one time.[1]

Of the European immigrants surging into the nation during these years, about a third stayed in New York City, but two-thirds pressed on, fanning out across the nation. Exhausted by the voyage across the Atlantic and by their uncertainty about being admitted at Ellis Island, bewildered in a strange land, they climbed on trains, to join relatives in a mysterious place called Chicago, to farm the rich land of Minnesota, to build sod huts on the Nebraska prairie, or to cross the vast expanses of the United States to the Far West.[2] Wherever they alighted, most immigrants sought better lives, for themselves, for their children.

The prospect of upward mobility was equally an article of faith among the native-born white population. Seeking it, large numbers of them moved, and moved again, women and men alike. Farm families moved to small towns; young people from small towns sought their fortunes in the cities; city dwellers took refuge in the peace and quiet of the countryside, transforming it into suburbia.

Of course some were stuck. Women were stuck all their lives scrabbling a bare living on a subsistence-level farm, with a new baby arriving every couple of years. Little girls put to work for 12 hours a day in cotton mills never learned of another way of life, let alone developed the energy to extricate themselves before they coughed their lungs out. Young women unlucky enough to become pregnant without a wedding ring were ostracized and doomed to degradation by an unforgiving society.

But poor people, as well as their luckier compatriots, shifted from place to place, job to job, now washing clothes, now running a boardinghouse, now prospecting for gold, now claiming a homestead—always aspiring.

Re-forming America

The optimistic, can-do spirit of the age inspired many well-to-do and middle-class women to improve the lot of others. Even desperately poor women lifted as they climbed. Amazing black women founded schools that changed the lives of thousands of children. Overworked, ill-nourished factory girls organized unions. Today one's hometown, tomorrow one's own state, next week the whole country could be spruced up, spring-cleaned, polished, and perfected.

Visions like these, whether for the prosperity of their own lives or for the welfare of the country, filled the heads of millions of American women. Human nature, certainly human behavior, they believed, could be changed for the better, by education, reform, improved housing, healthier working conditions, and large dollops of goodwill. They knew the recipe, and they could point with pride to the results they achieved when they followed it, from hot lunches for schoolchildren to rehabilitation for women prisoners.

These women used as their main instrument for the reform of society their heritage from their mothers, women's networks, informal or organized. But where their mothers had focused on educating and improving themselves and their families, Progressive Era women turned their gaze outward toward their communities and nation. There they found much to improve.

To this end they geometrically increased their numbers. They enlarged the membership of the clubs and societies to which their mothers had belonged, and they founded new associations. Then they meshed these organizations together nationally into large federations and linked one kind of organization to another through their own multiple memberships. This all happened spontaneously, without blueprints, as women convinced by experience that in union they had strength founded new groups for new purposes.

Sometimes, of course, all this proliferation produced duplication of effort, jealousy, and jurisdictional disputes. Women struggled for control within organizations. In Oregon Abigail Duniway fought epic battles with eastern suffragists. During World War I the National League for Woman's Service competed bitterly with the Woman's Committee of the Council for National Defense to coordinate women's volunteer war activities; neither succeeded.

But the organizational network also meant that women always knew where to go to get support for their projects. At will they could rally huge numbers. So in 1920 when the brand-new League of Women Voters proposed a Women's Joint Congressional Committee to forward legislative matters of special concern to women, they could quickly convene representatives of the General Federation of Women's Clubs, the National Council of Women, the Women's Christian Temperance Union, the National Women's Trade Union League, the National Congress of Mothers and Parent-Teacher Associations, the National Consumers' League, the American Home Economics Association, the National Federation of Business and Professional Women, and the American Collegiate Association. These organizations represented factory workers, department store workers, stenographers and file clerks, teachers, home economists, social workers, settlement workers and reformers, as well as millions of women who thought of themselves first as wives and mothers.

In this way women beat a new path to power. Only rarely, and then with little success, did they invade the traditionally masculine upper realms of political and economic power. Instead they cleverly exercised in the public sphere the moral suasion for which the 19th century had always praised them. Turning their attention, and their organizations, away from the self-education and the self-improvement for which their mothers had united, women in the Progressive Era flexed their moral and organizational muscles and did their effective best to make society behave.

Exercising Power

In their own organizations and in the society that those organizations helped to change so drastically, women enjoyed power, a distinctive kind of power. It worked well in part because women preserved a sense of themselves as women, different by nature from men. They based their power firmly on their traditional roles as nurturers and housekeepers, a kind of universally acknowledged "truth" that few dared challenge. They were, after all, just doing their duty, according to the lights that society had assigned them. Men might ridicule or groan, but they didn't feel threatened. As for the women themselves, they gained self-confidence, confirmed as finer, more sensitive, morally superior beings.

Suffrage was another matter—a clear invasion of men's sphere, a threat to men's political power. To win it, even the middle-of-the-road women in the National American Woman Suffrage Association adopted men's political techniques, lobbying, distributing propaganda, issuing press releases, parading.

Women like Alice Paul and Crystal Eastman, of course, went even further, picketing and demonstrating. To their methods other women reacted with horror, some men with cruelty and physical violence.

Among them all, the gentle and the bold, the persuasive and the confrontational, American women won the suffrage, slowly, painfully, at great expense of time, energy, patience, and personal suffering, against the active opposition of industry, many unions, and the economic and political establishments. Despite the female antisuffragists, women were more united in the suffrage movement than at any other time in American history.

The suffrage won, the coalition dissolved, and women reverted to working for the causes that had originally made them want the vote. They used the ballot, and through the new League of Women Voters they powerfully urged other women to use it. But they also held on to their own established organizations, which they could control, as their instruments of choice for political power.

Despite the call of Eleanor Roosevelt and Molly "More Women" Dewson for women to work within the political parties, the rank and file of activist women chose instead to work within their own organizations. For every woman who joined Alice Paul's Woman's Party in its support for the Equal Rights Amendment, a hundred or more carried on in the 1920s and 1930s the push for more reforms in the tradition of the Progressive Era.[3] Those few women who committed their lives to politics did so less to advance their own careers than to improve society. Down into the days of Roosevelt's New Deal, women reformers "constitute[d] a human bridge joining the indirect political influence of the settlement-house generation with the formal political practice of a reform administration in the 1930s."[4]

GREAT EXPECTATIONS. WOMEN GET THE NEWS THAT THEY HAVE WON THE VOTE. (NEW YORK PUBLIC LIBRARY PHOTO FILES)

Critics may cavil at the outcome of woman suffrage. Indeed many woman suffragists were disappointed, like Alice Stone Blackwell, who commented that not much had come from the ballot, "women being fools because God made them to match the men."[5] Of course woman suffrage has not transformed the United States into Eden, any more than it has led to the "communism, free love, and the nationalization of women" predicted by the antisuffragist organ the *Remonstrance*.[6] Nor do women typically vote as a block. To complain that the proponents of woman suffrage could not deliver on the prophecies some of them made in the heat of their campaign is naive. To assess the value of the suffrage, American women today need only ask themselves whether they would willingly give up the degree of control over society, their bodies, and their lives, that their votes represent.

The Quality of Life

Thanks in part to science and industry, in part to the spirit of the Progressive Era, and in large part to the women who lived in it, life was better for more American women in 1920 than it had been in 1900.

In 1900 many women's reproductive lives had sentenced them to the suffering, well-founded terror, and economic disaster of annual or biennial childbirth. By 1920 the birth control movement was beginning to deliver to poor women the contraceptive information that had been arbitrarily denied them, and twilight sleep was erasing the memory of childbirth pain for wealthier women. Women's health was improving as they discarded hobbling clothes and exercised more, replacing the image of the swooning, suffering victim with the ideal of the vigorous, self-confident New Woman.

Keeping house was easier in 1920, for the streets were cleaner, heating and cooking systems made less mess, electricity ran the household appliances that were dropping in price, and factory-prepared food saved time and energy. Fewer children meant lighter housework.

Fewer children also meant more time for mothers to spend with their children. Far fewer mothers had to see their children drooping from the fatigue of factory labor or crippled by dangerous machinery. Mothers enjoyed the mixed blessing of hearing from newly developed "experts" about how to raise healthier, better-educated children.

At work, women did better in 1920 than in 1900. Women in blue-collar jobs labored a little more safely, for fewer hours and at higher pay, thanks to their own efforts at organizing, the support of the Women's Trade Union League and the Consumers' League, the protective legislation that women's organizations had initiated and won, and the federal Women's Bureau that they had demanded. More opportunities were open to women who needed to earn money, in particular the millions of clerical jobs. Social workers, home economists, nurses, and teachers had professionalized themselves, setting themselves higher standards of education and performance.

Throughout most of the Progressive Era, women retained an acute sense of themselves as women, different from men, able to do some things men could not do, in some ways better than men. They defined themselves first as women. They associated themselves in groups with other women. And as women, they changed their world—and ours.

As women they learned to use the power of government to effect social and economic reform. Few of them, aside from Emma Goldman and the bohemians of Greenwich Village, wanted revolution. Almost all of the activists worked within the system to improve it.

They engaged in political action, lobbying, building spheres of influence, exerting political pressure through their organizations. But they had yet to penetrate the power structure of the political parties.

They learned to protect themselves as workers by invoking the powers of government, through protective legislation. But despite the Women's Trade Union League, the Consumer's League, and strikes like the Rising of the 20,000, women still had miles to go in unionization and labor negotiation.

They tackled social ills. Against problems like child labor they triumphantly advanced. But their attack on prostitution left prostitutes worse off than in the 19th century. And women barely recognized racism and nativism.

They evolved new ways of thinking about woman's sexuality, woman's relationship to the family, and motherhood—ways that weakened the ideal of woman as sacrificial saint and strengthened the concept of woman as individual.

They laid the groundwork for an equal rights amendment (proposed by Alice Paul in 1923). But activist women split over its underlying theory, asking questions still unresolved: With their unique capability of bearing children, do women need special protective legislation? Does protective legislation hamper women more than it helps them? Can women reconcile familial, economic, and public roles? In short, can women and men cooperate and compete on equal terms?

By the end of the Progressive Era, women were beginning to abandon the concept of woman's special virtue, which set her aside from or on a pedestal above men. Women's conduct in World War I brought the concept into question for pacifists like Jane Addams. And supporters of an equal rights amendment found it a handicap, since it conflicted with the idea of women's equality.

In area after area, risk-taking women had gained more control and more confidence. They had moved from women who shouldn't to women who could.

Source Notes

1. Florette Henri, *Black Migration: Movement North, 1900–1920* (Garden City, N.Y.: Anchor Press/Doubleday, 1975), p. viii.
2. For a notable description of an immigrant train, see (or rather, hear) Robert Louis Stevenson, *The Amateur Emigrant,* narrated by Donal Donnelly (Charlotte Hall, Md.: Recorded Books, n.d.).
3. Elisabeth Israels Perry notes that this concentration on causes other than feminism was reflected in the ambitions and ideals of individual women engaged in politics: ". . . the few models of successful political women available to younger women in the 1920s were women involved in politics less for the purpose of advancing their own careers than to promote ideals and programs." *Belle Moskowitz: Feminine Politics and the Exercise of Power in the Age of Alfred E. Smith* (New York: Oxford Univ. Press, 1987), p. xi.
4. William H. Chafe, *The Paradox of Change: American Women in the 20th Century* (New York: Oxford Univ. Press, 1991), pp. 36, 43. Carole Nichols makes an interesting argument that a correct assessment of the impact of women's voting depends on an evaluation of their achievements on the local and state levels. *Votes and More for Women: Suffrage and After in Connecticut* (New York: Haworth Press, 1983), p. 2. See also Anne Firor Scott's discussion of the postwar struggle in southern states to secure better child labor laws. *The Southern Lady: From Pedestal to Politics, 1830–1930* (Chicago: Univ. of Chicago Press, 1972), p. 188.
5. Robert Booth Fowler, *Carrie Catt: Feminist Politician* (Boston: Northeastern Univ. Press, 1986), p. 155.
6. William L. O'Neill, *Everyone Was Brave: The Decline and Fall of Feminism in America* (Chicago: Quadrangle Books, 1969), p. 228.

Bibliography

Abbott, Shirley. *Womenfolks: Growing Up Down South*. New Haven: Ticknor and Fields, 1983.

Abramovitz, Mimi. *Regulating the Lives of Women: Social Welfare Policy from Colonial Times to the Present*. Boston: South End Press, 1988.

Adams, Judith A. *The American Amusement Park Industry: A History of Technology and Thrills*. New York: Twayne, 1991.

Addams, Jane. *My Friend, Julia Lathrop*. New York: Macmillan, 1935.

———. *The Second Twenty Years at Hull House, September 1909 to September 1929*. New York: Macmillan, 1930.

———. *Twenty Years at Hull House, with Autobiographical Notes*. New York: Macmillan, 1924.

Addams, Jane, Emily G. Balch, and Alice Hamilton. *Women at the Hague: The International Congress of Women and Its Results*. 1915. Reprint. New York: Garland, 1972.

Akins, Zoe. *Cake Upon the Waters*. New York: Century, 1919.

Alland, Alexander, Sr. *Jessie Tarbox Beals, First Woman News Photographer*. New York: Camera/Graphic Press, 1978.

Allen, Frederick Lewis. *The Big Change*. New York: Harper, 1952.

Amott, Teresa, and Julie Matthaei. *Race, Gender, and Work: A Multicultural Economic History of Women in the United States*. Boston: South End Press, 1991.

Anderson, Harriet. "Woman." *Atlantic Monthly* 110 (August 1912):182.

Anderson, Margaret. *My Thirty Years' War: The Autobiography: Beginnings and Battles to 1930*. New York: Horizon Press, 1969.

Andre, Rae. *Homemakers: The Forgotten Workers*. Chicago: Univ. of Chicago Press, 1981.

Antler, Joyce. *The Educated Woman and Professionalization: The Struggle for a New Feminine Identity, 1890–1920*. New York: Garland, 1987.

———. *Lucy Sprague Mitchell: The Making of a Modern Woman*. New Haven: Yale Univ. Press, 1987.

Applegate, Shannon. *Skookum: An Oregon Pioneer Family's History and Lore*. New York: William Morrow, 1988.

Armitage, Susan, and Elizabeth Jameson, eds. *The Women's West*. Enid: Univ. of Oklahoma Press, 1987.

Arnold, Mary Ellicott, and Mabel Reed. *In the Land of the Grasshopper Song*. 1957. Reprint. Lincoln: Univ. of Nebraska Press, 1980.

Asbury, Herbert. *The Great Illusion: An Informal History of Prohibition.* Garden City, N.Y.: Doubleday, 1950.

Ashe, Elizabeth. *Intimate Letters from France during America's First Year of War.* San Francisco: Philopolis Press, 1918.

Atherton, Gertrude. *The Californians.* 1898. Reprint. Ridgewood N.J.: Gregg Press, 1968.

Austin, Mary. *Earth Horizon.* Boston: Houghton Mifflin, 1932.

————. *A Woman of Genius.* 1912. Reprint. Old Westbury, N.Y.: Feminist Press, 1985.

The Autobiography of a Happy Woman. 1915. Reprint. New York: Arno Press, 1974.

Ayer, Harriet Hubbard. *Harriet Hubbard Ayer's Book: A Complete and Authentic Treatise on the Laws of Health and Beauty.* 1902. Reprint. New York: Arno Press, 1974.

Baker, Estelle. *The Rose Door.* Chicago: Charles H. Kerr, 1911.

Banes, Ruth A. "Doris Ulmann and Her Mountain Folk,." *Journal of American Culture: Studies of a Civilization* 8 (Spring, 1985):29–42.

Banta, Martha. *Imaging American Women: Idea and Ideals in Cultural History.* New York: Columbia Univ. Press, 1987.

Barker-Benfield, G. J., and Catherine Clinton. *Portraits of American Women.* 2 vols. New York: St. Martin's, 1991.

Barrows, Esther G. *Neighbors All: A Settlement Notebook.* Boston: Houghton Mifflin, 1929.

Bataille, Gretchen M., and Kathleen Mullen Sands. *American Indian Women, Telling Their Lives.* Lincoln: Univ. of Nebraska Press, 1984.

Baum, Charlotte, Paula Hyman, and Sonya Michel. *The Jewish Woman in America.* New York: Dial, 1976.

Beam, Lura. *He Called Them by the Lightning: A Teacher's Odyssey in the Negro South, 1908–1919.* New York: Bobbs-Merrill, 1967.

Berk, Richard A., and Sarah Fenstermaker Berk. *Labor and Leisure at Home: Content and Organization of the Household Day.* Beverly Hills: Sage Publications, 1979.

Berman, Avis. *Rebels on Eighth Street: Juliana Force and the Whitney Museum of American Art.* New York: Atheneum, 1990.

Betts, Lillian Williams. *The Leaven in a Great City.* New York: Dodd, Mead, 1902.

Birmingham, Stephen. *The Grandes Dames.* New York: Simon and Schuster, 1982.

Birney, Mrs. Theodore. "The Twentieth-Century Girl: What We Expect of Her." *Harper's Bazaar* 33 (May 26, 1900): 224–27.

Black, Martha Louise. *My Ninety Years.* Edited by Flo Whyard. Anchorage: Alaska Northwest, 1976.

Blair, Karen J. *The Clubwoman as Feminist: True Womanhood Defined, 1868–1914*. New York: Holmes and Meier, 1980.

Blatch, Harriot Stanton. *Mobilizing Woman Power*. New York: Women's Press, 1918.

Blatch, Harriot Stanton, and Alma Lutz. *Challenging Years: The Memoirs of Harriot Stanton Blatch*. 1940. Reprint. New York: Hyperion, 1976.

Blewett, Mary H. *The Last Generation: Work and Life in the Textile Mills of Lowell, Massachusetts, 1910–1960*. Boston: Univ. of Massachusetts Press, 1991.

————. *Men, Women, and Work: Class, Gender, and Protest in the New England Shoe Industry, 1780–1910*. Urbana: Univ. of Illinois Press, 1988.

Blocker, Jack S., Jr. *Retreat from Reform: The Prohibition Movement in the United States, 1890–1913*. Westport, Conn.: Greenwood Press, 1976.

Blumberg, Dorothy Rose. *Florence Kelley: The Making of a Social Pioneer*. New York: Augustus M. Kelley, 1966.

Boardman, Mabel T. *Under the Red Cross Flag at Home and Abroad*. Philadelphia: Lippincott, 1915.

Bodnar, John, Roger Simon, and Michael Weber. *Lives of Their Own: Blacks, Italians, and Poles in Pittsburgh, 1900–1960*. Urbana: Univ. of Illinois Press, 1982.

Bordin, Ruth. *Woman and Temperance: The Quest for Power and Liberty, 1873–1900*. Philadelphia: Temple Univ. Press, 1981.

Boris, Eileen, and Cynthia R. Daniels, eds. *Homework: Historical and Contemporary Perspectives on Paid Labor at Home*. Chicago: Univ. of Illinois Press, 1991.

Brandon, Ruth. *The New Women and the Old Men: Love, Sex and the Woman Question*. New York: Norton, 1990.

Breckinridge, Mary. *Wide Neighborhoods: A Story of the Frontier Nursing Service*. New York: Harper, 1952.

Bristow, Edward J. *Prostitution and Prejudice: The Jewish Fight Against White Slavery, 1870–1939*. New York: Schocken Books, 1983.

Brooks, Thomas R. *Toil and Trouble: A History of American Labor*. New York: Delta, 1971.

Brooks, Van Wyck. *The Confident Years, 1885–1915*. New York: Dutton, 1952.

Brough, James. *Princess Alice: A Biography of Alice Roosevelt Longworth*. Boston: Little, Brown, 1975.

Brown, Dee. *The Gentle Tamers: Women in the Old Wild West*. Lincoln: Univ. of Nebraska Press, 1958.

Brown, Dorothy M. *Mabel Walker Willebrandt*. Knoxville: Univ. of Tennessee Press, 1984.

Brown, Harriet Connor. *Grandmother Brown's Hundred Years, 1827–1927*. New York: Little, Brown,, 1929.

Brown, Milton W. *American Painting from the Armory Show to the Depression.* Princeton, N.J.: Princeton Univ. Press, 1955.

———. *The Story of the Armory Show.* Washington, D.C.: The Joseph H. Hirshhorn Foundation, ca. 1963.

Bruns, Roger A. *The Damndest Radical: The Life and World of Ben Reitman, Chicago's Celebrated Social Reformer, Hobo King, and Whorehouse Physician.* Urbana: Univ. of Illinois Press, 1987.

Bryn Mawr, Class of 1907. "Carola Woerishoffen, Her Life and Work." Bryn Mawr, 1912.

Buechler, Steven M. *The Transformation of the Woman Suffrage Movement: The Case of Illinois, 1850–1920.* New Brunswick, N.J.: Rutgers Univ. Press, 1986.

Buell, Jennie. *One Woman's Work for Farm Women: The Story of Mary A. Mayo's Part in Rural Social Movements.* Boston: Whitcomb and Barrows, 1908.

Buffum, Herbert E., Ira Warren, William Thorndike, A. T. Lovering, A. E. Small, J. Heber Smith and Charles P. Lyman, *The Household Physician: A Twentieth Century Medica.* Boston: Woodruff, 1905, 1919.

Buhle, Mari Jo, and Paul Buhle, eds. *The Concise History of Woman Suffrage: Selections from the Classic Work of Stanton, Anthony, Gage, and Harper.* Urbana: Univ. of Illinois Press, 1978.

Buhler-Wilkerson, Karen. *False Dawn: The Rise and Decline of Public Health Nursing, 1900–1935.* New York: Garland, 1990.

———, ed. *Nursing and the Public's Health: An Anthology of Sources.* New York: Garland, 1989.

Bullough, Vern L. *The Subordinate Sex: A History of Attitudes Toward Women.* Urbana: Univ. of Illinois Press, 1973.

Bullough, Vern L., and Bonnie Bullough. *The Care of the Sick: The Emergence of Modern Nursing.* New York: Prodist (a division of Neale Watson Academic Publications), 1978.

Bunner, Henry Cuyler. *The Suburban Sage: Stray Notes and Comments on his Simple Life.* 1896. Reprint. Freeport N.Y.: Books for Libraries Press, 1969.

Bushman, Claudia, ed. *Mormon Sisters: Women in Early Utah.* Cambridge, Mass.: Emmeline Press, 1976.

Byerly, Victoria. *Hard Times, Cotton Mill Girls: Personal Histories of Womanhood and Poverty in the South.* Ithaca, N.Y.: ILR Press, 1986.

Byington, Margaret F. *Homestead, The Households of a Mill Town.* 1910. Reprint. Pittsburgh: The University Center for International Studies, Univ. of Pittsburgh, 1974.

Calhoun, Arthur W. *A Social History of the American Family from Colonial Times to the Present.* 3 vols. Cleveland: Arthur H. Clark, 1919.

Camhi, Jane Jerome. "Women Against Women: American Antisuffragism, 1880–1920." Ph.D. dissertation, Tufts Univ., 1973.

Campbell, Barbara Kuhn. *The "Liberated" Woman of 1914: Prominent Women in the Progressive Era*. Ann Arbor: Univ. of Michigan Research Press, 1979.

Cashman, Sean Dennis. *Prohibition: The Lie of the Land*. New York: Free Press, 1981.

Cather, Willa. *The Song of the Lark*. Boston: Houghton Mifflin, 1915.

Chafe, William H. *The Paradox of Change: American Women in the 20th Century*. New York: Oxford Univ. Press, 1991.

Chambers, Clarke A. *Paul U. Kellogg and The Survey: Voices for Social Welfare and Social Justice*. Minneapolis: Univ. of Minnesota Press, 1971.

Chopin, Kate. *The Awakening*. 1899. Reprint. New York: Avon Books, 1972.

Christian, Barbara. *Black Women Novelists: The Development of a Tradition, 1892–1976*. Westport, Conn.: Greenwood Press, 1980.

Churchill, Allen. *The Improper Bohemians*. New York: Dutton, 1959.

Clark, Judith Freeman. *Almanac of American Women in the 20th Century*. New York: Prentice-Hall, 1987.

Clark, Sue Ainslie, and Edith Wyatt. "Working-Girls' Budgets." *McClure's* 35 (October 1910): 595–614.

Clarke, Ida C. G. *American Women and the World War*. New York: Appleton, 1918.

Clarke, Robert. *Ellen Swallow: The Woman Who Founded Ecology*. New York: Follett, 1973.

Cleaveland, Agnes Morley. *No Life for a Lady*. 1920. Reprint. Lincoln: Univ. of Nebraska Press, 1988.

Cohen, Rose. *Out of the Shadow*. New York: Doran, 1918.

Cole, Margaret. "The Woman's Vote: What Has It Achieved?" *Political Quarterly* 33 (January 1962):74–83.

Coles, Robert. *Dorothy Day, A Radical Devotion*. Reading, Mass.: Addison-Wesley, 1987.

Collins, Elizabeth. *The Cattle Queen of Montana*. Spokane, Wash.: Dyer Printing, 1914.

Colvin, D. Leigh. *Prohibition in the United States: A History of the Prohibition Party and of the Prohibition Movement*. New York: Doran, 1926.

Commander, Lydia Kingsmill. *The American Idea*. 1907. Reprint. New York: Arno Press, 1972.

Connolly, Mark Thomas. *The Response to Prostitution in the Progressive Era*. Chapel Hill: Univ. of North Carolina Press, 1980.

Converse, Florence. *The Children of Light*. Boston: Houghton Mifflin, 1912.

Conway, Jill K. *The First Generation of American Women Graduates*. New York: Garland, 1987.

Cook, Blanche Wiesen. *Eleanor Roosevelt, 1884–1933*. New York: Viking, 1992.

Corey, Elizabeth. *Bachelor Bess: The Homesteading Letters of Elizabeth Corey, 1909–1919*. Edited by Philip L. Gerber. Iowa City: Univ. of Iowa Press, 1990.

Coss, Clare, ed. *Lillian D. Wald, Progressive Activist*. New York: Feminist Press, 1989.

Cott, Nancy, ed. *A Woman Making History: Mary Ritter Beard Through Her Letters*. New Haven: Yale Univ. Press, 1991.

Coughlin, Ellen K. Untitled article in the *Chronicle of Higher Education* (Jan. 23, 1991).

Cowan, Ruth Schwartz. *More Work for Mother: The Ironies of Household Technology from the Open Hearth to the Microwave*. New York: Basic Books, 1983.

Crary, Margaret. *Susette La Flesche—Voice of the Omaha Indians*. New York: Hawthorn Books, 1973.

Croswell, F. Elizabeth. "The Midwives of New York." *Charities and the Commons* 17 (1907):667.

Crow, Martha Foote. *The American Country Girl*. 1915. Reprint. New York: Arno Press, 1974.

Crunden, Robert. *Ministers of Reform: The Progressives' Achievement in American Civilization: 1889–1920*. New York: Basic Books, 1982.

Cummings, Richard Osborn. *The American and His Food: A History of Food Habits in the United States*. 1941. Reprint. New York: Arno Press and the *New York Times*, 1970.

Dana, Nathalie. *Young in New York: A Memoir of a Victorian Girlhood*. Garden City, N.Y.: Doubleday, 1963.

Dash, Joan. *A Life of One's Own. Three Gifted Women and the Men They Married*. 1973. Reprint. New York: Paragon House, 1988.

Davies, Margery W. *Woman's Place Is at the Typewriter: Office Work and Office Workers, 1870–1930*. Philadelphia: Temple Univ. Press, 1982.

Davis, Allen F. *Spearheads for Reform: The Social Settlements and the Progressive Movement, 1890–1914*. New York: Oxford Univ. Press, 1967.

Davis, Lenwood G. *The Black Woman in American Society*. Boston: G. K. Hall, 1975.

Degen, Mary Louise. *The History of the Women's Peace Party*. 1939. Reprint. New York: Burt Franklin Reprints, 1974.

Degler, Carl N. *At Odds: Women and the Family in America from the Revolution to the Present*. New York: Oxford Univ. Press, 1980.

Deland, Margaret. *The Awakening of Helena Richie*. New York: A. L. Burt, 1906.

———. "The Change in the Feminine Ideal." *Atlantic Monthly* 105 (March, 1910):289–302.

———. *The Iron Woman*. New York: Harper and Bros., 1911.

de Mille, Agnes. *Portrait Gallery*. New York: Houghton Mifflin, 1990.

de Wolfe, Elsie. *After All*. 1935. Reprint. New York: Arno Press, 1974.

Ditzion, Sidney. *Marriage, Morals and Sex in America: A History of Ideas*. New York: Octagon Books, 1969.

Dock, Lavinia L., Sarah Elizabeth Pickett, Clara D. Noyes, Fannie F. Clement, Elizabth G. Fox and Anna R. Van Meter. *History of American Red Cross Nursing*. New York: Macmillan, 1922.

Donovan, Frances R. *The Woman Who Waits*. 1920. Reprint. New York: Arno Press, 1974.

Dorr, Rheta Childe. *What Eight Million Women Want*. 1910. Reprint. New York: Kraus Reprint, 1971.

―――. *A Woman of Fifty*. 1924. Reprint. New York: Arno Press, 1980.

Dos Passos, John. *USA: The 42nd Parallel, Nineteen Nineteen, The Big Money*. New York: Random House (Modern Library ed.), 1937.

Douglas, Emily Taft. *Remember the Ladies: The Story of Great Women Who Helped Shape America*. New York: Putnam's, 1966.

Douglass, Gladys S. *Oh Grandma, You're Kidding, Memories of 75 Years in Lincoln*. Lincoln, Neb.: J and L Lee, 1983.

Douthit, Mary Osborn, ed. *The Souvenir of Western Women*. Portland, Oreg.: Anderson and Duniway, 1905.

Downey, Fairfax. *Portrait of an Era As Drawn by C. D. Gibson: A Biography*. New York: Scribner's, 1936.

Drake, Emma Frances Angell, M.D. *What a Young Wife Ought to Know*. Philadelphia: Vir, 1902.

Dreier, Mary E. *Margaret Dreier Robins: Her Life, Letters, and Work*. New York: Zenger Pub., 1950.

DuBois, Ellen Carol. *Feminism and Suffrage: The Emergence of an Independent Women's Movement in America 1848–1869*. Ithaca, N.Y.: Cornell Univ. Press, 1978.

DuBois, Ellen Carol, and Vicki L. Ruiz, eds. *Unequal Sisters: A Multicultural Reader in U.S. Women's History*. New York: Routledge, 1990.

Duffus, Robert L. *Lillian Wald: Neighbor and Crusader*. New York: Macmillan, 1938.

Dumont, Rosemary Ruhig, ed. *Women and Leadership in the Library Profession*. Special issue of *Library Trends* 34 (Fall 1985). Champaign: Univ. of Illinois, Graduate School of Library and Information Science.

Duniway, Abigail Scott. *Path Breaking: An Autobiographical History of the Equal Suffrage Movement in Pacific Coast States*. 1914. Reprint. New York: Schocken Books, 1971.

Duvall, Ellen. "A Point of Honor." *Atlantic Monthly* 88 (1901):253.

Dye, Nancy Schrom. *As Equals and As Sisters: Feminism, The Labor Movement, and the Women's Trade Union League of New York*. Columbia: Univ. of Missouri Press, 1980.

Eastman, Max. *Enjoyment of Living*. New York: Harper, 1948.

Edwards, Julia. *Women of the World: The Great Foreign Correspondents.* Boston: Houghton Mifflin, 1988.

Ehrenreich, Barbara, and Deirdre English. *Complaints and Disorders: The Sexual Politics of Sickness.* Old Westbury, N.Y.: Feminist Press, 1973.

————. *For Her Own Good: 150 Years of the Experts' Advice to Women.* New York: Anchor Press, 1979.

Ellis, Anne. *The Life of an Ordinary Woman.* 1929. Reprint. New York: Arno Press, 1974.

————. *Plain Anne Ellis: More About the Life of an Ordinary Woman.* 1931. Reprint. Lincoln: Univ. of Nebraska Press, 1984.

Erenberg, Lewis A. *Steppin' Out: New York Nightlife and the Transformation of American Culture, 1889–1930.* Chicago: Univ. of Chicago Press, 1981.

Ets, Marie Hall. *Rosa: The Life of an Italian Immigrant.* Minneapolis: Univ. of Minnesota Press, 1970.

Evans, James W., and Gardner L. Harding. *Entertaining the American Army: The American Stage and Lyceum in the World War.* New York: Association Press, 1921.

Evans, Sara M. *Born for Liberty: A History of Women in America.* New York: Free Press, 1989.

Ewen, Elizabeth. *Immigrant Women in the Land of Dollars: Life and Culture on the Lower East Side, 1890–1925.* New York: Monthly Review Press, 1985.

"The Experiences of a 'Hired Girl.'" *Outlook* 100 (April 6, 1912):778–780.

Fairbanks, Carol, and Bergine Haakenson, eds. *Writings of Farm Women 1840–1940: An Anthology.* New York: Garland, 1990.

Farnsworth, Martha. *Plains Woman: The Diary of Martha Farnsworth, 1882–1922.* Edited by Marlene Springer and Haskell Springer. Bloomington: Indiana Univ. Press, 1988.

Ferber, Edna. *Personality Plus: Some Experiences of Emma McChesney and Her Son Jock.* New York: Frederick A. Stokes, 1914.

Fisher, Dorothy Canfield. *A Montessori Mother.* New York: Henry Holt, 1916.

Fletty, Valborg. *Public Services of Women's Organizations.* New York: George Banta, 1951.

Flexner, Eleanor. *Century of Struggle: The Woman's Rights Movement in the United States.* Cambridge, Mass.: Belknap Press of the Harvard Univ. Press, 1968.

Florence, Lella Secor. *The Ford Peace Ship and After* in *We Did Not Fight.* 1935. Reprint. New York: Burt Franklin Reprints, 1974.

Foner, Philip S. *Women and the American Labor Movement, From Colonial Times to the Eve of World War I.* New York: Free Press, 1979.

Foote, Mary Hallock. *Edith Bonham.* Boston: Houghton Mifflin, 1917.

Forster, Margaret. *Significant Sisters: The Grassroots of American Feminism, 1839–1939.* New York: Knopf, 1985.

Fowler, Robert Booth. *Carrie Catt: Feminist Politician*. Boston: Northeastern Univ. Press, 1986.

Freedman, Estelle B. *Their Sisters' Keepers: Women's Prison Reform in America, 1830–1930*. Ann Arbor: Univ. of Michigan Press, 1981.

Freidel, Frank. *Over There: The Story of America's First Great Overseas Crusade*. Boston: Little, Brown, 1964.

Gacs, Ute D., Aisha Khan, Terrie McIntyre, and Ruth Weinberg, eds. *Women Anthropologists: Selected Biographies*. Champaign: Univ. of Illinois Press, 1989.

Gale, Zona. *Friendship Village*. New York: Macmillan, 1910.

———. *Heart's Kindred*. New York: Macmillan, 1915.

Gardener, Helen Hamilton. *Is This Your Son, My Lord?* Boston: Arena, 1890.

Gates, Eleanor. *Apron-Strings*. New York: Sully and Kleinteich, 1917.

Gibbs, Margaret. *The DAR*. New York: Holt, Rinehart and Winston, 1969.

Giddings, Paula. *When and Where I Enter: The Impact of Black Women on Race and Sex in America*. New York: Bantam Books, 1984.

Giele, Janet Z. "Social Change in the Feminine Role: A Comparison of Woman's Suffrage and Woman's Temperance, 1870–1920." Doctoral dissertation, Radcliffe College, 1961.

Gilman, Charlotte Perkins. *What Diantha Did*. New York: Charlton, 1910.

Glasgow, Ellen. *Virginia*. Garden City, N.Y.: Doubleday, Page and Co., 1913.

Glaspell, Susan. *Plays*. Boston: Small, Maynard and Co., 1920.

Gluck, Sherna, ed. *From Parlor to Prison: Five American Suffragists Talk About Their Lives*. New York: Vintage, 1976.

Godwin, Inez A. "Ten Weeks in a Kitchen." *Independent* 53 (Oct. 17, 1901):2459–2464.

Golden, Claudia. *Understanding the Gender Gap: An Economic History of American Women*. New York: Oxford Univ. Press, 1990.

Goldmark, Josephine. *Impatient Crusader: Florence Kelley's Life Story*. Champaign: Univ. of Illinois Press, 1953.

Golin, Steve. *The Fragile Bridge: Paterson Silk Stike, 1913*. Philadelphia: Temple Univ. Press, 1988.

Gordon, Jean, and Jan McArthur. "American Women and Domestic Consumption, 1800–1920: Four Interpretative Themes." *Journal of American Culture: Studies of a Civilization* 8 (Fall, 1985):35–46.

Gordon, Linda. "Voluntary Motherhood: The Beginnings of Feminist Birth Control Ideas in the United States." In *Clio's Consciousness Raised: New Perspectives on the History of Women*. Edited by Mary Hartman and Lois W. Banner. New York: Harper and Row, 1974.

———. *Woman's Body, Woman's Right: A Social History of Birth Control in America*. New York: Penguin Books, 1977.

Gordon, Lynn D. *Gender and Higher Education in the Progressive Era*. New Haven: Yale Univ. Press, 1990.

Gover, C. Jane. *The Positive Image: Women Photographers in Turn-of-the-Century America.* Albany: State Univ. of New York Press, 1988.

Grant, Robert. *Unleavened Bread.* 1915. Reprint. Ridgewood, N.J.: Gregg Press, 1968.

Green, James, ed. *Workers' Struggles, Past and Present: A "Radical America" Reader.* Philadelphia: Temple Univ. Press, 1983.

Green, Martin. *New York 1913: The Armory Show and the Paterson Strike Pageant.* New York: Collier/Macmillan, 1988.

Greenwald, Maurine Weiner. *Women, War and Work: The Impact of World War I on Women Workers in the United States.* Westport, Conn.: Greenwood Press, 1980.

Gridley, Marion E. *American Indian Women.* New York: Hawthorn Books, 1974.

Grittner, Frederick K. *White Slavery: Myth, Ideology, and American Law.* New York: Garland, 1990.

Groneman, Carol, and Mary Beth Norton, eds. *"To Toil the Livelong Day": America's Women at Work, 1780–1980.* Ithaca, N.Y.: Cornell Univ. Press, 1987.

Gusfield, Joseph R. *Symbolic Crusade: Status Politics and the American Temperance Movement.* 1963. Reprint. Westport, Conn.: Greenwood Press, 1980.

Gutek, Barbara A. *Sex and the Workplace.* San Francisco: Jossey-Bass, 1985.

Hall, Jacquelyn Dowd. *Revolt Against Chivalry: Jessie Daniel Ames and the Women's Campaign Against Lynching.* New York: Columbia Univ. Press, 1979.

Hamilton, Alice. *Exploring the Dangerous Trades: The Autobiography of Alice Hamilton, M.D.* 1943. Reprint. Boston: Northeastern Univ. Press, 1985.

Hamilton, Olivia E. Papers. Schlesinger Library, Radcliffe College.

Hampsten, Elizabeth. *Read This Only to Yourself: The Private Writings of Midwestern Women, 1880–1910.* Bloomington: Indiana Univ. Press, 1982.

———. *To All Inquiring Friends: Letters, Diaries, and Essays in North Dakota, 1880–1910.* Grand Forks: Department of English, Univ. of North Dakota, 1979.

Hancock, Joy Bright. *Lady in the Navy: A Personal Reminiscence.* Annapolis: Naval Institute Press, 1972.

Handlin, Oscar. *This Was America.* Cambridge: Harvard Univ. Press, 1949.

Hareven, Tamara K.; and Ralph Langenbach. *Amoskeag: Life and Work in an American Factory City.* New York: Pantheon Books, 1978.

Harland, Marion. *The Distractions of Martha.* New York: Scribner's, 1906.

Harley, Sharon, and Rosalyn Terborg-Penn, eds. *The Afro-American Woman: Struggles and Images.* Port Washington, N.Y.: Kennikat Press, 1978.

Harris, Seale, with the collaboration of Frances Williams Browin. *Woman's Surgeon: The Life Story of J. Marion Sims.* New York: Macmillan, 1950.

Hart, James D. *The Popular Book: A History of America's Literary Taste.* Berkeley: Univ. of California Press, 1963.

Hartman, Mary S., and Lois Banner, eds. *Clio's Consciousness Raised: New Perspectives on the History of Women.* New York: Harper and Row, 1974.

Hasanovitz, Elizabeth. *One of Them: Chapters from a Passionate Autobiography.* Boston: Houghton Mifflin, 1918.

Haskin, Sara Estelle, *Women and Missions in the Methodist Episcopal Church, South.* Nashville: Methodist Pub. House, 1920.

Hayden, Dolores. *The Grand Domestic Revolution: A History of Feminist Designs for American Homes, Neighborhoods, and Cities.* Cambridge: MIT Press, 1981.

Haynes, Elizabeth Ross. "Negroes in Domestic Service in the United States." *Journal of Negro History* 8 (October 1923):384–442.

Henri, Florette. *Black Migration: Movement North 1900–1920.* Garden City, N.Y.: Anchor Press/Doubleday, 1975.

Herrick, Robert. *Together.* 1908. Reprint. Greenwich, Conn.: Fawcett, 1962.

Hershey, Burnet. *The Odyssey of Henry Ford and the Great Peace Ship.* New York: Taplinger, 1967.

Hill, Joseph A. *Women in Gainful Occupations, 1870 to 1920.* Census Monographs 9. Washington, D.C.: Government Printing Office, 1929.

Hobson, Barbara Meil. *Uneasy Virtue: The Politics of Prostitution and the American Reform Tradition.* New York: Basic Books, 1987.

Hofstadter, Richard. *The Age of Reform, from Bryan to F.D.R.* New York: Vintage, 1955.

Hooks, Janet M. *Women's Occupations Through Seven Decades.* U.S. Dept. of Labor, Women's Bureau, *Bulletin* #218. Washington, D.C.: Government Printing Office, 1947.

Hoppin, Laura B., ed. *History of the World War Reconstruction Aides: Being an account of the activities and whereabouts of Physio Therapy and Occupational Therapy Aides who served in U.S. Army Hospitals in the United States and in France during the World War.* Milbrook, N.Y.: W. Tydsley, 1933.

Horton, Isabelle. *High Adventure: Life of Lucy Rider Meyer.* New York: Garland, 1928.

Hughes, Lora Wood. *No Time for Tears.* Boston: Houghton Mifflin, 1946.

Hymowitz, Carol, and Michaele Weissman. *A History of Women in America.* New York: Bantam Books, 1978.

Indiana Univ. Institute for Sex Research. *Sexual Behavior in the Human Female.* Philadelphia: W. B. Saunders, 1953.

Ione, Carol. *Pride of Familyh: Four Generations of American Women of Color.* New York: Summit Books, 1991.

Irwin, Inez Haynes. *Angels and Amazons: A Hundred Years of American Women.* 1933. Reprint. New York: Arno Press, 1974.

————. *The Story of the Woman's Party*. 1921. Reprint. New York: Kraus, 1971.

Ise, John. *Sod and Stubble*. 1936. Reprint. Lincoln: Univ. of Nebraska Press, 1967.

Jastrow, Marie. *Looking Back: The American Dream Through Immigrant Eyes*. New York: Norton, 1986.

————. *A Time to Remember: Growing Up in New York Before the Great War*. New York: Norton, 1979.

Jensen, Joan M. *Promise to the Land: Essays on Rural Women*. Albuquerque: Univ. of New Mexico Press, 1991.

————, ed. *With These Hands: Women Working on the Land*. Old Westbury, N.Y.: Feminist Press; New York: McGraw-Hill, 1981.

Johnston, Annie Fellows. *The Land of the Little Colonel: Reminiscences and Autobiography*. Boston: L. C. Page, ca. 1929.

Jones, Jacqueline. *Labor of Love, Labor of Sorrow: Black Women, Work and the Family from Slavery to the Present*. New York: Basic Books, 1985.

Katzman, David M. *Seven Days a Week: Women and Domestic Service in Industrializing America*. New York: Oxford Univ. Press, 1978.

Kaufman, Polly Welts. *Women Teachers on the Frontier*. New Haven: Yale Univ. Press, 1984.

Kearney, Belle. *A Slaveholder's Daughter*. St. Louis: The St. Louis Christian Advocate Press, 1900.

Kelley, Edith Summers. *Weeds*. 1923. Reprint. Carbondale and Edwardsville: Southern Illinois Univ. Press, 1972.

Kellogg, Clara Louise. *Memoirs of an American Prima Donna*. New York: Putnam's, 1913.

Kendall, Elaine. *Peculiar Institutions: An Informal History of the Seven Sister Colleges*. New York: Putnam's, 1975–76.

Kennedy, David M. *Birth Control in America: The Career of Margaret Sanger*. New Haven: Yale Univ. Press, 1970.

Kerr, K. Austin. *Organized for Prohibition: A New History of the Anti-Saloon League*. New Haven: Yale Univ. Press, 1985.

Kessler-Harris, Alice. *Out to Work: A History of Wage-Earning Women in the United States*. Oxford: Oxford Univ. Press, 1982.

————. *A Woman's Wage: Historical Meanings and Social Consequences*. Lexington: Univ. of Kentucky Press, 1990.

————. *Women Have Always Worked: A Historical Overview*. New York: Feminist Press, 1981.

Knapp, Richard F., and Charles F. Hartsoe. *Play for America: The National Recreation Association 1906–1965*. Arlington Va.: National Recreation Association, 1979.

Kraditor, Aileen. *The Ideas of the Woman Suffrage Movement, 1890–1920*. New York: Columbia Univ. Press, 1965.

————. *The Radical Persuasion: Aspects of the Intellectual History and the Historiography of Three American Radical Organizations*. Baton Rouge: Louisiana State Univ. Press, 1981.

Kraft, Barbara S. *The Peace Ship: Henry Ford's Pacifist Adventure in the First World War*. New York: Macmillan, 1978.

Lagemann, Ellen Condliffe. *A Generation of Women: Education in the Lives of Progressive Reformers*. Cambridge: Harvard Univ. Press, 1979.

Laird, Carobeth. *Encounter with an Angry God: Recollections of My Life with John Peabody Harrington*. Morongo Indian Reservation, Banning, Calif.: Malki Museum Press, 1975.

Lamb, May Wynne. *My Life in Alaska: The Reminiscences of a Kansas Woman, 1916–1919*. Edited by Dorothy Wynne Zimmerman. Lincoln: Univ. of Nebraska Press, 1988.

Landgren, Marchal E. *Years of Art: The Story of the Art Students League of New York*. New York: Robert McBride, 1940.

Lane, Rose Wilder. *Old Home Town*. 1935. 2d reprint. Lincoln: Univ. of Nebraska Press, 1985.

Lash, Joseph P. *Eleanor and Franklin: The Story of Their Relationship*. New York: Norton, 1971.

Laughlin, Clara E. *The Keys of Heaven*. New York: Doran, 1918.

Leavitt, Judith Walzer. *Brought to Bed: Childbearing in America, 1750 to 1950*. New York: Oxford Univ. Press, 1986.

————, ed. *Women and Health in America: Historical Readings*. Madison: Univ. of Wisconsin Press, 1984.

Le Guin, Charles A., ed. *A Home-Concealed Woman: The Diaries of Magnolia Wynn Le Guin, 1901–1913*. Athens: Univ. of Georgia Press, 1990.

Leider, Emily Wortis. *California's Daughter: Gertrude Atherton and Her Times*. Stanford, Calif.: Stanford Univ. Press, 1991.

Lerner, Gerda, ed. *Black Women in White America*. New York: Random House, 1972.

Levenstein, Harvey A. *Revolution at the Table: The Transformation of the American Diet*. New York: Oxford Univ. Press, 1988.

Lewis, Lucy Biddle. Papers. Biddle MSS, Friends' Historical Library, Swarthmore, Pa.

Lewis, Sinclair. *The Job: An American Novel*. New York: Grosset and Dunlap, 1917.

Litoff, Judy Barrett. *American Midwives, 1860 to the Present*. Westport, Conn.: Greenwood Press, 1978.

Lobsenz, Johanna. *The Older Woman in Industry*. 1929. Reprint. New York: Arno Press, 1974.

London, Jack. *The Iron Heel*. New York: Macmillan, 1908.

Lopata, Helena Z. "The Life Cycle of the Social Role of Housewife." *Sociology and Social Research* 51 (October 1966):5–22.

Lutz, Alma, coll. and ed. *With Love, Jane: Letters from American Women on the War Fronts*. New York: John Day, 1945.

Lynd, Robert, and Helen Lynd. *Middletown: A Study in American Culture*. New York: Harcourt Brace, 1929.

McCarthy, Kathleen D, ed. *Lady Bountiful Revisited: Women, Philanthropy, and Power*. New Brunswick, N.J.: Rutgers Univ. Press, 1990.

Macdonald, Anne L. *No Idle Hands: The Social History of American Knitting*. New York: Ballantine Books, 1988.

Macdonell, Mrs. R. W. *Belle Harris Bennett: Her Life Work*. 1938. Reprint. New York: Garland, 1987.

Madeleine: An Autobiography. New York: Harper and Bros., 1919.

Malkiel, Theresa S. *The Diary of a Shirtwaist Striker*. 1910. Reprint. Ithaca, N.Y.: ILR Press, 1990.

Mark, Joan. *A Stranger in Her Native Land: Alice Fletcher and the American Indians*. Lincoln: Univ. of Nebraska Press, 1988.

Marriot, Alice. *Maria, the Potter of San Ildefonso*. Norman: Univ. of Oklahoma Press, 1948.

Marsh, Margaret. *Surburban Lives*. New Brunswick, N.J.: Rutgers Univ. Press, 1990.

Martin, Theodora Penny. *The Sound of Our Own Voices: Women's Study Clubs, 1860–1910*. Boston: Beacon Press, 1987.

Matthews, Glenna, *"Just a Housewife": The Rise and Fall of Domesticity in America*. Oxford: Oxford Univ. Press, 1987.

May, Elaine Tyler. *Great Expectations: Marriage and Divorce in Post-Victorian America*. Chicago: Univ. of Chicago Press, 1980.

May, Henry F. *The End of American Innocence: A Study of the First Years of Our Own Time, 1912–1917*. New York: Oxford Univ. Press, 1959.

Mayo, Edith, curator. "From Parlor to Politics: Women and Reform in America, 1890–1925." Exhibit at the Museum of American History, the Smithsonian Institution.

Milkman, Ruth, ed. *Women, Work and Protest: A Century of US Women's Labor History*. London: Routledge and Kegan Paul, 1985.

Mills, Nettie Elizabeth. *The Lady Driller: Autobiography of Nettie Elizabeth Mills*. New York: Exposition Press, 1955.

Mintz, Steven, and Susan Kellogg. *Domestic Revolutions: A Social History of American Family Life*. New York: Free Press, 1988.

Moffatt, Mary Jane, and Charlotte Painter, eds. *Revelations: Diaries of Women*. New York: Vintage, 1975.

Montgomery, James. *Liberated Woman: A Life of May Arkwright Hutton*. Spokane, Wash.: Gingko House, 1974.

Morgan, Wallace. "Every Night at Midnight." *McClure's* 45 (June 1915):26.

Morrison, Theodore. *Chautauqua: A Center for Education, Religion, and the Arts in America*. Chicago: Univ. of Chicago Press, 1974.

Mourning Dove: A Salishan Autobiography, ed. Jay Miller. Lincoln: Univ. of Nebraska Press, 1990.

Moynihan, Ruth Barnes. *Rebel for Rights: Abigail Scott Duniway*. New Haven: Yale Univ. Press, 1983.

Moynihan, Ruth Barnes, Susan Armitage, and Christine Fischer Dichamp, eds. *So Much to Be Done: Women Settlers on the Mining and Ranching Frontier*. Lincoln: Univ. of Nebraska Press, 1990.

Nathan, Maud. *The Story of an Epoch-Making Movement*. Garden City, N.Y.: Doubleday, Page and Co., 1926.

Nestor, Agnes. *Woman's Labor Leader: The Autobiography of Agnes Nestor*. Rockford, Ill.: Bellevue Books Publishing, 1954.

Neverdon-Morton, Cynthia. *Afro-American Women of the South and the Advancement of the Race, 1895–1925*. Knoxville: Univ. of Tennessee Press, 1989.

Nichols, Carole. *Votes and More for Women: Suffrage and After in Connecticut*. New York: Haworth Press, 1983.

Nichols, J. L., and William H. Crogman. *Progress of a Race*. 1920. Reprint. New York: Arno Press and the *New York Times*, 1969.

Niederman, Sharon. *A Quilt of Words; Women's Diaries, Letters and Original Accounts of Life in the Southwest, 1860–1960*. Boulder, Colo.: Johnson Books, 1988.

Notable American Women 1607–1950: A Bibliographical Dictionary. Edited by Edward T. James, Janet Wilson James, and Paul S. Boyer. 3 vols. Cambridge, Mass.: Belknap Press of Harvard Univ. Press, 1971.

Notable American Women: The Modern Period: A Bibliographical Dictionary. Edited by Barbara Sicherman and Carol Hurd Green, with Ilene Kantrov and Harriette Walker. Cambridge, Mass.: Belknap Press of Harvard Univ. Press, 1980.

Odegard, Peter H. *Pressure Politics: The Story of the Anti-Saloon League*. 1928. Reprint. New York: Octagon Books, 1966.

Ogden, Annegret S. *The Great American Housewife: From Helpmate to Wage Earner*. Westport, Conn.: Greenwood Press, 1986.

O'Hagan, Anne. "The Confessions of a Professional Woman." *Harper's Bazaar* 41 (September 1907):848–54.

Oldfield, Sybil. *Women Against the Iron Fist: Alternatives to Militarism, 1900–1989*. Cambridge, Mass.: Basil Blackfield, 1989.

O'Neal, Hank. *"Life Is Painful, Nasty & Short . . . In My Case It Has Only Been Painful & Nasty, Djuna Barnes", 1978–1981*. New York: Paragon House, 1990.

O'Neill, William L. *Divorce in the Progressive Era*. New Haven: Yale Univ. Press, 1967.

———. *Everyone Was Brave: The Decline and Fall of Feminism in America*. Chicago: Quadrangle Books, 1969.

Parry, Albert. *Garrets and Pretenders: A History of Bohemianism in America.* New York: Covici-Friede, 1933.

Paulson, Ross Evans. *Women's Suffrage and Prohibition: A Comparative Study of Equality and Social Control.* Glenview, Ill.: Scott, Foresman, 1973.

Peiss, Kathy. *Cheap Amusements: Working Women and Leisure in Turn-of-the-Century New York.* Philadelphia: Temple Univ. Press, 1986.

Perry, Elisabeth Israels. *Belle Moskowitz: Feminine Politics and the Exercise of Power in the Age of Alfred E. Smith.* New York: Oxford Univ. Press, 1987.

Peters, Margot. *The House of Barrymore.* New York: Knopf, 1990.

Proceedings of the Fifth Biennial Convention of the National Women's Trade Union League of America, New York City, June 7–12, 1915.

Putnam, Emily James. *The Lady: Studies of Certain Significant Phases of Her History.* 1910. Reprint. Chicago: Univ. of Chicago Press, 1969.

Randall, Mercedes M. *Improper Bostonian: Emily Greene Balch.* New York: Twayne, 1964.

Reinehr, Frances Grace. *Bloody Mary: Gentle Woman.* Lincoln, Neb.: Foundation Books, 1989.

Rich, Adrienne. *Of Woman Born: Motherhood as Experience and Institution.* New York: Norton, 1976.

Richards, Clarice E. *A Tenderfoot Bride: Tales from an Old Ranch.* 1920. Reprint. Lincoln: Univ. of Nebraska Press, 1988.

Richards, Linda. *Reminiscences of Linda Richards: America's First Trained Nurse.* Boston: Whitcomb and Barrows, 1911.

Richardson, Dorothy. *The Long Day: The Story of a New York Working Girl* 1905. Reprint. Charlottesville: Univ. of Virginia Press, 1990.

Rideout, Walter B. *The Radical Novel in the United States, 1900–1954: Some Interrelations of Literature and Society.* Cambridge: Harvard Univ. Press, 1956.

Roberts, Mary. *American Nursing: History and Interpretation.* New York: Macmillan, 1954.

Robertson, Janet. *The Magnificent Mountain Women: Adventures in the Colorado Rockies.* Lincoln: Univ. of Nebraska Press, 1990.

Robins, Elizabeth. *The Convert.* 1907. Reprint. Old Westbury, N.Y.: Feminist Press, 1980.

Roderick, Mary Louise Rochester. *A Nightingale in the Trenches.* New York: Vantage, 1966.

Rogers, Agnes. *Women Are Here to Stay.* New York: Harper, 1949.

Rogers, Anna A. "Why American Marriages Fail." *Atlantic Monthly* 100 (September 1907):292.

Rollyson, Carl. *Nothing Ever Happens to the Brave: The Story of Martha Gellhorn.* New York: St. Martin's, 1990.

Root, Waverly, and Richard de Rochemont. *Eating in America: A History*. New York: William Morrow, 1976.

Rose, Hilda. "The Stump Farm: A Chronicle of Pioneering." *Atlantic Monthly* (February 1927):145–52; (March 1927):334–42; (April 1927):512–18.

Rose, Phyllis. *Jazz Cleopatra: Josephine Baker in Her Time*. New York: Vintage, 1991.

Rosen, Ruth. *The Lost Sisterhood: Prostitution in America 1900–1918*. Baltimore: Johns Hopkins Univ. Press, 1982.

Rosen, Ruth, and Sue Davidson, eds. *The Maimie Papers*. Old Westbury, N.Y.: Feminist Press with the Schlesinger Library of Radcliffe College, 1977.

Rotella, Elyce J. *From Home to Office: U.S. Women at Work, 1870–1930*. Ann Arbor: Univ. of Michigan Research Press, 1981.

Rothman, Sheila M. *Woman's Proper Place: A History of Changing Ideals and Practices, 1870 to the Present*. New York: Basic Books, 1978.

Sandler, Martin W. *As New Englanders Played*. Chester, Conn.: Globe Pequot Press, 1979.

Sandoz, Mari. *Son of the Gamblin' Man: The Youth of an Artist*. 1960. Reprint. Lincoln: Univ. of Nebraska Press, 1976.

Santmyer, Helen Hooven. *". . . and Ladies of the Club."* New York: Putnam's, 1984.

———. *The Fierce Dispute*. New York: St. Martin's, 1987.

———. *Herbs and Apples*. New York: St. Martin's, 1987.

Sapiro, Virginia. *The Political Integration of Women: Roles, Socialization, and Politics*. Champaign: Univ. of Illinois Press, 1983.

Scharff, Virginia. *Taking the Wheel: Women and the Coming of the Motor Age*. New York: Free Press, 1991.

Schlissel, Lillian. *Women's Diaries of the Westward Journey*. New York: Schocken Books, 1982.

Schneider, Dorothy, and Carl J. Schneider. *Into the Breach: American Women Overseas in World War I*. New York: Viking, 1991.

Schor, Juliet B. *The Overworked American: The Unexpected Decline of Leisure*. New York: Basic Books, 1992.

Schwarz, Judith. *Radical Feminists of Heterodoxy: Greenwich Village 1912–1940*. Rev. ed. Norwich, Vt.: New Victoria, 1986.

Scott, Anne Firor. *The Southern Lady: From Pedestal to Politics 1830–1930*. Chicago: Univ. of Chicago Press, 1972.

Scott, Anne Firor, and Andrew MacKay Scott. *One Half the People: The Fight for Woman Suffrage*. Champaign: Univ. of Illinois Press, 1982.

Scott, Evelyn. *Escapade: An Autobiography*. 1923. Reprint. New York: Carroll and Graf, 1987.

Sears, Elizabeth. "Business Women and Women in Business." *Harper's Monthly* 134 (January 1917).

Seawell, Molly Elliot. "The Ladies' Battle." *Atlantic Monthly* 106 (September 1910):303.

Shaw, Anna Howard, with Elizabeth Jordan. *The Story of A Pioneer.* 1915. Reprint. New York: Kraus Reprint, 1990.

Sicherman, Barbara, ed. *Alice Hamilton: A Life in Letters.* Cambridge: Harvard Univ. Press, 1984.

Sillia, Helene M, ed. *Lest We Forget . . ., A History of Women's Overseas Service League.* N.p., 1978.

Simkhovitch, Mary K. *Neighborhood: My Story of Greenwich House.* New York: Norton, 1938.

Sinclair, Andrew. *The Emancipation of American Women.* New York: Harper and Row, 1965.

Sinclair, Upton. *The Jungle.* New York: Doubleday, Page and Co., 1906.

Snitow, Ann, Christine Stansell, and Sharon Thompson. *Powers of Desire: The Politics of Sexuality.* New York: Monthly Review Press, 1983.

Sochen, June. *Herstory: A Woman's View of American History.* New York: Alfred, 1974.

———. *Movers and Shakers: American Women Thinkers and Activists 1900–1970.* Chicago: Quadrangle Books, 1973.

Solomon, Barbara Miller. *In the Company of Educated Women: A History of Women in Higher Education in America.* New Haven: Yale Univ. Press, 1985.

Solomon, Hannah G. *Fabric of My Life: The Autobiography of Hannah G. Solomon.* New York: Bloch, 1946.

Sparkes, Boyden, and Samuel Taylor Moore. *The Witch of Wall Street: Hetty Green.* Garden City, N.Y.: Doubleday, Doran and Co., 1935.

Stadum, Beverly. *Poor Women and Their Families: Hard-Working Charity Cases, 1900–1930.* Albany: State Univ. of New York Press, 1991.

Stein, Leon. *The Triangle Fire.* Philadelphia: Lippincott, 1962.

Steinson, Barbara J. *American Women's Activism in World War I.* New York: Garland, 1982.

Stephenson, Charles, and Rober Asher, eds. *Life and Labor: Dimensions of American Working-Class History.* Albany, State Univ. of New York Press, 1986.

Sterling, Dorothy. *Black Foremothers, Three Lives.* Old Westbury, N.Y.: Feminist Press, 1979.

Stern, Elizabeth G. *My Mother and I.* 1917. Reprint. New York: Macmillan, 1941.

Stern, Jane, and Michael Stern. "Neighboring." *The New Yorker,* April 15, 1991.

Stevens, Doris. *Jailed for Freedom.* New York: Schocken Books, 1976.

Stevenson, Robert Louis. *The Amateur Emigrant.* Narrated by Donal Donnelly. Charlotte Hall, Md.: Recorded Books, n.d.

Stewart, Elinore Pruitt. *Letters of a Woman Homesteader*. 1913. Reprint. Boston: Houghton Mifflin, 1988.

———. *Letters on an Elk Hunt by a Woman Homesteader*. 1915. Reprint. Lincoln: Univ. of Nebraska Press, 1979.

Stilgoe, John R. *Borderland: Origins of the American Suburb, 1820–1930*. New Haven: Yale Univ. Press, 1988.

Stokeley, Edith K., and Marian K. Hurd. *Miss Billy: A Neighborhood Story*. Boston: Lothrop, Lee and Shepard Co., 1905.

Strasser, Susan. *Never Done: A History of American Housework*. New York: Pantheon Books, 1982.

Stratton, Joanna L. *Pioneer Women: Voices from the Kansas Frontier*. New York: Simon and Schuster, 1981.

Sway, Marlene. *Familiar Strangers: Gypsy Life in America*. Urbana: Univ. of Illinois Press, 1988.

Taeuber, Irene B., and Conrad Taeuber. *People of the United States in the Twentieth Century*. Washington, D.C.: Bureau of the Census, 1971.

Talbot, Marion, and Lois Kimball Mathews Rosenberry. *The History of the American Association of University Women, 1881–1931*. Boston: Houghton Mifflin, 1931.

Tanner, Annie Clark. *A Mormon Mother: An Autobiography*. Salt Lake City: Tanner Trust Fund, Univ. of Utah, 1976.

Tarbell, Ida. *The Business of Being a Woman*. N.Y.: Macmillan, 1912.

Tax, Meredith. *The Rising of the Women: Feminist Solidarity and Class Conflict, 1880–1917*. New York: Monthly Review Press, 1980.

———. *Rivington Street*. New York: William Morrow, 1982.

Ticknor, Caroline, "The Steel-Engraving Lady and the Gibson Girl." *Atlantic Monthly* 88 (1901):108.

Tilly, Louise A., and Patricia Gurin, eds. *Women, Politics, and Change*. New York: Russell Sage Foundation., 1990.

Timberlake, James H. *Prohibition and the Progressive Movement, 1900–1920*. New York: Oxford Univ. Press, 1979.

Townsend, Harriet A. *Reminiscences of Famous Women*. Buffalo, N.Y.: Evans-Penfold, 1916.

True, Ruth S. *The Neglected Girl*. New York: Survey Associates, 1914.

Truman, Margaret. *Women of Courage from Revolutionary Times to the Present*. New York: William Morrow, 1976.

Tucker, Cynthia Grant. *Prophetic Sisterhood: Liberal Women Ministers of the Frontier, 1880–1930*. Boston: Beacon Press, 1990.

Turner, Florence. *At the Chelsea*. New York: Harcourt Brace Jovanovich, 1987.

U.S. Department of Commerce and Labor, Bureau of the Census, *Statistics of Women at Work*. Washington, D.C.: Government Printing Office, 1907.

Van Horn, Susan Householder. *Women, Work, and Fertility, 1900–1986*. New York: New York Univ. Press, 1988.

Van Vorst, Mrs. John, and Marie Van Vorst. *The Woman Who Toils, Being the Experiences of Two Gentlewomen as Factory Girls.* New York: Doubleday, Page and Co., 1903.

Varese, Louise. *Varese: A Looking Glass Diary,* vol. 1 (1883–1920). New York: Norton, 1972.

Wallace, Phyllis A. *Black Women in the Labor Force.* Cambridge: MIT Press, 1980.

Walsh, Correa Moylan. *Feminism.* New York: Sturgis & Walton, 1917.

Ware, Caroline R. *Greenwich Village, 1920–1930: A Comment on American Civilization in the Post-War Years.* Boston: Houghton Mifflin, 1935.

Ware, Susan. *Partner and I: Molly Dewson, Feminism, and New Deal Politics.* New Haven: Yale Univ. Press, 1987.

Weinberg, Sydney Stahl. *The World of Our Mothers: The Lives of Jewish Immigrant Women.* New York: Schocken Books, 1988.

Weiner, Lynn Y. *From Working Girl to Working Mother: The Female Labor Force in the United States, 1820–1980.* Chapel Hill: Univ. of North Carolina Press, 1985.

Weitzenhoffer, Frances. *The Havemeyers: Impressionism Comes to America.* New York: Harry N. Abrams, 1986.

Wells, Ida B. *Crusade for Justice: The Autobiography of Ida B. Wells.* ed. Alfreda M. Duster. Chicago: Univ. of Chicago Press, 1970.

Wertheimer, Barbara Meyer. *We Were There: The Story of Working Women in America.* New York: Pantheon Books, 1977.

Wertz, Richard W., and Dorothy C. Wertz. *Lying-In: A History of Childbirth in America.* New York: Free Press, 1977.

Wesley, Charles H. *The History of the National Association of Colored Women's Clubs: A Legacy of Service.* Washington, D.C.: The Association, 1984.

Wharton, Edith. *The House of Mirth.* New York: Scribner's, 1908.

White, Deborah Gray, *Ar'n't I a Woman? Female Slaves in the Plantation South.* New York: Norton, 1984.

The Whole Family: A Novel by Twelve Authors. 1908. Reprint. New York: Ungar, 1987.

Winslow, Helen M. *The President of Quex: A Woman's Club Story.* Boston: Lothrop, Lee and Shepard, 1906.

Woloch, Nancy. *Women and the American Experience.* New York: Knopf, 1984.

Woods, Robert A., and Albert J. Kennedy. *The Settlement Horizon.* New York: Russell Sage Foundation, 1922. Reprint. New York: Arno Press, 1970.

——, eds. *Young Working Girls: A Summary of Evidence from Two Thousand Social Workers.* Boston: Houghton Mifflin, 1913.

Young, Ann Eliza. *Wife No. 19, or The Story of A Life in Bondage. Being a Complete Expose of Mormonism, and Revealing the Sorrows, Sacrifices and Sufferings of Women in Polygamy*. 1875. Reprint. Salem, NH: Ayer, 1986.

Young, Carrie. *Nothing to Do but Stay: My Pioneer Mother*. Ames: Univ. of Iowa Press, 1991.

Zurier, Rebecca. *Art for the Masses: A Radical Magazine and Its Graphics, 1911–1917*. Philadelphia: Temple Univ. Press, 1988.

Index